THE WOMAN AND THE HOUR

Harriet Martineau
and Victorian Ideologies

Harriet Martineau. From 'Gallery of Literary Characters No. xlii: Miss Harriet Martineau,' by Alfred Croquis (Daniel Maclise). *Fraser's Magazine* 8 (Nov. 1833): 576.

THE WOMAN AND THE HOUR

*Harriet Martineau
and Victorian Ideologies*

CAROLINE ROBERTS

UNIVERSITY OF TORONTO PRESS
Toronto Buffalo London

© University of Toronto Press Incorporated 2002
Toronto Buffalo London
Printed in Canada

ISBN 0-8020-3596-5

∞

Printed on acid-free paper

National Library of Canada Cataloguing in Publication Data

Roberts, Caroline, 1970–
    The woman and the hour : Harriet Martineau and Victorian ideologies

    Includes bibliographical references and index.
    ISBN 0-8020-3596-5

    1. Martineau, Harriet, 1802–1876.   2. Authors, English – 19th century –
Biography.   3. Women social reformers – Great Britain – Biography.
I. Title.

PR4984.M5Z78 2002   823'.8   C2001-903537-3

University of Toronto Press acknowledges the financial assistance to its
publishing program of the Canada Council for the Arts and the Ontario Arts
Council.

This book has been published with the help of a grant from the Humanities
and Social Sciences Federation of Canada, using funds provided by the
Social Sciences and Humanities Research Council of Canada.

University of Toronto Press acknowledges the financial support for its
publishing activities of the Government of Canada through the Book
Publishing Industry Development Program (BPIDP).

For my parents

Contents

Acknowledgments

The research for this book was funded by the Rhodes Trust and by the Social Sciences and Humanities Research Council of Canada. I am grateful for the support of these institutions and also wish to thank for their friendly help the staff of the Bodleian Library, the Radcliffe Science Library, the British Library, and the University of Toronto Library.

Among those friends and colleagues who have been of invaluable assistance, I wish to thank in particular Mary Carpenter, Shirley Foster, Patricia Ingham, and the late Don McKenzie. Kristen Pederson has been an excellent editor, and I thank her warmly. I owe a special thanks to David Shaw for his meticulous reading of the manuscript and for his insightful advice. I am also grateful to Jill Matus for many fine lunches and a title. Kate Flint, whose exacting scholarship is inspirational, has been tremendously supportive. My gratitude to her cannot be adequately expressed here. Finally, I wish to thank my husband, Ben Quine, for his encouragement and love.

THE WOMAN AND THE HOUR

Introduction:
Contexts and Controversies

This study has its inception in an observation by Harriet Martineau (1802–76) in her posthumously published *Autobiography* (1877):

> On five occasions in my life I have found myself obliged to write and publish what I entirely believed would be ruinous to my reputation and prosperity. In no one of the five cases has the result been what I anticipated. I find myself at the close of my life prosperous in name and fame, in my friendships and in my affairs.[1]

Harriet Martineau was one of the nineteenth century's most prolific writers, whose articles for the *Daily News* alone number in excess of one thousand, and her isolation of five texts, singular for their anticipated ruin of her name and career, provides a useful focus. This study examines these five texts, exceptional in Martineau's literary output for their highly controversial status: her *Illustrations of Political Economy* (1832–4), *Society in America* (1837), *Letters on Mesmerism* (1844), *Eastern Life, Present and Past* (1848), and the *Letters on the Laws of Man's Nature and Development* (1851). It also examines Martineau's two published novels, *Deerbrook* (1839) and *The Hour and the Man: A Historical Romance* (1841), which, although excluded from her list of her most inflammatory work, were also highly provocative for their unusual choice of hero – a middle-class apothecary in *Deerbrook* and, in *The Hour and the Man*, Toussaint L'Ouverture, the black hero of the revolution (1791) in St Domingo (Haiti).

My purpose is to situate these texts historically in order to understand why they were controversial, for Harriet Martineau's assessment of her work was not unfounded. Investigation of the reception of her texts at the time of their publication reveals that she inspired some of the most hostile and, at times, virulent reviews to be published in the periodical press in the first half of the nineteenth century. This study draws heavily on these reviews as valuable records of their effect on her first readers. It also attempts to situate her texts in their larger historical framework, again making extensive use of periodical literature as an important indicator of public, middle-class ideology at the time. By 'ideology' I do not mean concerted propaganda, but rather Victorian society's shared view of political, economic, and social relations, commonly understood then as 'natural.' I investigate Martineau's texts in relation to, and as part of, Victorian ideology, although, as the title of my study suggests, 'ideologies' may be more exact. In her ground-breaking book, *Uneven Developments: The Ideological Work of Gender in Mid-Victorian England*, Mary Poovey observes that

> to describe an ideology as a 'set' of beliefs or a 'system' of institutions and practices conveys the impression of something that is internally organized, coherent, and complete ... [but] the middle-class ideology we most often associate with the Victorian period was both contested and always under construction; because it was always in the making, it was always open to revision, dispute, and the emergence of oppositional formulations.[2]

My contextualizing examination of Martineau's texts supports the view that ideology is not stable and fixed but fractured, contradictory, and constantly changing. However gradual these changes may be, they are reflected, nonetheless, in the contrast between Martineau's view of her publications as potentially 'ruinous' and the fact of her continued prosperity. Her most controversial works never destroyed her career. However outraged her readers were by any one publication, they invariably greeted its successor with keen interest.

Martineau's steady and widespread appeal to the public means that her works are an important gauge of prevailing beliefs, opinions, and attitudes within her society. She was adroit at establishing herself as a prominent speaker in many of her society's most vexing debates, and the topics of her publications addressed issues of general concern, such as political economy, the status of women, slavery, mesmerism, phrenology, and atheism. This representative quality of Martineau's works is indicated by their noisy reception: if her interests had been tangential to the concerns of her society, her works would have been marginalized, which was not the case. Rather, her intellectual fearlessness, fine journalistic sense of timing and of the topical, and clear, forceful prose combined to facilitate her self-appointed role as national educator and popularizer of progressive social views and reforms. Martineau believed that an author should be of his or her age, as I shall indicate more fully in chapter 1. She also recognized that individuals were overdetermined by cultural influences, so that an author was also necessarily of his or her age.

Martineau's own cultural overdetermination has meant that posterity has tended to forget her. The immersion of her work in the immediate interests of her society has led to its being perceived as belonging to an age, rather than being of more enduring interest. As a consequence, she has appeared as a relatively minor figure in literary criticism of the Victorian period, although critical interest is growing as more literary and cultural historians rediscover her. Valerie Sanders has expertly examined the influences of Martineau's texts on later writers, and there have been excellent biographies by R.K. Webb and, more recently, by Valerie Kossew Pichanick. Gillian Thomas has evaluated Martineau's significance in relation to the Victorian literary world, and Shelagh Hunter examines her 'moral independence' – a Wordsworthian moral psychology uniting religion, politics, and self-development.[3] However, there has been no sustained analysis of Martineau's most important texts. This study aims to supply this deficiency by historical analysis, by close reading, and by considering Martineau's texts in relation to more recent theorizing on the construction and ordering of knowledge in the nineteenth century. Foucault's work is significant in this last endeavour and is often illuminated and sometimes qualified by Martineau's and her society's epistemological assumptions and anxieties.

To say that this study constitutes a departure from the biographies that have dominated criticism of Martineau to date is not to suggest that biography is irrelevant to my work or that matters of biography can ever be fully separated from matters of ideology. Martineau's highly successful writing career, following the collapse of her father's textile manufacturing business in Norwich, was itself a departure from and a challenge to the ideals of feminine behaviour that structured her society's separate, gendered spheres. Moreover, biographical information is indispensable when determining the operations of particular texts: for example, *Letters on Mesmerism*, in which Martineau publicly proclaims her recovery from severe gynaecological ailments by mesmerism, cannot be understood either in its own terms or in terms of its effect on her readers without also considering the five-year illness which debilitated her after the publication of *Deerbrook* in 1839. Similarly, the religious scepticism of *Eastern Life, Present and Past* and the evident atheism of *Letters on the Laws of Man's Nature and Development* are not fully appreciated without the knowledge that Martineau was raised a Unitarian and that her writing career began in 1830 with three prize-winning essays for the Unitarian Association. Unitarianism, which attracted many Victorian intellectual radicals and provincial freethinkers, affirmed the Unity of God, the humanity (as opposed to the divinity) of Jesus, and the eternal salvation of souls. At different times in her life, Martineau was a deeply religious person, which made her eventual 'conversion' to atheism all the more distressing to the public. That said, the emphasis of this study is on Martineau's texts and nineteenth-century culture rather than on her life. Chapter 1 considers her *Illustrations of Political Economy* (1832–4), particularly her 'Populations numbers': she wrote several stories illustrating the desirability of the Malthusian 'preventive check' on overpopulation, and public responses to these stories indicate that her popularization of Malthus challenged Victorian establishment views. Chapter 1 examines these challenges and also engages in a debate with recent critics who claim that Martineau was empowered by her appropriation of traditionally 'masculine' discourses.

After completing her *Illustrations of Political Economy,* Martineau spent the next two years travelling in America. On her return to England, she published *Society in America* (1837) and *Retrospect of Western Travel* (1838). *Society in America* compares the existing state of American society with its founding principles in the Declaration of Independence and argues that the status of women and slaves in America indicates the deferral of constitutional ideals. It argues for the enfranchisement of women and slaves and was sharply criticized in both England and America. Chapter 2 examines this text and the issues it raised.

In 1839 Martineau published her first novel, *Deerbrook*, the subject of chapter 3. *Deerbrook* was controversial in departing from 'silver-fork' literary conventions and featuring a middle-class hero, Edward Hope. Hope, who is called a 'village apothecary,' has a working knowledge of anatomy that provides a focus for his neighbours' prejudices against anatomical practices – prejudices that were common in England both before and after the passing of the Anatomy Act in 1832. Hope also signals a development in the education of medical men in the early part of the nineteenth century, and chapter 3 examines *Deerbrook* in relation to these developments. *Deerbrook* also invites consideration in relation to recent critical views on nineteenth-century realism, and this chapter explores the operations of clinical discourse within the novel and suggests (unlike virtually all readings of the novel to date) that *Deerbrook* is a feminist text.

Chapter 4 examines Martineau's second novel, *The Hour and the Man: A Historical Romance* (1841), which traces the life of the Haitian leader Toussaint L'Ouverture. *The Hour and the Man* has received little attention from twentieth-century critics, but it was the first English novel to feature a black hero (after Behn's *Oroonoko* ca. 1688) and greatly distressed many of its first readers. I indicate that the novel raises significant questions about historical meaning and addresses problems surrounding the knowledge and representation of history, the alliance of history and romance, the experience of history by the colonized subject, and the relation between history and women.

Chapter 5 considers Martineau's five-year illness described in *Life in the Sick-Room* (1844) and her announced cure by mesmerism. Martineau had been under considerable stress since the beginning of her literary career. Her mother had initially opposed her choice of career and maintained a strained relationship with her famous daughter. Martineau had also suffered from the rigours of her fast-paced literary production. Like many Victorian women (and men), she sought respite from life's conflicts in a sickroom, and her proclaimed recovery by mesmerism surprised and offended many observers. My chapter investigates the status of mesmerism in England in the 1830s and 1840s, qualifies the notion that mesmerism was regarded simply as quackery (as many recent commentators have supposed), and explores the ideological implications of Martineau's cure. In particular, the chapter focuses on perceived sexual displays by female somnambulists and the threats that these displays posed for medical practitioners seeking professional respectability at the time.

Chapter 6 addresses *Eastern Life, Present and Past* (1848) and the conflict between religious faith and nineteenth-century historical consciousness. The importance of history as an emergent field of study in the nineteenth century has become a commonplace in Victorian cultural studies. That this new, professional historiography lacked universal acceptance is not, however, always recognized. Martineau's efforts to trace the historical origins of Christianity in ancient Egypt were seen to deny scriptural authority and to reduce religious mysteries to the status of romantic legends. This chapter considers the ambivalent status of historical research for both Martineau and her readers.

My final chapter looks at Martineau's joint publication with Henry George Atkinson, *Letters on the Laws of Man's Nature and Development* (1851).[4] This text was arguably the most controversial of Martineau's career, for it made an explicit declaration of atheism. Her promotion of phrenology as an empirical basis of scientific rationalism also raised social and political questions of a potentially revolutionary nature. Indeed, the *Letters* provoked an uproar, and this chapter considers the text's ideological implications that, once again, placed Martineau at the centre of controversy.

Martineau's greatest challenge to modern scholarship is posed by her eclecticism. The texts considered here reflect such a diversity of interests that they defy complete integration; they incorporate a sufficiently diffuse range of genres to frustrate strict methodological consistency. The hostile criticism generated by these texts is, of course, a significant unifying principle, and, given the preoccupation of each text with vital Victorian concerns, it may be said of Martineau that her work is paradoxically most subversive where it is also most representative of the Victorian age.[5] It is also important to recognize that, notwithstanding the range of her interests, certain issues preoccupied Martineau and recur in different works throughout her career. Her doubts about Christianity, for example, are incorporated into *Society in America*, *The Hour and the Man*, and *Eastern Life*, and culminate in the explicit atheism of *Letters on the Laws of Man's Nature and Development*. Developing concurrently with Martineau's evolving atheism is her interest in accepted and 'alternative' sciences, beginning with the *Illustrations of Political Economy* and advancing to a radical materialism informed by her Eastern researches and experiments in mesmerism and phrenology. An examination of Martineau's major works illuminates important debates in Victorian society; it also sheds light on the intellectual development of one of that society's eminent figures. Constant throughout Martineau's career was her unflagging optimism regarding necessary social change. She believed that she lived in an age of transition and that popular education was essential for social development. She regarded authorship as a social imperative and herself as duty-bound to declare her opinions to a mass audience: 'My business in life has been to think and learn, and to speak out with absolute freedom what I have thought and learned' (*HMA* 1:133). Most of her considered views relate to ameliorating the condition of marginal-ized social groups. Perhaps above all else, Martineau was an egali-tarian, and the texts considered here variously reflect her life-long opposition to all forms of social oppression based on sex, race, class, and creed.

Chapter One

Gendered Discourses
and a Sociology of Texts:
Illustrations of Political Economy (1832–4)

In February 1832, Harriet Martineau's life 'burst suddenly into summer' with the success of her *Illustrations of Political Economy* (1832–4), a collection of twenty-five tales published in monthly numbers, exemplifying the theories of Smith, Bentham, Ricardo, Malthus, McCulloch, and James Mill (*HMA* 1:180).[1] The stories aim to teach readers political economy by exhibiting its principles 'in their natural workings in selected passages of social life' and were inspired by Jane Marcet's *Conversations on Political Economy* (*HMA* 1:138).[2] Martineau believed that her series was 'craved by the popular mind,' and, indeed, the astonishing popularity of her tales suggests her proficiency with principles of supply and demand: 'The entire periodical press, daily, weekly, and, as soon as possible, monthly, [initially] came out in my favour; and I was overwhelmed with newspapers and letters, containing every sort of flattery' (*HMA* 1:160, 178). The success of the *Illustrations* established Martineau's fame and released her from all financial cares, but she was nonetheless aware of her work's inherent limitations. In an autobiographical memoir, published in the *Daily News* two days after her death, she writes of the *Illustrations* that, beyond initiating 'a multitude of minds' into the nature and significance of political economy, 'there is no merit of high order in the work. It did not pretend to offer discoveries, or new applications or elucidations of prior discoveries. It popularized, in a fresh form, some doctrines and many truths long before made public by others.'[3] To some feminist critics, Martineau's assessment of her *Illustrations* seems like traditionally feminine self-deprecation.[4] These critics also maintain that since the doctrines she illustrates are those of male theorists of political economy, the success of Martineau's work derives from her legitimization of the political ideas of men. In many respects, these views are compelling, but they are not historically comprehensive. By highlighting her 'feminine' self-deprecation, they pass over Martineau's general scepticism about human autonomy and authorial genius. By insisting on her appropriation of 'masculine' discourse, they underestimate the importance of 'feminine' discourse in her work. Because, in effect, these critics endorse the valorization of 'masculine' over 'feminine' rhetoric, they overlook the ways in which the *Illustrations* overturn this hierarchy or, when the reception of her work is considered, threaten to collapse it altogether. This chapter engages in the debate on the operations of discourses in the *Illustrations*. More especially, it focuses on the controversial status of particular numbers of the *Illustrations* for Martineau's readers. In addition to establishing Martineau as a significant literary figure, the *Illustrations* also established her reputation as a polemical writer.

To emphasize the historicity of a text is to consider the historical circumstances of its production, distribution, and reception – an appropriate emphasis for Martineau's *Illustrations*, perhaps, since she organized her tales to exemplify matters of production, distribution, and consumption.[5] The historicization of her tales also involves a shift away from a focus on the author as solitary genius – a Romantic conception of the author that differs fundamentally from Martineau's own understanding of authorship. Certainly in her own case, Martineau always rejected imputations of genius, insisting to her American friend Maria Chapman that 'I am pained and ashamed when anybody I care for talks of my possessing genius' (*HMA* 3:76). The fact that, for Chapman, Martineau's assessment of her work derived from 'her want of general self-esteem' rather than from her questioning of the notion of genius itself, suggests the ideological operation of Romantic conceptions of authorship in Martineau's culture, although, as we shall see, such conceptions did not reflect Martineau's own experience. (Chapman maintains: 'All the reviews of this period, hostile as well as friendly, took for granted the fact of her great genius. Unquestioned as it was by the world, by herself it was always steadily denied, not only at this time, but ever afterwards' [*HMA* 3:75].) That these conceptions still prevail is suggested by the agreement of recent critics with Chapman's position. For Linda Peterson, Martineau's claim that she had 'nothing approaching to genius' looks like 'conventional feminine behaviour.' Peterson aligns her view with Deirdre David's opinion that

Martineau displays 'conventionally feminine qualities of passivity and acquiescence' (Peterson 182; David 32).

Martineau's views on authorial genius were not, however, simply self-referential. On the contrary, although accepting Maria Chapman's definition of genius as 'that inspiration of great thoughts and great things which instantly distinguishes from the crowd and arrays inferiority against itself' (*HMA* 3:75), Martineau claimed never to have witnessed its manifestation. In an article entitled 'Literary Lionism' in the *London and Westminster Review* (April 1839), she notes a general absence of genius among her contemporaries. Whereas a monastic author might be regarded as 'holier or wiser than other people,' the class of 'literary lions' in her own society testified to the prevailing mediocrity of writers: 'If, at any one time, there is a *class* of persons to whom the public are grateful for intellectual excitement, how *médiocre* must be the quality of the intellectual production!'[6] Martineau does not, however, advocate cultivation of literature in monastic seclusion. Rather, she emphasizes 'the mischief' of artists' 'separation from others who live and think' (*HMA* 1:285). For Martineau, the artist must 'live as others live, in order to see and feel, and to sympathize in human thought' (*HMA* 1:286). The successful artist must be of his society, and if he 'deliberately believes that his thoughts are so far beyond his age, or his feelings so universal and so felicitously expressed as that he is even now addressing a remote posterity, no further proof of his ignorance and error is needed' (*HMA* 1:289–90).

Martineau recognized that few authors outlive their age, because they cannot express universal ideas but are inscribed in and informed by their historical situations. This recognition is consistent with her larger belief that all individuals lack autonomy, a belief which, however paradoxically, invokes presumed universal laws. Convinced herself of the truth of necessarian doctrine, of the determination of men and women by 'eternal and irreversible laws,' Martineau thought that the 'smallest amount of science' would convince anyone that 'the constitution and action of the human faculty of Will are determined by influences beyond the control of the possessor of the faculty' (*HMA* 1:110–11). Moreover, Martineau felt that this truth was the basis of all activity: 'All human action proceeds on the supposition that all the workings of the universe are governed by laws which cannot be broken by human will' (*HMA* 1:110).[7] For Martineau, this determinism was the 'mainspring' of her own work (*HMA* 1:111).

In her consideration of Martineau's feminist politics, Deirdre David suggests that Martineau's necessarianism implicitly subverts male power by 'welcoming dependence on certain laws which control the lives of both women *and* men.' Furthermore, it is this subversiveness that, for David, 'redeems her from an essentially uninteresting endorsement of dominant ideologies' (David 45). David's position requires further consideration. On the one hand, David suggests that Martineau's feminism is contained in her recognition that no one (men included) is free. On the other hand, it is because Martineau is not free that her work is 'essentially uninteresting.' David applauds Martineau for 'celebrating the dying of superstitious belief in self-originating power' and, at the same time, relegates her work to the status of 'auxiliary usefulness' to a patriarchal culture because she does not originate meaning (David 45, 31). A better understanding of the paradox of David's position results from seeing it as analogous to, or as part of, a larger conflict between feminism and 'new historicism.' One might suppose a stable relation to exist between these two critical positions, given their shared insistence that there is no transhistorical human nature, that human subjectivity is socially constructed along with gender differences, and that literature participates in this process of social construction, but some feminists criticize new historicism because it apparently fails to allow for change. Although feminists recognize that representations, writers, and readers are socially determined, some would like feminist writers to originate new subject positions in any historical moment. David regards Martineau as merely reiterating the patriarchal ideologies of her time, and for this reason she does not 'celebrate' her work 'for the sake of sentimental feminist convenience' (David 32):

> Martineau's career is primarily devoted to a kind of safe elaboration, repeating in its fully developed form the repetition of received text that she performed as a child when she recited Milton's poetry. Political theory replaces poetry, yet Martineau remains a dutiful intellectual daughter, repeating, in one way or another, the words of her intellectual fathers. (David 35)

Linda Peterson, in her study of Martineau as a 'sage writer,' seems to share David's views: 'Either women must embrace traditional forms of discourse, call them "public" or "masculine," or women must explore alternate "feminine" approaches and accept the possibility of exclusion from mainstream thought.' According to Peterson, Martineau consistently chooses the former approach, and although Peterson believes that this choice is empowering for her, she adds that it is difficult to justify Martineau's 'obsession with theory' (Peterson 180).

Both David and Peterson are interested in Martineau's relation to a male-dominated culture; accordingly, both focus on her use of 'masculine' discourse in the *Illustrations*, or rather on what is '*supposed* to be masculine,' as one of Martineau's reviewers in the *Tatler* put it.[8] In the eighteenth and nineteenth centuries, science and its theories were regarded as masculine domains, whereas literature and art were generally seen as 'feminine.' As David Simpson notes, 'the aftermath of the French Revolution saw in Britain both a reemphasis on the feminized identity of the literary and the aesthetic (of which the poetry of Keats would become a prime example) and a corresponding remasculinization of the vocabulary of theory and method.'[9] By defining Martineau's career in terms of her relation to the 'masculine,' however, critics enforce a hierarchy of gendered discourses: 'masculine' discourse becomes the standard which determines the status of Martineau's work. For David, Martineau's elaboration of the political and cultural beliefs of men results in her 'acquiescent labour' (David 31); for Peterson, Martineau's effectiveness as a 'sage writer' derives from her appropriation of 'masculine' language (Peterson 172). As was suggested at the outset of this chapter, however, these critics' concern with the 'masculine' eclipses Martineau's use of 'feminine' strategies and the inversion of gender hierarchy in her work. Their focus on gender also deflects attention from materialist considerations of class.

Martineau's competence using 'masculine' discourse undoubtedly contributed to her initiation into public literary life.[10] As Jerome McGann observes, the initiation of a text's authority 'takes place within the conventions and enabling limits that are accepted by the prevailing institutions of literary production.'[11] Communication cannot take place independently of social circumstances, which means that literary institutions share authority for literary production with authors. As a young woman facing poverty (following the collapse of her father's manufacturing business), there is no question that Martineau had to conform to prevailing conventions and limits in order to make money, and that, in the early 1830s, this meant using the discourse of the dominant sex and class.[12] But this alone is not sufficient to explain the extraordinary success of Martineau's volumes, whose circulation had reached ten thousand in England before Martineau returned in August 1836 from her visit to America (*HMA* 1:267). What enabled Martineau to enjoy an unprecedented success was a problem with the dominant discourse itself, that is, with the language of upper-class men.

The problem was that the theoretical language of male political economists seemed boring and obscure. As a writer for the *Spectator* remarked, catechisms of political economy had no charm and 'had cut a dry mass into still drier shreds.' As a result, the principles of political economy were not 'part of the ordinary information of a useful and respectable citizen.'[13] A gap existed between those who lectured on political economy at Oxford and everybody else, or between the upper and educated classes and the rest of society.[14] Martineau attempted to bridge this gap by making economic principles accessible to the common reader: because political economy had been 'mystified by the use, and as frequent abuse, of high-sounding scientific terms, such as superfecundity, law of population, geometrical and arithmetical ratios, inverse variation, and a hundred others,' as Poulett Scrope complained in the *Quarterly Review*,[15] she wrote stories to illustrate the meanings of these mystified terms. Martineau demystified upper-class, 'masculine' language, and she achieved this by introducing 'feminine' language to it. By publishing narratives that made economic principles comprehensible to the average reader, Martineau demonstrated that theory was deficient without narrative and, in the process, toppled the hierarchy of 'masculine' and 'feminine' language initially taken for granted by her contemporaries and by recent critics. Indeed, her retention of awkward-sounding economic jargon in the mouths of her characters testified to the awkwardness of 'masculine' discourse itself and was necessary for the demystification of this discourse and the instruction of her readers. As Christian Johnstone observed in his review of the *Illustrations* in *Tait's*, 'if it is of importance that all classes of society should become familiarized with such discussions, it is also of importance that they should be accustomed from the first to conduct them in precise and definite, that is, in technical language.'[16] The success of Martineau's narratory didacticism is suggested by a contemporary reviewer, William Empson:

> We have heard more political economy during the last three months, than we believe was ever before heard out of the Political Economy Club. It has flowed smoothly, too, from off the tongues of people so very unlikely to trouble themselves with such investigations, that [Martineau's] own ficti-tious personages, whether they be retired sergeants, or village sextons,

who speak as professors of the science, can now no longer appear to us a romance.[17]

Martineau's use of narrative clarified obscure language, facilitated her entry into literary life, and made her works immensely popular. In short, Martineau was empowered by her imposition of 'feminine' discourse on 'masculine' preserves and modes.

There was undoubtedly a need for demystified economic theory, and it is unlikely that the *Illustrations* would have been so widely distributed if they had not contained narrative. Initially, however, Martineau faced extraneous difficulties arising from a cholera epidemic and the Reform Bill of 1832 in finding a publisher for her works. Political conditions affected the sales of books, and the Reform Bill caused such a stagnation of the book trade that it became the subject of a pamphlet by 'Mercurius Rusticus' (Thomas Frognall Dibdin).[18] Martineau finally accepted unreasonable terms from Charles Fox, the brother of William Johnson Fox, who was Martineau's friend and the editor of the *Monthly Repository*. The work was to be published by subscription with Charles Fox receiving half the profits plus the usual bookseller's commission and privileges (*HMA* 1:167). Charles Fox's printer was William Clowes, who was the first to print cheap periodical literature, including the *Penny Magazine*.[19] With Clowes as her printer, the *Illustrations* were able to sell at the low price of 1s. 6d. per volume, but low costs were in themselves no guarantee of sales.[20] According to Charles Knight, the editor of the *Penny Magazine*, the public had a taste for works of amusement rather than instruction.[21] However, Martineau's mixture of instruction and narrative held irresistible appeal for the public and ensured her great success.

Despite the importance of fiction for Martineau, critics contend that she subordinates narrative to theory (Peterson 181; David 42). This is mostly owing to Martineau's inclusion of a 'Summary of Principles' with each story. For Peterson, these summaries mean that theoretical texts 'control and master Martineau's imaginative work' (Peterson 181). Her opinion invites consideration of Martineau's method of composition as described in her autobiography. Martineau began each tale by writing down her own ideas on the topic in question. She then read books on the topic, making notes and restraining herself from considering the scene and nature of her story 'till it should be suggested by [her] collective didactic materials' (*HMA* 1:194). She then wrote her 'Summary of Principles,' which she considered the hardest part of her work, by which time she perceived her story's scene. She embodied her principles in characters whose interaction supplied the story's action. On the third day, she outlined chapters, composed an extensive 'Table of Contents,' and then as to the 'actual writing – I did it as I write letters' (*HMA* 1:195).

The writing process Martineau describes here is clearly a highly mechanical one but does not necessarily entail the conclusion that theory mastered her fiction. It is important to notice, for instance, that Martineau offers competing accounts of her writing method and, at times, denies a necessary connection between her didactic materials and her story's scene, or even any connection at all. For example, her choice of scene for an anti-monopoly story, 'Cinnamon and Pearls,' had nothing to do with didactic materials or with a 'Summary of Principles': 'I feared an opium story might prove immoral, and I did not choose to be answerable for the fate of any Opium-eaters. Salt was too thirsty a subject for a July number. Cinnamon was fragrant, and pearls pretty and cool: and these, of course, led me to Ceylon for my scenery' (*HMA* 1:245). It seems that authorship could involve arbitrary decisions for Martineau, and, as a consequence, it may be more accurate to associate her writing process with her scepticism about genius rather than with any subordination of 'feminine' to 'masculine.' Once again, it may be that recent critics question Martineau's feminism because they fail to examine critically Romantic conceptions of the author. In the Romantic view, as exemplified by Shelley, literary production begins with a mystical moment in which the artist apprehends synthesises which he then seeks to express in language; in Ralph Waldo Emerson's view, the thought and the form emerge simultaneously. For both Shelley and Emerson, thought and form are necessarily connected. As Paul de Man asserts, there is 'an intimate unity between the image that rises up before the senses and the supersensory totality that the image suggests.'[22] This is a view of creativity that Martineau ridiculed. Owning that she has suffered from 'absence of "inspiration," and all that,' she claimed that by just sitting down with a pen in hand she could be in 'full train' in fifteen minutes. She was thus 'relieved, in a great measure, from those embarrassments and depressions which I see afflicting many an author who waits for a mood instead of summoning it, and is the sport, instead of the master, of his own impressions and ideas' (*HMA* 1:190). Martineau did not believe that forms and meanings were intimately or necessarily linked. That this view, which might align itself with some feminists' concerns with constructed meanings, institutions, and even human subjectivity, should instead be regarded as complicit with or subordinate to patriarchal culture is, perhaps, paradoxical.

At the time of their publication, Martineau's narratives were not at all regarded as subordinate to 'masculine' theory. William Empson suggested that Martineau's 'Summary of Principles,' instead of controlling and mastering her fiction, had merely a vestigial function: 'The political-economy moral is stitched on, and becomes the *purpureus pannus* of an apparently independent fable' (Empson 12). In fact, Empson considered Martineau's narratives so powerful that he feared readers would become enthralled by her fictions and miss the political economy in her tales altogether:

> The charm of the composition is so great, that the first welcome duty of a critic is to request their reader to be sure during the perusal to keep in mind that object [serious reading], in order that he may fully understand their value. Unless he puts a little moral restraint of this kind upon himself, the usefulness of the several stories may be injured by their beauty; and the importance of the end lost sight of in the agreeableness of the means employed for its attainment. (Empson 3–4)

Empson sees Martineau's Horatian end potentially thwarted by her Eve-like tendency to entice and misdirect the reader: 'The poetical nature of her fictions, the field which they open to a fertile imagination, the rapidity and fervour with which, at an exciting crisis, her spirit warms and rushes forward, expose her to much greater risks than those of purely didactic writers' (Empson 13).

Notwithstanding Empson's enthusiasm, it is worth noting that sales of the *Illustrations* went down after they were reviewed favourably in a Whig magazine. The opinion that Martineau wrote compelling narratives was, however, widespread. According to Maria Chapman, Martineau's stories were read only for their fiction in America, where, in Chapman's patriotic view, the lessons of political economy 'were not then so much needed' (*HMA* 3:67). In England, one reviewer for the *Tatler* anticipated that when the tales outlived their usefulness they would not be read the less, but rather the more 'for the sake of that fine vein of humanity and those graphic sketches of external nature and human life, with which they all more or less abound.'[23] Martineau's tales were seen to provide realistic pictures of humanity and, in particular, of the lower classes. In *The Other Nation*, Sheila Smith examines representations of the poor in a selection of novels of the 1840s and 1850s – works by Dickens, Disraeli, Gaskell, and others.[24] Smith argues that these novelists participated in the novel's development as a serious art form by representing the poor realistically to their readers. Although she excludes Martineau's *Illustrations* from her argument, the tales also contributed to the development Smith identifies.[25] Consider, for example, an opening scene from 'A Manchester Strike,' in which the hero of the tale, William Allen, follows his daughter, Martha, home from the factory where both are employed:

> He saw her before him for some distance, and observed how she limped, and how feebly she made her way along the street, (if such it might be called,) which led to their abode. It was far from easy walking to the strongest. There were heaps of rubbish, pools of muddy water, stones and brickbats lying about, and cabbage-leaves on which the unwary might slip, and bones over which pigs were grunting and curs snarling and fighting ... By this time they had reached the foot of the stairs which led up to their two rooms in the third story of a large dwelling which was occupied by many poor families. Barefooted children were scampering up and down these stairs at play; girls nursing babies sat at various elevations, and seemed in danger of being kicked down as often as a drunken man or an angry woman should pass; a thing which frequently happened.[26]

Such representations of poverty abound in the *Illustrations* and were praised by readers. One review of 'Homes Abroad' in the *Spectator* commended Martineau's 'intimate knowledge of the condition of the lower ranks of society,' and another asserted that 'Miss Martineau is the real painter of the poor: she has all the truth of Crabbe, with more hope and more reason.'[27] That Martineau's representations of the poor impressed her reviewers reflects both her role in directing the reader's attention to the lower classes and the importance of her narratives in the positive reception of the *Illustrations*.[28] Martineau's fictions were not considered subordinate to the principles of economics. On the contrary, as one contemporary reviewer of 'Cinnamon and Pearls' maintained, 'the science is subordinate to the story.'[29]

By emphasizing the importance of narrative in the *Illustrations*, I have suggested that Martineau's tales overturn the hierarchy of 'masculine'/'feminine' discourse. It may be the case, however, that her stories collapse this distinction altogether. In her consideration of

Martineau as a 'sage writer,' Peterson outlines three positions that feminists usually choose among in relation to women's writing: first, that writing is genderless; second, that women have a distinctive way of writing; and, third, that 'feminine' writing is any that expresses 'the disruption of authority' or 'the disruption of the rational.'[30] For Peterson, Martineau's practice is defined by the first position: her competence with theory demonstrates that rational discourse is not the prerogative of men. I should like to suggest that the *Illustrations* also conform to the third view of 'feminine' writing, that which expresses the disruption of authority and of the rational, and that it is her use of 'masculine' discourse which entails this classification. All individuals are culturally determined, as Martineau herself recognized, and her use of 'masculine' discourse was undoubtedly required by the limits and conventions of institutionalized literary production. At the same time, by using the political discourse of men (and thereby testifying to the illusory 'unity of any one "contained" text'),[31] Martineau's writing manifests contradictions within that discourse. Catherine Belsey's work is instructive here. According to Belsey, if one accepts that ideology is contradictory and that discourses are informed by ideology, then it follows that discourses will also be contradictory and that all literature, by participating in ideology, may be expected to reproduce its contradictions.[32] That Martineau's use of men's discourse participates in precisely such a disruption becomes evident when considering further the contemporary reception of her tales. According to Elaine Freedgood, classical political economy rationalized the often harsh effects of industrial capitalism, and the *Illustrations*, in particular, tranquillized readers like 'short-acting drugs': 'The intense but short-lived popularity of the *Illustrations* attests to their ability to provide helpful explanations [of social problems] and short-term consolations to a wide variety of readers' (Freedgood 36); but whatever consolation the *Illustrations* offered readers was undermined by the controversial status of particular stories. These stories reproduced contradictions and tensions in economic theories and vexed Martineau's readership.

Martineau's anti-slavery story, 'Demerara,' seems an obvious example of a text which exposes a contradiction in the political and economic ideas of men, by its demonstrating that man cannot hold property in man. Not only is it impossible for a man to own another man's reason, making slave labour less valuable than brute labour, Martineau argues, but 'property is held by conventional, not natural right. As the agreement to hold man in property never took place between the parties concerned, *i.e.*, is not conventional, Man has no right to hold Man in property.'[33] For some readers, these views threatened to destabilize the whole notion of private property. In his review, William Empson felt the need to uphold the legality of slavery while conceding its immorality – 'Under whatever formal sanction a property in man may be legally instituted, it can never stand on that original and continuous moral right, which sanctifies a property in things' (Empson 25). In another review, John Wilson Croker thrashed Martineau's subversive 'notion': 'Why, by this rule, *what* have we a right to hold in property?'[34] For Croker, Martineau's idea was 'as foolish as it is dangerous. Has Miss Martineau ever read Blackstone? or does she write works on the principles of legislation in total ignorance of all that has previously been said on the subject?' (Croker 140). Because Martineau exposed the false premise of the argument for slavery, she was seen to challenge the conventional arrangements behind one of her society's most important institutions.

'Demerara,' however, did not create the most furore amongst Martineau's readers. The sarcasm of Croker's remarks on her anti-slavery story is greatly exceeded by the violence of his response to her stories concerned with overpopulation: 'A *woman* who thinks child-bearing a *crime against society*! An *unmarried woman* who declaims against *marriage*!! A *young woman* who deprecates charity and a provision for the *poor*!!!' (Croker and Scrope 151). The stories in question are 'Weal and Woe in Garveloch,' 'Cousin Marshall,' 'A Manchester Strike,' and 'Ireland.' 'Ireland' looks at that country's economic difficulties as described in governmental 'Blue-books' (*HMA* 1:218). 'A Manchester Strike,' referred to above, was inspired by documents from Manchester operatives and illustrates the nature of wages and the operations of strikes. 'Cousin Marshall' portrays the evils of indiscriminate charity and derives its materials from 'a brother who was a Guardian, and from a lady who took an interest in workhouse management' (*HMA* 1:218).[35] 'Weal and Woe in Garveloch' continues the story of 'Ella of Garveloch,' which traces the origin and progress of rent on an island in the Hebrides described in Macculloch's *Highlands and Islands of Scotland* (*HMA* 1:197). In 'Weal and Woe in Garveloch' the island suffers from overpopulation. In textual terms, if not strictly compositional terms, all of these stories share a tendency towards collaborative status. They also share a recommendation to lower the population. 'A Manchester Strike' declares that the conditions of labourers may be best improved '*by adjusting the proportion of population to capital*'

(MS 136). 'Ireland' advises against the establishment of poor laws as promoting undesired growth in that country. Similarly, 'Cousin Marshall' argues against charity as a means of decreasing the number of indigents. In 'Weal and Woe in Garveloch,' a preventive check on population growth is urged and exemplified by the decision of two characters, Ronald and the widow Cuthbert, not to marry although they are in love and are financially solvent. It was his disgust with these ideas that led Croker to boast at a dinner party of his 'tomahawking Miss Martineau in the Quarterly' in an article which Martineau's printers, who also printed the *Quarterly,* described as 'the filthiest thing that had passed through the press for a quarter of a century' (*HMA* 1:205). Croker's attack was not, however, unique. Even in his largely favourable review, Empson was compelled to ask, 'If Ronald is not to marry, who is? Are the burden and drudgery of population to be thrown on the thoughtless only? Are the charms of domestic life to be given by preference to those who will feel them least?' (Empson 27). More vicious was a review of 'Cousin Marshall' in *Fraser's Magazine*: 'What a frightful delusion is this, called, by its admirers, Political Economy, which can lead a young lady to put forth a book like this! – a book written by a *woman* against the *poor* – a book written by a *young woman* against *marriage!*'[36] Like Croker, this reviewer sought to destroy Martineau by associating her with sexual vice. If the reviewer was indeed William Maginn (as suggested by the *Wellesley Index*), he took a different line of attack in *Fraser's* 'Gallery of Literary Characters.' Supplying an unflattering plate depicting Martineau with a somewhat sexualized cat perched on her buttocks and stretching up to her neck, he offered to 'assist' the reader with

> the delineation of her countenance, figure, posture, and occupation, which will be found on the opposite plate. He [the reader] will readily agree with us, after proper inspection, that it is no great wonder that the lady should be pro-Malthusian; and that not even the Irish beau, suggested to her by a Tory songster, is likely to attempt the seduction of the fair philosopher from the doctrines of no-population.[37]

The viciousness of the attacks on Martineau and her population stories is explained by recognizing that these stories express an ideological contradiction capable of destabilizing an increasingly important element in nineteenth-century society. The domestic ideal was central to the division of the public and private spheres; it was the prize of the middle classes and the goal of the working man. By arguing for the postponement of marriage and for the necessity of 'the preventive check,' Malthus had challenged prevailing ideologies of the middle class, and by writing stories illustrating Malthus's arguments, Martineau participated in this challenge. On the one hand, the domestic ideal should be in everybody's reach. On the other, the population was reproducing itself beyond the means of subsistence. In short, attempts to achieve the 'ideal' of a marriage, a home, and a family were resulting in poverty, sickness, and death. Readers of Martineau's stories feared an attack on their society's organization, as Maginn's review of 'Cousin Marshall' makes clear: 'The cottage system, which Miss M. utterly condemns, does this [elevates people]. It gives hope and courage to the labourer; it places comfort and independence within his reach: he learns to respect himself; he wishes to have a wife and family worthy of his regard' (Maginn 408). Maginn feared that Martineau's proposals would abolish the working classes' incentive to work. Of course, it was not just the working classes who were threatened by the Malthusian scheme. Referring to the middle classes, John Ham asserted in 'The Prudential Check – Marriage or Celibacy' that 'for every male who postpones the period of marriage, a female is left nearly unemployed and often unprotected.'[38] Not all middle-class women, however, would be left unemployed by remaining single. As Ham also perceived, some would move into the public sphere in their search for an occupation and an independent income.

Naturally, these outcomes had to be prevented. People looked for other solutions to the population problem, notably through the importation of food by the repeal of the Corn Laws and through increased emigration. Martineau herself illustrated the advisability of these schemes in 'Sowers Not Reapers' and 'Homes Abroad,' but she also continued to stress the importance of voluntarily limiting the population, as in one of her last stories, 'The Farrers of Budge Row.' For others, who did not support 'the preventive check,' importation, emigration, and technological advancement were the only means of dealing with the perceived population crisis. As the review in the *Quarterly* observes, 'the preventive check' is Martineau's 'primary topic of instruction,' while her '*secondary* remedies' (emigration and comprehensive national improvements) 'we have always advocated as the primary, the true, and the only modes of putting an end to the misery and turbulence of the poor natives' (Croker 147). It is likely that this opinion was not originally Croker's but Poulett Scrope's, who collaborated with Croker by providing economic theory to supplement Croker's abuse. Certainly these are views Scrope puts forward in an earlier article in the *Quarterly*, 'Malthus and Sadler: Population and Emigration.' Objecting to the 'misery and extreme want' which, according to Malthus, 'is, in the long run, the natural and necessary condition of human existence,' Scrope stresses 'the *local* pressure' against food supplies. Whereas Malthus considered emigration a merely temporary expedient, Scrope emphasizes the adequacy of emigration coupled with mechanical improvements to carry men into the foreseeable future. To check the population's increase 'lest, at the end of centuries, subsistence should run short for mankind, and Eternal Wisdom be at last found wanting' amounts, in Scrope's eyes, to 'presumption, combined with folly' (Scrope 108).[39]

It is, perhaps, Martineau's tendency to look centuries ahead that constitutes her most powerful disruption of the status quo. In *The Order of Things*, Michel Foucault describes three consequences of the modern focus on labour as the origin of all value, which he identifies in Ricardo's works.[40] The first consequence is the emergence of a linear series of production, which replaces a circular causality based on exchange and introduces the historicity of economics. The second consequence is a displacement of represented needs by what Foucault calls 'an anthropology of natural finitude' (*OT* 258). Labour originates in the land's scarcity. When land can no longer spontaneously supply the means of subsistence for growing numbers, people apply labour to the land and clear new lands to evade death. The third consequence is the possibility of conceiving the immobilization of history. Ricardo argues that the 'rent of land' indicates the 'avarice' of the land rather than its fruitfulness – an idea illustrated in Martineau's 'Ella of Garveloch.' As population increases, less fertile land is cultivated, requiring increased production costs, which is to say, increased labour. Inevitably, the quantity of labour will outstrip the quantity of food it produces, at which point excess population, or excess labour, dies. In Foucauldian terms, 'history will have led man's finitude to that boundary-point at which it will appear at last in its pure form; it will have no more margin permitting it to escape from itself, it will have no more effort to make to provide a future for itself, and no new lands to open up for future men' (*OT* 260); or, as in the terms of Poulett Scrope, 'Eternal Wisdom [will] be at last found wanting.' Like the theories of Ricardo and Malthus, Martineau's stories made it possible to imagine the impossibility of limitless history. By insisting on the necessity of 'the preventive check,' Martineau suggested to her readers that emigration and the cultivation of new soils could not be permanent solutions to the population problem. By illustrating the discourse of male economic theorists, she not only advocated a disruption of the patriarchal status quo by advising against the domestic ideal, she also intimated a disruption of masculine rationality by gesturing to the moment when history would 'do nothing but stop, quiver for an instant upon its axis, and immobilize itself forever' (*OT* 259). In fact, as she concedes in her autobiography, the repeal of the Corn Laws, agricultural improvements, and improved emigration eased the overpopulation problem significantly (*HMA* 1:210). Notwithstanding, Martineau compels the reader of her stories to look forward to the stasis of history. It is, perhaps, not surprising that readers like Croker wanted 'to tomahawk' her.

Historical consideration of the *Illustrations* indicates that Martineau's stories did not simply endorse patriarchal ideologies and that she herself was not solely empowered by her appropriation of 'masculine' discourses. Although her tales articulated the political ideas of men, it was her use of narrative that made these ideas accessible to readers and that precipitated the series' extensive circulation. At the same time, by clarifying the political and cultural ideas of men, she exposed tensions and contradictions within those ideas capable of disrupting the fabric of her society. Reception of the *Illustrations* by Martineau's contemporaries was very different from their reception by recent feminist critics. For David, the *Illustrations* perform a textual service to a male-dominated culture. Yet for that culture, Martineau's texts were subversive. Martineau's own experience illustrated that subversiveness could mean fame, and this was a lesson she would continue to exemplify throughout her career. When Martineau had completed the *Illustrations of Political Economy*, she crossed the Atlantic to assess the theory and practice of society in America, and her published conclusions confirmed her status as a popularizer of controversy.

Chapter Two

The Linguistic Structure of American Society

In 1834, having completed her *Illustrations of Political Economy,* Harriet Martineau boarded a sailing packet in Liverpool and headed to New York. She spent the next two years travelling through America, armed with letters of introduction to prominent Americans, spending time in New York, Baltimore, Washington, Boston, Charleston, and New Orleans. She attended weddings and orations, visited prisons and factories, stayed at Southern plantations, and witnessed slave auctions. Having achieved fame with her *Illustrations,* she was 'Lafayetted.' Wherever she went, doors were opened, and she was abundantly provided with information. She dined with President Jackson and stayed with the Madisons at Montpelier, Virginia. Throughout her travels she took notes, and although she had declared before and during her journey that she did not intend to write a book, few were surprised when *Society in America* and *Retrospect of Western Travel* were published in 1837 and 1838 respectively. The content of *Society in America,* however, startled many readers and outraged many more. When *Society in America* is situated in its cultural milieux on both sides of the Atlantic and considered in relation to other English 'travel books' on America, the disturbing nature of its content for its first readers becomes readily apparent.

'There is but one method by which most nations can express the general mind: by their literature. Popular books are the ideas of the people put into language by an individual. To a self-governing people there are two methods open: legislation is the expression of the popular mind, as well as literature.'[1] For Martineau, national literature is sufficiently informed by a country's beliefs and morals to be the same as national speech. However, at the time of her two-year journey in America, from 1834 to 1836, she did not think that Americans yet had a literature of their own: 'If the American nation be judged of by its literature, it may be pronounced to have no mind at all.' As a consequence, she turned to America's Constitution and, in particular, to the principles spelled out in the Declaration of Independence, to find an expression of the nation's prevalent concerns: 'If the national mind of America be judged of by its legislation, it is of a very high order' (*SA* 3:206). A consideration of American legislation gave rise to what she thought was an 'indisputable' way of judging the country (*SA* 1:viii). By comparing the existing state of American society with its professedly founding principles, she avoided arbitrary standards and the prejudices inherent in a comparison of a foreign country and 'home.' In certain areas, Martineau found that the theory and practice of American society coincided, but in others, constitutional ideals were clearly deferred. An examination of legislation rather than literature revealed, nonetheless, that American society was characterized by what we might now call the 'linguistic structure.' Gaps were apparent between America's founding principles and the social realities those principles were supposed to represent. The widest gaps were evident in the status of women and slaves.

Twentieth-century critics may be surprised by Martineau's apparent disdain for early nineteenth-century American literature. Certainly her contemporary American critics were shocked by her belief that there was no national literary 'utterance,'[2] leading her reviewer in the *American Quarterly Review*, for example, to speculate that Washington Irving had 'chanced to affront the lady.'[3] For Martineau, Irving had shed 'some gentle, benignant, and beguiling influences' on people's lives but seemed unlikely to achieve anything more. When she turned away from literature to a consideration of legislation, however, it is evident that Martineau believed American literature and legislation to be related, or at least metaphorically connected:

I regard the American people as a great embryo poet: now moody, now wild, but bringing out results of absolute good sense: restless and wayward in action, but with deep peace at his heart: exulting that he has caught the true aspect of things past, and at the depth of futurity which lies before him, wherein to create something so magnificent as the world has scarcely begun to dream of. There is the strongest hope of a nation that is capable of being possessed with an idea; and this kind of posses-

sion has been the peculiarity of the Americans from the first day of their
national existence till now. (*SA* 1:39)

The idea which possesses America is that of self-government, and the
rationale of this government, as stated in the Declaration of Independence, is 'that all men are created equal; that they are endowed by their
Creator with certain inalienable rights; that among them are life, liberty, and the pursuit of happiness; that to secure those rights, governments are instituted among men, deriving their just powers from the
consent of the governed' (quoted in *SA* 1:4). These are also the principles by which Martineau judges American society.

In many respects, Martineau found that American society measured
up to its founding standards. She was pleased with American manners[4] and felt that the 'striking effect' of observing for the first time
absence of poverty, gross ignorance, servility, and insolence could not
be exaggerated (*SA* 1:27). In these views, she distanced herself from
previous travellers to America and, in particular, from Fanny Trollope,
who not only had to bear the insolence of being continually referred to
as 'old woman,' but generally found American manners intolerable.[5]
For Trollope, who went to America as a Whig and returned a Tory, the
greatest difference between England and America was 'want of refinement' (*DMA* 33).[6] It is not strange, Trollope concluded, 'that those who
have lived in the repose of order, and felt secure that their country
could go on very well, and its business proceed without their bawling
and squalling, scratching and scrambling to help it, should bless the
gods that they are not republicans' (*DMA* 304–5). In contrast, Martineau delighted in the absence of the 'aristocratic insolence' that characterized England: 'Nothing in American civilisation struck me so
forcibly and so pleasurably as the invariable respect paid to man, as
man. Nothing since my return to England has given me so much pain
as the contrast there' (*SA* 3:27).

Although American egalitarianism pleased Martineau, the absence
of clearly defined class differentiations contributed, in her opinion,
to individuals' status anxiety and to a tendency to social conformity
that most writers on America were also quick to discern. Alexis de
Toqueville, whose *Democracy in America* was published in 1836, during
Martineau's travels, claimed that no country suffered from so little
freedom of thought and expression as America.[7] For Francis Grund,
'the continual fears and apprehensions in which even the "most
enlightened citizens" of the United States seem to live with regard to

their next neighbours, lest their actions be condemned by their fellow creatures,' were contemptible.[8] Martineau too felt that America was characterized by a 'worship of Opinion,' which she saw as superseding worship of wealth, and she located the origin of this evil in reliance on human opinion as the only grounds of distinction, or 'honour,' in a society defined by an absence of class hierarchies (SA 3:10). Seymour Martin Lipset describes this phenomenon as 'status anarchy': achievement and status are conferred only by others' esteem when individuals are urged to compete but without defined reference points to mark their success.[9]

Martineau believed that this reliance on others' good opinion showed itself in ostentation, in fear of imputation of poverty, in fear of imputation of cowardice, and in fear of vengeance, the last of which apparently caused newspapers to preserve an editorial silence on matters of personal and public outrage rather than face retaliation from offended parties. There was also 'an almost insane dread of responsibility' that made individuals unwilling to depart from majority opinion (SA 1:160). Martineau maintained that this unwillingness led, in turn, to political apathy, and in this view she flatly contradicted representations of Americans by earlier travel writers, especially Fanny Trollope. Trollope was greatly irritated by 'the election fever which is constantly raging through the land. Had America every attraction under heaven that nature and social enjoyment can offer, this electioneering madness would make me fly it in disgust. It engrosses every conversation, it irritates every temper, it substitutes party spirit for personal esteem; and, in fact, vitiates the whole system of society' (DMA 186). In contrast, Martineau perceived not only indifference or political scepticism among citizens but, worse, that some were actually afraid to vote. Although citizens voted by ballot, and could vote secretly, many did not avail themselves of this protection and were, as a consequence, afraid to demonstrate singularity. English reviewers of Society in America realized that Martineau, in drawing attention to political apathy, had undone a popular construction of Americans: 'This is the very opposite of our English ideas of the bawling, bustling, vociferous patriots of America, continually overwhelmed in politics.'[10] Martineau recognized this too: 'So far is it from being true that all Americans are the bustling politicians the English have been apt to suppose' (SA 1:158).

One stereotype that Martineau did not undermine was that of the 'tyrant majority' that reigned in America. Unrelenting oppression by the majority not only featured in de Toqueville's description of America, who claimed that '[in] America there is no security whatever against the tyranny of the majority,' but held a prominent place in the aspersions generally cast on democratic institutions by English Tories (*DA* 2:125). For example, John Wilson Croker, reviewing Dickens's *American Notes for General Circulation*, selected Dickens's account of censorship of public opinion to argue that '[we] see in [the Americans] the result of their political and municipal institutions – the fruits, in short, of a *despot-democracy*, which we believe to be essentially hostile to the advance of civilisation.'[11] Archibald Alison also cited the multiple abuses of the 'tyrant majority' when demonstrating the failure of all democratic governments 'in all nations and ages of the world.'[12] However, although Martineau recognized the power of the majority in America and, furthermore, embraced the idea that 'the majority is always right,' she was nevertheless able to identify a process by which civilization could advance and by which change could occur within that society. The view that 'the majority is always right' seems to be necessarily true for Martineau. Because the majority wills a particular measure, that measure becomes law and is therefore right, although this does not mean that the majority always wills the best measures. It may happen that the majority wills unwisely with respect to some belief or course of action on the basis of incomplete or mistaken knowledge. Martineau claims that when this happens, 'the people learn, and act upon their learning,' thereby ultimately willing the best. 'The case proves only that out of ignorance come knowledge, conviction, and action,' she contends, and this belief enables her to accept the possibility of social change (*SA* 1:32). Of course, this theory also assumes that the majority will be represented by the best men, which Martineau believed was often far from the case. Candidates who could best flatter their hearers and best prostitute 'moral sentiment' were most likely to get elected (*SA* 1:134). For her reviewer in the *North American Review*, this opinion was 'the unkindest cut of all'; even Montesquieu, who thought that republicans might not choose the best measures, had at least supposed they might excel in choosing the best representatives.[13] Given the bitter responses of Martineau's American reviewers, her belief in Americans' indifference to foreign criticism is ironic: 'the generality of Americans seem to see clearly enough that it is yet truer with regard to nations than individuals that, though it is very pleasant to have the favourable opinion of one's neighbours, yet, if one is good and happy within oneself, the rest does not much matter' (*SA* 3:26).[14]

If Americans were offended by Martineau's opinions on contemporary politics and politicians, they were generally gratified by her views of many social institutions. In particular, Martineau found that the regulation of prisons and the treatment of criminals in America coincided precisely with constitutional ideals: 'In the treatment of the guilty, America is beyond the rest of the world, exactly in proportion to the superiority of her political principles' (SA 3:181). Martineau was especially pleased with the treatment of prisoners in the Philadelphia penitentiary, where the principle of punishment was seclusion from other inmates. Prisoners here felt they were treated 'with respect,' which struck Martineau as signalling due attention to human rights. For this reason, and because prisoners had a good chance in society following their discharge, Martineau thought that the solitary system with labour was the best method of punishment that had yet been tried. Moreover, with regular visits from friendly (non-criminal) visitors, she felt that the moral health of criminals could be more or less completely restored (SA 3:182-4). Martineau did not think that the same could be said of inmates subject to the silent system in the Auburn prison at New York, where criminals were prohibited from speech. Talking, she maintained, was an innocent and necessary act, and it was impossible to expect reformation from persons forced to be silent. Moreover, Martineau greatly objected to the panopticism used to preserve silence: the spying, the 'loop-holes to peep through, and the moccasins which are made to make the tread of the spies as stealthy as that of a cat' were all deeply insulting (SA 3:186).[15] Later, when Dickens visited America and found it intensely disappointing compared with his high expectations, formed in part by Society in America, he took care to define his opinions of the solitary and silent systems in opposition to Martineau. In his chapter entitled 'Philadelphia and Its Solitary Prison,' he remonstrated against the solitary system as 'cruel and wrong': 'I hold this slow and daily tampering with the mysteries of the brain, to be immeasurably worse than any torture of the body' (AN 146-7). For Dickens, the silent system at Auburn was immeasurably better.[16]

Martineau maintained that the solitary system surpassed not only the silent system, but also the 'herding' in older prisons 'copied from those of Europe,' a claim that calls attention to debates concerning penal reform in England at the time of Martineau's travels. The 'herding' of which she speaks characterized many English prisons, where men and women were placed together without regulated conduct, and often without sufficient food and clothes. The Third Report of Inspectors of Prisons (1838) describes typical conditions in a Borough Compter:

> The association of the untried with the convicted, the facilities for occasional conversation with the sexes ... the exaction of 'chummage,' the number and almost constant presence of visitors, many of whom are persons of the worst character, the encouragement to drunkenness, by the unlimited quantity of beer permitted to be consumed by convicted as well as untried prisoners, the constant desecration of the Sabbath, the absence of any separate accommodation for the sick, and the want of an apartment for the decent performance of divine worship; these are among the more prominent features of a prison, which is exceedingly discreditable to the court under whose jurisdiction it is placed.[17]

Such conditions inspired experiments with the solitary and silent systems in England, whose respective merits were much in dispute. Some thought the silent system provided a welcome check to base communications; others objected to the complicated machinery necessary to maintain silence (DeMorgan 175–6). All agreed that labour was essential for prisoners' health – a consensus consistent with work-ethic ideology and middle-class individualism. However, some feared that with labour, food, clothes, and hygiene, prisons would not inspire sufficient dread to deter crime, and argued that until new systems could be perfected, capital punishments would be indispensable.[18] This was a view that Basil Hall held and that Martineau staunchly opposed. In her *How to Observe Morals and Manners*, written for Charles Knight while on her way to America, Martineau argued that capital punishment was inconsistent with prevailing ideological norms. Newgate could not be understood as the 'expressed decision of the English people' regarding the treatment of criminals:

> Its existence is to be interpreted, not as a token of the cruelty and prolifigacy of the mind of society, but of its ignorance of the case, or of its bigoted adherence to ancient methods, or of its apathy in regard to improvements to which there is no peremptory call of self-interest. Any one of these is enough, Heaven knows, for any society to have to answer for; enough to yield, by contrast, surpassing honour to the philanthropy which has pulled down the pillory, and is labouring to supersede the hangman, and to convert every prison in the civilised world into an hospital for the cure of moral disease.[19]

For Martineau, capital punishment was inconsistent with society's professed concern for the individual.[20]

If Americans were gratified by Martineau's view of their prisons, they could also applaud her commendations of their institutions for the deaf, mute, and blind. Martineau's own hearing had been impaired since adolescence, obliging her to carry an ear-trumpet, and she thought well of the Pennsylvania Institution and the New York Institution, founded in 1821 and 1818 respectively, where deaf pupils were occupied with school exercises and other labours, such as needlework. Consistent with her view on the reformation of criminals, Martineau believed that employments for the impaired were of incalculable importance, although she doubted whether the best means had yet been discovered for reaching the minds of the deaf and mute. The education of the blind was more cheering. Martineau expressed great satisfaction with the New England Institution for the Education of the Blind, directed by Samuel Gridley Howe, but was interested more in the Philadelphia Asylum for the Blind, which was then flourishing. At both institutions, cultivation of the individual's mind was the chief object. What Martineau objected to was an unfounded view of the impaired as a 'favoured class, gifted with a keener apprehension, a more subtile reason, and a purer spirituality than others.'[21] This was a tendency to which Dickens inclined when describing Laura Bridgman, a blind, deaf, and mute pupil at the Perkins Institution for the Blind in Boston (formerly the New England Institution for the Education of the Blind), and again, differing from Martineau, Dickens applauded the Perkins Institute and the Massachusetts Asylum for the Blind above all others.[22]

Although Martineau felt that democratic principles and social practices were consistent in some social institutions, she was profoundly disturbed by what she considered a fundamental violation of democratic principles: the status of women in American society. For Martineau, 'the condition of that half of society over which the other half has power' is the test of civilization, and examining American civilization by this standard, she found that it fell short not only of its democratic principles, but also of conditions in some parts of the Old World (*SA* 3:105). Fanny Trollope had commented on the 'seven-fold shield of habitual insignificance' which guarded American women, but Martineau phrased the point in more explicit terms: 'While woman's intellect is confined, her morals crushed, her health ruined, her weakness encouraged, and her strength punished, she is told that her lot is cast in the paradise of women' (*DMA* 48; *SA* 3:106). With respect to women's intellect, Martineau perceived that the education of women in America was essentially the same as in England.[23] A woman learned just enough to divert her harmlessly and to make her minimally companionable to her husband. Margaret Fuller later remonstrated against the view that women were to be educated *'for men,'* to make them better wives and mothers.[24] Women's having the power of intellect, she argued, was sufficient justification for its full cultivation. Martineau perceived, however, that women's scanty education was perfectly 'natural,' since they were barred from pursuits for which men were prepared (*SA* 3:108). The sole purpose of women's education was to teach them that marriage was their only object in life.[25]

The subject of separate spheres for the sexes preoccupied Martineau. Trollope and Dickens both acknowledged the great courtesy paid to women in the United States, but Martineau was alone in recognizing the full effects of this 'chivalry': 'One consequence, mournful and injurious, of the "chivalrous" taste and temper of a country with regard to its women is that it is difficult, where it is not impossible, for women to earn their bread. Where it is a boast that women do not labour, the encouragement and rewards of labour are not provided. It is so in America' (*SA* 3:147). As she would do at various times throughout her career, Martineau catalogued those few jobs available to women. Teaching, needlework, and the running of hotels and boarding houses she considered more traditional women's employments, while printing and compositorial work, work in mills, folding, and stitching were open to them since the advent of factories.[26] She also alluded to hazards connected with these employments: the philanthropist would do well to examine the physical ailments of seamstresses and the mental illness of governesses. Fuller would later cite such hazards when arguing for women's participation in politics: those who considered the female constitution as a deterrent to political activity did not think it 'impossible for the negresses to endure field work, even during pregnancy, or the sempstresses to go through their killing labours' (*WNC* 24).

As it was, women heard speeches 'about wives and home' and apostrophes to 'woman.' Indeed, a woman's 'husband's hair stands on end at the idea of her working,' and, for Martineau, the consequence was not only the crushing of her intellect, but also the destruction of her morals. Deprived of most careers, women were prevented from learning and embracing the principles and laws of duty. In short, a woman was like a slave: 'Her case differs from that of the slave, as to the principle, just so far as this; that the indulgence is large and universal, instead of petty and capricious' (*SA* 3:106). And, of course, those women who broke their shackles to step into public and moral domains were severely castigated. Certainly this was true for American female abolitionists, such as Angelina Grimké, who, having allied herself with radical abolitionism in 1835, was condemned two years later for her unbiblical interference in public reforms both in Catherine E. Beecher's *An Essay on Slavery and Abolitionism with Reference to the Duty of American Females Addressed to Miss A.E. Grimké* and in a Pastoral Letter by the Congregational Ministers of Massachusetts.[27] It was also true for Martineau. She was attacked in American periodicals, such as the *American Quarterly Review*, for her speech to the Boston Ladies' Anti-Slavery Society in 1835, which showed a commitment to principles that could destroy the Union,[28] and she was attacked by reviewers on both sides of the Atlantic for her advocacy of sexual equality, which was no less unbiblical than Grimké's public activities. The *American Quarterly Review* assailed her for 'frustrating the designs of an all-wise Legislator, who so strongly drew the line between the pursuits and occupations of the two sexes.'[29] *Fraser's Magazine* scorned 'her individual self as a crowning example of the equality of the sexes' and her egalitarian principles.[30] 'Marriage could not exist if the parties concerned in it were on an absolute equality,' the reviewer argues, explaining that

> it was in the knowledge of this fact in the nature of the human species, that the Omniscient Creator, instead of calling at once into existence two beings of equal strength, and of like faculties, began by forming one man in his own image, and then drew from that man another being, to be a help meet for him – endowing her with feelings and passions unknown to his sterner nature, which should make her dependent upon him for happiness ...[31]

The Omniscient Creator 'shackled the independence of [woman's] intellect,' to fit her for 'honorable' household affairs.[32]

For Martineau, it was not only women who suffered from the division of spheres. Because a man did not want his wife to work, he toiled 'to indulge her with money' (*SA* 3:106). As a consequence, not even American merchants, who might be supposed to be happy, were so. Instead, 'they are shackled, careworn, and weary as the slave' (*SA* 3:46). Martineau describes a day in the life of a merchant, one that easily represents a day for any middle-class citizen, to suggest his toil and unhappiness:

> ... these gentlemen rise early, snatch their breakfasts, hurry off two or
> three miles to their counting-houses, bustle about in the heat and the dust,
> noise and traffic of Pearl Street all the long summer's day, and come home
> in the evening, almost too wearied to eat or speak; while their wives, for
> whose sake they have been thus toiling after riches, have had the whole
> day to water their flowers, read the last English novel, visit their acquain-
> tance, and amuse themselves at the milliner's; paying, perhaps, 100 dol-
> lars for the newest Paris bonnet. (*SA* 3:46–7)

If women were satisfied with these conditions, it indicated only their
degradation, but it was more likely that both women and men were
'restless and dissatisfied' with this way of life. Furthermore, the middle classes were not alone in this dissatisfaction. The mechanic and
farming classes were also unhappy with a system that required them
to spend most of their waking hours providing for their external
wants, and Martineau believed that 'they would most thankfully agree
to work in their vocation for the community for a short portion of
every day, on condition of being spared all future anxiety about their
physical necessities' (*SA* 3:49). Here, modifying her earlier commitment to laissez-faire economics in the *Illustrations of Political Economy*,
Martineau espouses socialist theory.[33] Confirming Godwin's belief in
the importance of leisure for the individual, she declares that 'there is
no way of securing perfect social liberty on democratic principles but
by community of property' and maintains that although it would take
a long time to effect such a reform in England, because of the intricacy
of English property-right protection, it could be more speedily accomplished in America, where democratic principles were more conducive
to change (*SA* 3:39, 50). Not surprisingly, these views were not well
received in either America or England. The *North American Review*
hoped the experiment would be confined to England; *Fraser's* dismissed her argument as 'beyond the range of mortal pedantry.'[34]

Valerie Pichanick has observed that Martineau's altered view of
socialism was a concession to Owenism.[35] What should be added to
this observation is that Martineau's comparison of workers and slaves
may be aligned with specific arguments by factory reformers in
England. In particular, critics of industrialism had appropriated the
comparison of slaves and white 'free' labourers from pro-slavery writers who had used the analogy to point to the superior status of the
slave. In the hands of a pro-slaverite and social reformer like William
Cobbett, the identification exposed the hypocrisy of the English aboli-

tionist movement. When used by Robert Owen, it emphasized the need for centralized economics in place of free-market operations to liberate 'slaves of necessity.' In 1830, when Richard Oastler used the comparison in his *Leeds Mercury* letter, he began the Ten Hours Movement.[36] Martineau's description of the slavery of American workers, or their 'universal servitude to worldly anxiety,' participates in a rhetoric of freedom informed by the unstable relationship between abolitionism and industrial reform (*SA* 3:51). Moreover, by extending the analogy to encompass the merchant, 'weary as the slave,' she suggests another metaphor – one that identifies slavery and the middle class, galled by the separation of spheres. For men, this enslavement took the form of endless toil for money. For women, it meant the substitution of indulgence for justice:

> The truth is, that while there is much said about 'the sphere of woman,' two widely different notions are entertained of what is meant by the phrase. The narrow, and, to the ruling party, the most convenient notion is that sphere appointed by men, and bounded by their ideas of propriety; – a notion from which any and every woman may fairly dissent. The broad and true conception is of the sphere appointed by God, and bounded by the powers which he has bestowed. This commands the assent of man and woman; and only the question of powers remains to be proved. (*SA* 1:206)

Women had been unfairly 'caged' in one small corner of the universe (*SA* 2:340).

Martineau's distinction between an arbitrary, male-assigned 'sphere of woman' and a God-given sphere to which man and woman should assent, signals the main thrust of her argument regarding the status of women. It is a rights-based argument. In a chapter entitled 'Political Nonexistence of Women,' she compares women's condition to principles set out in the Declaration of Independence and finds a major discrepancy between democratic ideals and social reality. According to the Declaration, the just powers of governments derive from the consent of the governed, but since women did not have the opportunity to consent to governments' powers, it was unjust that they should be taxed, fined, imprisoned, and sometimes executed by those governments. Martineau acknowledges that in some states, as in New Jersey, women have acquiesced to having their voting rights stripped away, but, for Martineau, such cases only demonstrated these women's degradation. In acknowledging that women are sometimes responsible for their own injuries, she rejects the assumptions of those feminist discourses that invariably portray women as victims. Instead, she makes an unequivocal, personal declaration:

> I, for one, do not acquiesce. I declare that whatever obedience I yield to the laws of the society in which I live is a matter between, not the community and myself, but my judgement and my will. Any punishment inflicted on me for the breach of the laws, I should regard as so much gratuitous injury; for to those laws I have never, actually or virtually, assented. I know that there are women in England who agree with me in this – I know that there are women in America who agree with me in this. The plea of acquiescence is invalidated by us. (*SA* 1:204)

Following the same principles, she asserts that any legal protection that women enjoyed was to be regarded, not as tacit consent to all laws, but merely as a favour conferred on them by those in power. To the widespread argument that women's exercise of political duties would interfere with the discharge of their other, household duties, Martineau responds that women are best able to judge what their duties should be. She contends that 'God has given time and power for the discharge of all duties; and, if he had not, it would be for women to decide which they would take, and which they would leave' (*SA* 1:203). This argument, of course, also calls attention to the uncertain role played by God in the definition of human rights.

In 'Sex, Slavery and Rights in Mary Wollstonecraft's *Vindications*,' Jane Moore examines the status of rights arguments in *A Vindication of the Rights of Man* (1790) and *A Vindication of the Rights of Woman* (1792).[37] In neither of these texts does Wollstonecraft aim to problematize the principle of rights, but rather, particularly in *A Vindication of the Rights of Woman*, she hopes to add the individual and civil rights of women to the universal category. Wollstonecraft's belief in universal rights is inseparable from and relies upon her belief in God. God is the Transcendental Signified, or Logos, Who secures the connection between the prior concept, or logos (otherwise and usually a problematic hypostasis), and the signifier. In other words, God fixes all meanings and therefore 'the *truth* of rights' (Moore 22). With God in place as a guarantor of rights, Wollstonecraft can distinguish between inviolable rights originating with God and laws formed by political and individual interests: Edmund Burke's national rights, for example, are not necessarily the universal rights of mankind. The difficulty (as well as the advantage) in fixing the truth of rights in an extralinguistic Being is that such truths cannot be examined, but only repeated. This gives rise to 'citational knowledge' in Wollstonecraft – where sacred rights can only be asserted and not demonstrated – but it does enable her to evade the problem of the arbitrariness of rights produced in language, where rights become subject to the play of the signifier (Moore 27). This is a problem that Martineau confronts directly.

Martineau's interest in the arbitrariness of signification is evident in what may be fairly called her deconstruction of a passage from James Mill's 'Essay on Government': 'One thing is pretty clear; that all those individuals, whose interests are involved in those of other individuals, may be struck off without inconvenience ... In this light, women may be regarded, the interest of almost all of whom is involved, either in that of their fathers or in that of their husbands' (quoted in *SA* 1:202). Martineau points out that no two persons' interests can be, or be thought to be, identical according to democratic principles. Simultaneously, she focuses on the word 'almost' in Mill's second clause. This word unravels Mill's proposal since as long as there are women without fathers and husbands, 'his proposition remains an absurdity.' Moreover, as long as laws exist to protect women from fathers and husbands, their interests can never be said to be the same. Martineau recognizes that rights are informed by analyticity, not logical necessity: they depend on definitions of persons and contexts, rather than on logical truths. Furthermore, universal rights and laws formed by political and individual interests are not distinct, as they are for Wollstonecraft, but rather interanimating. Laws made to protect women should also rescue them from exclusion from the right to representation.

It is important to observe that Martineau's approach to linguistic problems surrounding rights and laws regarding the status of women exemplifies her general approach to controversial subjects, and, indeed, for Martineau the structure of general government in America was fraught with linguistic difficulty. The general objects of government had been stated, and the jurisdictions of federal and state powers had been 'drawn out upon paper,' but the application of the instrument was necessarily problematic. The problem resided in the signification of abstract concepts, which can never be transparent. Instead, Martineau perceived infinite room for 'varieties of construction' since no two men's abstractions are discoverably alike: 'Of course, the profession in this case is, that words are to be taken according to their just and natural import; that there is to be no straining; that they are to be judged of according to common sense; and so on. The old jests against etymologists are enough to prove how far men are from agreeing what straining is' (*SA* 1:47). According to Martineau, the only way to overcome these difficulties was through compromise. An example of the difficulties inherent in bridging the 'awful chasms of compromise,' and one which further reveals that Martineau's linguistic approach to women's rights is indicative of a more general methodology, can be found in her assessment of debates over 'internal improvements,' which she considered to be of the utmost importance in the United States. The first appropriation made by Congress for internal improvements occurred in 1802 under Jefferson's administration, when a law was passed making appropriations for road-works in the northwest territory. Improvements continued under Madison and received their first check by Monroe, who vetoed a levy toll for road-works as unconstitutional. Improvements continued under Adams, and were regarded inconsistently by Jackson.[38] To be brief, Martineau summed up the arguments of those for and against internal improvements. Those in favour saw Congress as constitutionally authorized by such clauses as those that permitted Congress to make post-roads, to regulate commerce between the states, and to provide for the general welfare of the country. Those against improvements argued that to read into these clauses an authorization for the expenditure of public funds for any object that the present government may proclaim to be for the general good 'is an obvious straining of the instrument' (*SA* 2:213). Recourse to the intentions of the framers of the Constitution was of no help since 'there is no evidence of its having occurred to any one, in the early days of the republic, to inquire whether the general government should have power to institute and carry on public works, all over the States' (*SA* 2:209). Martineau suggests that the only way to settle the matter is through language, by amending the Constitution, or by a multiplication of signifiers: '... the truly honest and patriotic mode of proceeding would be to add to the constitution by the means therein provided; instead of straining the instrument to accomplish an object which was not present to the minds of its framers' (*SA* 2:214).

Martineau's approach to problems surrounding internal improvements is consistent with her approach to the problem of women's rights. Like Wollstonecraft, Martineau hopes to add women's rights to the category of the universal rights of mankind, but she is less inclined to appeal to an extralinguistic Being as the origin and guarantor of these rights. Instead, in *Society in America*, we see the beginning of a metaphysical uncertainty that would later cause her to renounce Christianity. Martineau has no faith in 'the existence of this Pure Reason' and believes that 'if it did universally exist, ultimate principles could admit of no dispute' (*SA* 3:211). Since principles were very much in dispute, and since both rights and laws seemed determined not by God, but by interested parties, Martineau insists that a woman should 'represent her own interests' (*SA* 1:206). Her declaration that 'I, for one, do not acquiesce' is a recognition of the arbitrariness of rights and of the limited interests represented by rights at that time. It resembles Lacan's recognition that rights have no essential truth:

> What is called logic or law is never more than a body of rules that were laboriously drawn up at a moment of history duly certificated as to time and place, by agora or forum, church, even party. I shall expect nothing therefore of those rules except the good faith of the Other, and, as a last resort, will make use of them, if I think fit or if I am forced to, only to amuse bad faith.[39]

Like Lacan, Martineau perceives that rights have no fixed meaning, and she is willing to wage the battle for rights on linguistic ground, at the site where meanings and rights are determined. She not only deconstructs Mill, she contests Jefferson. Jefferson excludes from democratic deliberations:

1. Infants, until arrived at years of discretion;
2. Women, who, to prevent depravation of morals, and ambiguity of issue, could not mix promiscuously in the public meetings of men;
3. Slaves, from whom the unfortunate state of things with us takes away the rights of will and property.[40]

Martineau maintains that 'if the slave disqualification, here assigned, were shifted up under the head of Women, their case would be nearer the truth than as it now stands' (*SA* 1:201). She not only calls for the inclusion of women in democratic deliberations but recognizes the arbitrariness of reasons cited for their exclusion from those deliberations. Moreover, by perceiving that women are best defined by conditions relating to slaves, Martineau again suggests an analogy between the two groups. Her revision of Jefferson is precisely metaphorical. It is a carrying across of the clause on slaves to the category of women.

By using the metaphor of women and slaves, Martineau's discourse participates in a tradition of women's abolitionist rhetoric in England that began in the late seventeenth century, when women writers projected their anxieties about their own subordination onto their representations of slaves.[41] Women's dependence on men, their lack of education, and their lack of political representation caused them to refer obliquely to themselves as slaves throughout the period of colonial protest, making feminist agitation the logical entailment of abolitionism following the ratification of the Emancipation Bill in 1834. However, there were hazards associated with use of the metaphor. In particular, the description of various forms of oppression as kinds of 'slavery' detracted from the horrors of the institution of slavery itself.[42] Moreover, since women's displacement of anxieties about themselves was, for the most part, unconscious, they tended to regard the slave as different, or other, objectifying slaves as a totalized, homogeneous group.[43] A formula describing the voiceless slave, or the 'collective they,'[44] was used in anti-slavery poems by such writers as Maria and Harriet Falconer and Helen Maria Williams and continued even in the abolitionist efforts of radical women after the French Revolution, albeit to a lesser extent. Although writers such as Wollstonecraft and Mary Hays still relegated slaves to the status of 'other,' their rights-based arguments were informed by humanitarian principles that narrowed the gap between subjects and slaves.[45] These late eighteenth-century female radical polemicists also contested social and evangelical mandates that stressed women's commitment to the domestic sphere. Female abolitionists before the French Revolution advanced sentimental arguments for improved conditions for slaves and stressed the fracture of family life under the system of slavery. These women were also loathe to advocate slave rebellion and insisted on the importance of converting slaves both to Christianity and to a Christian way of life, in which women assumed a sacred role.[46] The public stance of polemicists after the French Revolution, who insisted on human equality, contested, but 'without an overt confrontation,' traditional beliefs about women's appropriate speech and behaviour (Ferguson 197).

Following the passage of the Emancipation Bill in 1833, the power that women abolitionists had enjoyed became diffused, and their activities decreased (Ferguson 273). As it turned out, this diminishing of energies was premature, since an apprenticeship system replaced slavery after the bill was passed, under which 'apprentices' were at least as badly treated as slaves had been under the previous system: not only did colonial legislatures take from 'apprentices' such allowances as had been conceded to them as slaves, such as food and clothing, while at the same time insuring that their workload was not diminished, they also enacted new laws increasing penalties and punishments of 'workers.' Moreover, they initiated a new Asiatic slavery, whereby Asiatics called 'Hill Coolies' were shipped to colonies like British Guyana from Bengal to compete for labour with emancipated blacks.[47] Notwithstanding these conditions, much abolitionist activity stopped after 1833. Martineau continued her efforts, however, by agitating against slavery in America, and her efforts differ from those of women abolitionists who preceded her, and which I have attempted to outline above, in a number of important ways: Martineau does not objectify slaves; she is willing to advocate rebellion; she does not believe in the conversion of slaves to Christianity; and she does not hold up a Christian way of life in which women assume a sacred role, but instead overtly confronts traditional beliefs about women's roles and behaviour, as has been already seen. Because Martineau remonstrates against the status of women, she does not encourage slaves' conversion to a religious ideology which also restricts women's roles. Finally, Martineau's use of the metaphor identifying women and slaves does not cause her to detract from the horrors of slavery or from the aims of abolitionism. Instead, Martineau unravels the metaphor at the same time that she evokes it. She identifies two separate systems of oppression that are alike, but independent.

Consistent with her arguments respecting the status of women, Martineau perceived the institution of slavery as being fundamentally inconsistent with democratic ideals. Slavery constituted another linguistic gap in American society, another gap between democratic principles and the social conditions those principles were supposed to represent. Again, like her arguments for women, her arguments for the slave are rights-based: the present population recoils at the idea of suffrage being given to slaves, yet 'this is what must be done' (SA 2:163). She argues that indulgence cannot atone for the injustice of withheld rights and that the 'restoration of two millions and a half of people to their human rights will be as great a deed as the history of the world will probably ever have to exhibit' (SA 2:170). Martineau also recognized that the problems surrounding the withheld rights of slaves were linguistic problems: whether Congress had the authority to abolish slavery in the District of Columbia was 'a disputed point of construction' that might well make statesmen 'uneasy about the stability of their work' (SA 1:52).[48]

Martineau's anti-slavery opinions were well known to Americans before her travels by means of her anti-slavery story, 'Demerara,' written as part of her *Illustrations of Political Economy.*[49] In this tale, she demonstrated that slavery is morally, socially, and economically indefensible. She also became increasingly convinced of the uselessness of the colonization scheme instituted by the American Colonization Society. The Society, established in 1817, had been supported by such key abolitionists as Garrison and Wilberforce, and Martineau had considered writing a tale about their efforts to transport emancipated slaves to Liberia. She abandoned the plan after receiving information about the program from Elliott Cresson, and by the time she arrived in America, she realized that the scheme was a complete failure. In twenty years, the Society had transported only two to three thousand people, while the annual increase of the slave population was estimated at sixty thousand, and the population of free blacks exceeded three hundred and sixty thousand (SA 2:110). Moreover, were it successful, the scheme would have depleted southern states of labour, which needed rather to be augmented by converting slave labour to free labour.[50] Martineau also became sensitive to the moral implications of removing blacks from the country that had become their home. Her hopes for a post-emancipation society, distinguished by social and economic integration, were undermined, however, by her awareness of racism: 'Mr. Madison told me, that if he could work a miracle, he knew what it should be. He would make all the blacks white; and then he could do away with slavery in twenty-four hours' (SA 2:153). Such, she perceived, was 'the hatred which is borne to an irremovable badge' (SA 2:154).

Moira Ferguson has explored Martineau's representations of self-determining and rebellious slaves in 'Demerara' but not in *Society in America.*[51] Here, Martineau adopts a strategy of portraying slaves that differs dramatically from the approach taken in her anti-slavery story. In the preface to 'Demerara,' she writes:

While endeavouring to preserve the characteristics of Negro minds and manners, I have not attempted to imitate the language of slaves. Their jargon would be intolerable to writer and readers, if carried through a volume. My personages, therefore, speak the English which would be natural to them, if they spoke what can be called English at all.[52]

In 'Demerara,' Martineau replaced the language of slaves with the discourse of the dominant culture. Our first indication that she takes a different view in *Society in America* occurs when she first sees a company of slaves travelling westwards. Asked where they were going, the company offers 'the answer commonly given by the slaves': 'Into Yellibama' (*SA* 1:291). Martineau emphasizes the gaiety of the group, and in suggesting the attractiveness of their appearance, she departs from a tendency to superimpose the features of whites onto blacks – a practice adopted by many anti-slavery writers to make blacks more appealing to white readers.[53] Martineau has observed the blank, unheeding look of the depressed slave, but this roadside group demonstrates that this look has nothing to do with 'negro nature; although no such proof is needed by those who have seen negroes in favourable circumstances, and know how pleasant an aspect those grotesque features may wear' (*SA* 1:292).

Instead of overwriting the language and manners of slaves, Martineau satirically points out that slaves often parody their masters' conventionalisms and that, as a consequence, slaveholders 'have before their eyes, in the manners of the coloured race, a perpetual caricature of their own follies' (*SA* 3:99). Not only did black footmen wear stiff cravats and perform 'eye-catching flourishes,' but slave women invited to balls wore satin, muslin, and white kid gloves, albeit faded and torn. Couples engaged in courtship rituals copied from the whites, and even their funeral customs imitated those of the dominant race; the epitaph of a black baby at Savannah, for example, begins 'Sweet blighted lily!' (*SA* 3:101).[54] Such imitation narrows the division between the masterly subject and the objectified slave. By copying the mannerisms of the white race, slaves resist being relegated to the status of 'other.' Rather than occupy the position of object, these slaves provide, in Martineau's opinion, 'a *mirror* of conventionalism from which they [the masters] can never escape' (*SA* 3:99; emphasis added). By reflecting the manners of whites, slaves invert the operations of objectification.

Unlike most women abolitionists before her, Martineau is willing to advocate slave resistance, and rebellion if need be. In portraying voiced slaves, she endorses those slaves' rebellious inclinations. For example, she reports a conversation between a Virginian gentleman and his head slave, referring to a massacre in Southampton in which over seventy whites were killed:

'You hear,' said he, 'that the negroes have risen in Southampton.'

'Yes, massa.'

'You hear that they have killed several families, and that they are coming this way.'

'Yes, massa.'

'You know that, if they come here, I shall have to depend upon you all to protect my family.'

The slave was silent.

'If I give you arms, you will protect me and my family, will you not?'

'No, massa.'

'Do you mean, that if the Southampton negroes come this way, you will join them?'

'Yes, massa.'

When he went out of the room, his master wept without restraint. (*SA* 2:149)

For Martineau, the moral of the story is '[the] more confidence in the man [that is, the slave], the less in the system' (*SA* 2:150). Martineau believes in 'the necessity of immediate action, either by resistance or flight,' and allies herself with those who resist unjust oppression (*SA* 2:147).

As is consistent with her opinions regarding resistance and rebellion, Martineau does not promote the conversion of slaves to Christianity. Rather, she believes that 'abject, unintelligent adoption of the devotional language of whites' is greatly inferior to their own spontaneous utterance. She notes the errors of instilling in slaves white notions of Christian spirituality whose hypocrisy the slaves easily detect, taunting their mistresses: '"You no holy. We be holy. You in no state o' salvation"' (*SA* 2:159). Religion, she argues, is 'worse than useless' to people with no rights and duties, and she believes that slaves are right to resist conversion to the dominant religion:

'Harry,' said his master, 'you do as badly as ever. You steal and tell lies. Don't you know you will be punished in hell?'

'Ah, massa, I been thinking 'bout that. I been thinking when Harry's head is in the ground, there'll be no more Harry, – no more Harry.'

'But the clergyman, and other people who know better than you, tell you that if you steal you will go to hell, and be punished there.'

'Been thinking 'bout that too. Gentlemen *be* wise, and so they tell us 'bout being punished, that we may not steal their things here: and then we go and find out afterwards how it is.' (*SA* 2:159)

Harry speaks with discursive determination, resisting inscription by the dominant religious discourse. Far from the nameless, voiceless slaves of earlier abolitionist writing, he insists on his identity, his agency, and his refusal to be constructed in his master's and the clergyman's terms. He will not locate his identity only in his soul and not in his body, or his 'head' – a distinction insisted on by patriarchal authority to command greater control over the latter. The consolation of a spiritual realm in which atonements are made for trials suffered on earth does not beguile Harry, nor is he afraid of the eternal punishments with which ministers frighten slaves into obeying their masters. Harry's resistance coincides with Martineau's own growing doubts about Christianity: 'There are no true religious sanctions of slavery. There will be no lack of Harrys to detect the forgeries put forth as such' (*SA* 2:160). She perceives that Christianity has been detached from principles of justice and liberty: '... it will have to be cast out as a rotten branch' (*SA* 3:233).[55]

Martineau's acceptance of bodily identity enables her to be more explicit about rape and sexual abuse of slaves than previous abolitionist writers, and she does not shrink from offering the details of stories about little girls who are raped, murdered, and then mutilated to conceal the violence done to them (*SA* 2:142–3). Similarly, she remonstrates against 'gentlemen who, by their own licentiousness, increase the number of slave children whom they sell in the market' (*SA* 2:155). Earlier abolitionists had also expressed concern about the violent treatment of slave women; however, evangelical sensibilities dictated that many atrocities be left unstated, and attention was largely focused on the flogging of female slaves. Of course, this itself was a landmark. Male abolitionists were unwilling to denounce flogging of either male or female slaves, but, for women, outrage at women's beatings and forced indecency involved a projection of fury 'against a male-oriented dispensation' (Ferguson 263). On the other hand, female abolitionists who drew attention to the flogging of scantily clad female slaves were also able to repress their own sexuality and to regard slave women as different.[56] Martineau obstructs this displacement. By describing the management of female slaves, who become mothers at fifteen to fill their masters' purses, she outlines a practice that makes the wife of a planter 'the chief slave of the harem' (*SA* 2:328). Martineau narrows the gap between a pitying subject and an abused, objectified other. The wife's and the slave's sexual degradation are the same. Amalgamation assists in closing this gap: planters' repeated abuse of slave women produced increasingly fairer-skinned children, and yet planters 'dare to raise the cry of "amalgamation" against the abolitionists' (*SA* 2:328–9). Quadroons are three-quarters white and mark two generations of miscegenation, and it was with these women that New Orleans white men had affairs, sometimes for life: 'Every Quadroon woman believes that her partner will prove an exception to the rule of desertion. Every white lady believes that her husband has been an exception to the rule of seduction' (*SA* 2:327). Martineau emphasizes the threat to domestic peace and security caused by these affairs. She recognizes that the domestic ideal is a strong weapon against both promiscuity and slavery, since slavery disrupts the marriages of both whites and slaves. Martineau was told that society in the South was '"always advancing towards orientalism,"' that is, towards a state of dependence on men by both black and white women, and that neither genius nor calamity could check its progress. Genius '"is too rare a circumstance ... and may heaven avert the last,"' one man declared. Martineau differs: 'O, may Heaven hasten it! would be the cry of many hearts, if these be indeed the conditions of woman's fulfilling the purposes of her being' (*SA* 2:340). Martineau is against 'orientalism,' as popularly conceived. She is against a harem of slaves with a wife as its chief. However, this does not mean that she desexualizes women or reopens a gap between blacks and whites. Martineau instead accepts the designation of 'amalgamationist' and supports interracial marriages.[57] Asked 'whether I would not prevent, if I could, the marriage of a white person with a person of colour ... I replied that I would never, under any circumstances, try to separate persons who really loved' (*RWT* 139–40). For Martineau, the body is the site where feminist and abolitionist agendas converge.

Martineau's anti-slavery arguments stand out among considerations of the subject by other English writers on America. Fanny Trollope, for example, scarcely treated the subject at all and could say that she was 'at [her] ease' in slave states. Moreover, she felt that slavery was 'far less injurious to the manners and morals of the people than the fallacious ideas of equality' (*DMA* 132). In contrast, Dickens devotes his penultimate chapter to the topic, but this chapter consists of lists of runaway slaves taken largely from a contemporary pamphlet entitled *American Slavery As It Is*.[58] Furthermore, some readers of *American Notes* were not convinced by his contention that slavery was responsible for all violence in America.[59] Certainly Martineau's is the more penetrating analysis, and yet it is noteworthy that most reviewers of *Society in America* paid very little attention to her slavery arguments. In both England and the northern states of America, this may have something to do with preaching to the converted, but it may also be the case that conservative English reviewers who were against slavery and who pointed to its existence in America as another indication of the failure of democracy, passed quickly over the evils of the system because Martineau had compared it with the condition of women. This comparison suggested that for English humanitarians who had already abolished slavery, improving women's status was the next logical step, and conservatives who were against this argument minimized its premise. Thus the reviewer for *Fraser's* devotes one small paragraph to the topic, regretting 'that our space will not permit us to give a lengthened summary of this part of the book,' while he spends several pages attacking Martineau's arguments for women's rights.[60]

The difference between Martineau's analysis of slavery and Trollope's and Dickens's approaches to the system points to overall differences between these authors' works. Trollope does not consider the workings of American political institutions at all. Instead, she offers this disclaimer:

> I am in no way competent to judge of the political institutions of America; and if I should occasionally make an observation on their effects, as they meet my superficial glance, they will be made in the spirit, and with the feeling of a woman, who is apt to tell what her first impressions may be, but unapt to reason back from effects to their causes ... but there are points of national peculiarity of which women may judge as ably as men, – all that constitutes the external of society may be fairly trusted to us. (*DMA* 32)

Trollope's stance is consistent with Elizabeth Eastlake's opinion that the 'charm' of a woman's travel writing is its 'very *purposelessness* resulting from the more desultory nature of her education.'[61] Trollope's overriding concern is to parade her acculturation before a comprehending English audience in order to recover a sense of her station, which had been unacknowledged in America, and, with this end in view, she punctuates her text with descriptions of sublime and picturesque vistas.[62]

Dickens had no need to parade his acculturation, and yet he was no less susceptible than Trollope to charges of superficiality. Dickens frustrated all of his reviewers with his too frequent descriptions of street life and low life: 'Surely, a little reflection might have taught him that a very different order of qualifications, natural and acquired, from those which enabled him to please the town with his monthly and weekly effusions touching Cockneys and the peculiar regions, physical and moral, in which they flourish, was required for the author of a work on the United States of America,' the reviewer for *Fraser's* complained.[63] Croker went so far as to provide a table breaking down Dickens's discussion of Boston into topics and the numbers of pages allotted to irrelevant items.[64] *American Notes* suggested *'purposelessness,'* but even Eastlake would have been dissatisfied: 'What is the use of plain Mrs. Anybody's getting into courts and harems, and scraping acquaintance with all sorts of illustrious strangers? They cannot tell us *who they are like!* or, if they do, it is somebody that nobody knows anything about' (Eastlake 121). Dickens was not Mrs Anybody, but his unwillingness to relate any information about the good society to which he had been admitted in America frustrated many of his readers.

Martineau's investigation of the theory and practice of American society set her work apart from that of other writers. Both Trollope and Dickens were seen to provide descriptions of American social life that only skimmed the surface of that society,[65] whereas hers is an early sociological text rather than a compilation of notes on manners. Another way of defining this difference is to see Martineau's text as the work of a traveller, rather than that of a tourist – a distinction that emerges in the nineteenth century, and one which James Buzard has thoroughly charted.[66] Martineau's study evidently participates in what Buzard refers to (without reference to Martineau) as the 'post-picturesque': the 'America' it describes is 'better able to cope with historicity, change, and the "everydayness" of social and political life' (Buzard 210). Subject to a range of interpretative strategies, travel writing, or sociological study, becomes the site of textualization for Martineau, who ultimately resists interpretative closure. Deferring a final analysis, she once again describes America in literary terms: 'American society itself constitutes but the first pages of a great book of events, into whose progress we can see but a little way; and that but dimly. It is too soon yet to theorise; much to soon to speak of conclusions even as to the present entire state of this great nation' (*SA* 3:297). After *Society in America* was completed, she turned her attention to less theoretical subjects. First, she published a more personal account of her visit to America in *Retrospect of Western Travel* (1838). Subsequently, she published a novel, *Deerbrook* (1839), which is considered in the next chapter.

Chapter Three

Realism and Feminism:

Deerbrook (1839)

Six weeks before Harriet Martineau began to write *Deerbrook*, she learned that John Murray was interested in publishing her novel. Since Murray had entertained no applications to publish a novel since Scott's, his willingness to publish hers appeared to her 'a remarkable fact' (*HMA* 2:114).[1] At the last moment, Murray withdrew his interest: friends of John Gibson Lockhart had disclosed that the novel's hero was an apothecary. Happily, others were not so cautious, and Edward Moxon published two large editions of *Deerbrook* without meeting the demand for it. If *Deerbrook*'s middle-class setting distressed many of its first readers, this focus, however, is the novel's chief attraction for some recent critics: 'It is here that the novel gains an interest beyond laboured imitation,' Deirdre David contends (David 80). Even so, the novel's middle-class characters, and especially its apothecary-hero, have received little critical attention, particularly in relation to historical events of the 1830s.[2] It is part of the purpose of this chapter to consider how Martineau's apothecary-hero both reflects and promotes the professionalization of medical practitioners. The chapter next proceeds to examine the function of clinical discourse in the novel, which is inherent in the novel's thematic content and complicates its promotion of clinical medicine. Finally, I indicate that *Deerbrook* is a feminist text, which other critics of the novel deny. In my view, *Deerbrook*'s feminist strategies derive from the operations and status of clinical discourse in the text and from the novel's disrupted realism and narrative authority.

Martineau chose to write about the middle class 'because it was my own, and the one that I understood best' (*HMA* 22:115). Inscribed in the middle class herself, she was able to provide convincing descriptions of middle-class life. Responding favourably to Martineau's choice of a setting, G.S. Venables argued in his review for *Blackwood's* that 'the lower station would not have admitted of sufficient refinement; and one which was much higher, would perhaps not have given so favourable an opportunity of introducing the domestic details in which she so peculiarly excels.'[3] In addition to introducing details of middle-class life, Martineau was well situated to transmit middle-class ideologies, beginning her novel with a picture of the ideal middle-class home as seen from the outside, from the perspective of a traveller on the stage-coach which had begun to run through Deerbrook:

> Every town-bred person who travels in a rich country region, knows what it is to see a neat white house planted in a pretty situation, – in a shrubbery, or commanding a sunny common, or nestling between two hills, – and to say to himself, as the carriage sweeps past its gate, 'I should like to live there,' – 'I could be very happy in that pretty place.' Transient visions pass before his mind's-eye of dewy summer mornings, when the shadows are long on the grass, and of bright autumn afternoons, when it would be luxury to saunter in the neighbouring lanes; and of frosty winter days, when the sun shines in over the laurustinus at the window, while the fire burns with a different light from that which it gives in the dull parlours of a city.[4]

The picture is a pastoral fantasy in which the peace of country living is contrasted with the city's 'dull parlours,' but it is also a surface description of the Greys' 'tempting white house' (Thomas 96; 1:2). Martineau begins her novel by proffering an external view of an idealized, domestic setting.

Hester and Margaret Ibbotson, two Dissenting sisters from Birmingham, arrive at the Greys (their cousins), and the plot unfolds. Edward Hope, the apothecary-hero, falls in love with Margaret but is himself loved by Hester. Mrs Grey persuades Hope to marry Hester on the grounds that he has paid her sufficient attention to require their union. Hope also knows that Margaret loves Philip Enderby, the brother of the novel's villain, Mrs Rowland. Mrs Rowland, bitter at Hope's affiliation with the Greys, frustrates Philip's and Margaret's union, and Margaret moves in with her sister and Hope after their marriage. In her *Autobiography*, Martineau indicates that she borrowed her plot from real life: a friend of the family had been compelled by a match-making lady to marry the sister of the woman he loved (*HMA* 22:113). In this respect, the novel's triangle conforms with Martineau's Aristotelian view that the best plots are 'taken bodily from life' (*HMA* 1:130) – a view which, for Deirdre David, signals Martineau's failure as a novelist. Consistent with her criticism of Martineau's *Illustrations of Political Economy*, David condemns Martineau for failing to be 'the sovereign authorizer of her own text' (David 76). Concerning the *Illustrations*, I have argued that Martineau's reproduction of received ideas results in a reproduction of the ideological contradictions underpinning those ideas.[5] In *Deerbrook*, Martineau's borrowed triangle allows her to proffer and withdraw the domestic ideal and, at the same time, to expose a discrepancy between the requirements of the public and the private spheres.

At the time the novel commences, Hope has been in Deerbrook for five years. He has managed to build a successful practice for himself, as Mrs Enderby makes clear: 'He was extremely busy, as everybody knew – had [*sic*] very large practice now; but he always contrived to find time for everything' (1:48). In keeping with Hope's achievements, it is desirable that he should marry. By mid-century, a wife was considered 'almost a necessary part of a physician's professional equipment' both because she represented status and because women could be hesitant about receiving medical attention from a bachelor.[6] It may be for this reason that Hope's marital prospects interest the villagers: 'If one could overhear the talk in every house along the village, I dare say some of it is about Mr. Hope winning one of these young ladies,' the governess, Maria Young, muses, adding: 'Every one wishes to see Mr. Hope married' (1:68). Driven to marry Hester, Hope becomes optimistic about his circumstances. He considers himself 'a perfectly happy man' and is bemused by the struggle he underwent to accept his present lot (1:266). Preparations of the conjugal home, or the 'corner-house,' are also described in ideal terms:

> On this table, and by this snug fireside, will the cheerful winter breakfast go forward, when each is about to enter on the gladsome business of the day; and that sofa will be drawn out, and those window-curtains will be closed, when the intellectual pleasures of the evening – the rewards of the laborious day – begin ... and the shaded parlour will be the cool retreat of the wearied husband, when he comes in to rest from his professional toils. (1:263)

The Hopes' home will be a haven from the trials of professional life.

Hester's 'blushing bashfulness' when she first plays the mistress before her husband completes what David calls a 'cloying' picture of domestic bliss (1:326–7; David 88).

The ideal is advanced, however, only to be taken away. Forced to acknowledge that he has indeed married the wrong sister and that his affection for Margaret is not of a brotherly kind, Hope perceives the corner-house as a bitter parody of the domestic dream it is supposed to fulfil: '"So this is home!" thought [Hope] as he surveyed the room, filled as it was with tokens of occupation, and appliances of domestic life.' For Hope, a gap exists between the signs of domesticity and the happiness those signs are meant to represent, suggesting both the iconographic construction and destruction of the idealized middle-class haven: 'At [his] own table, by [his] own hearth,' Hope is 'in bondage' every moment that he spends at home (2:63). In addition to 'tokens,' language is understood to construct the ideal: 'I like those words, Morris,' Margaret says to their servant; 'I like to hear you speak of your master and mistress, it has such a domestic sound! Does it not make one feel at home, Maria?' (1:295). The narrative recognizes that the domestic ideal is linguistically constituted. As Margaret concedes at a cowslip gathering, regarding a spider's web: 'I rather think ... the word "nest" itself has something to do with my liking for what I have been looking at' (1:78).

Problems in the corner-house are compounded by Hester's temperament. She is jealous of Margaret's friendship with Maria and worries about Hope when he visits distant patients. Wretched in domestic life herself, she earnestly counsels Margaret to avoid it altogether: '"You are kinder to me than I deserve," murmured Hester: "but, Margaret, mind what I say! never marry, Margaret! Never love, and never marry, Margaret!"' (2:55). What apparently allows Hester to surmount her wretchedness is the destruction of Hope's career. The public and the private spheres, which should be mutually enhancing, are set apart by opposed teleologies: the Hopes' home seems to be happy only when Hope's practice fails.

Hope's professional troubles begin with a controversial vote in the general election. He votes against the candidate supported by the local magistrate, Sir William Hunter, with severe consequences for his livelihood. For instance, Hope's almshouse practice is at stake – 'Lady Hunter had asked whether it was possible that Mr. Hope had forgotten under whose interest he held his appointment to attend the almshouses and the neighbouring hamlet' – and is eventually lost (2:36).

Furthermore, most of the villagers turn against Hope for defying the Hunters' will. It is because of repercussions like these that medical men in the nineteenth century tended to avoid voting in elections at all. In villages, where reports of unpopular behaviour were disseminated widely and quickly, a medical man's failure to conform to social norms put his practice at risk. Indeed, the same vulnerability to public opinion that made a medical man wary of voting in elections also made him careful about his personal appearance and manners (Peterson 128–9). That Hope is described as 'a great favourite' with everybody at the beginning of the novel is no surprise to Hester and Margaret when they see him: 'He was not handsome; but there was a gaiety of countenance and manner in him under which the very lamp seemed to burn brighter' (1:17). Hope is appraised by non-professional standards and was once told 'that I seemed to be half whistling as I walked up the street in the mornings; and that it was considered a practice too undignified for my profession' (1:333). The success of a man's practice had little to do with his medical knowledge or skill, reflecting widespread ignorance about medical science at the time.

That Hope's practice suffers from his vote for Mr Lowry is not merely a sign of the dependence of medical men on lay opinion; it also points to the larger problem concerning bribery and intimidation at elections, which increased significantly following the passing of the Reform Bill as a means of maintaining support for an anti-popular party. 'Wealth and influence are at their command, and the corrupt employment of these advantages is their only hope, and our only fear,' Arthur Buller wrote in 1836 when arguing for the secret ballot.[7] Buller wonders at 'the number of families ruined at the last election on account of obnoxious votes' and laments the divisions among friends and the sacrifices of integrity caused by the buying and selling of partisanship. Mrs Grey, whose husband promises Sir William to abstain from voting, echoes Buller's concerns when she asserts: 'I am sure, I wish there were no such things as elections – in country places, at least. They make nothing but mischief' (2:14). This mischief frequently included mob violence, in which dependent electors reacted to their invaded freedom by breaking panes of glass and heads. In Deerbrook, however, the mob attacks the Hopes instead of the Hunters as a result of rumours that circulate about Hope's medical investigations.

These rumours begin when Hope's surgery pupil sends a big toe in an envelope to a boy in the village, who opens the package at dinner: 'You may imagine the conjectures as to where it came from, and the revival of stories about robbing churchyards, and of prejudices about dissection,' Maria tells Margaret (2:149). Mrs Rowland, unable to forgive Hope for marrying into the Grey family (Mrs Rowland and Mrs Grey nourish a mutual antagonism), becomes involved in the gossip with 'dark hints' about what she has heard in the churchyard and has seen from her window at night – hints which feed the fear or ignorance of the people. The problem in distinguishing fear from ignorance is that the date of the action in Deerbrook is unspecified. The Anatomy Act (ensuring a sufficient availability of bodies for anatomical research) was passed in 1832.[8] Before this time, although the importance of pathological anatomy was stressed by such figures as Matthew Baillie, surgeons received only murderers' bodies for study.[9] Indeed, dissection was part of a murderer's sentence, making the surgeon identifiable with the hangman and anatomy with murder.[10] This created a general horror of anatomy among the public, but what was worse was that there were not enough murderers' bodies to go around. To supply this deficiency, 'Resurrection-men,' or 'Resurrectionists,' illegally exhumed bodies[11] and sold them for two to ten, or sometimes as much as sixteen, guineas.[12] That such prices could be an incentive to murder is exemplified by the famous case of Burke and Hare, who suffocated their victims, leaving no marks of internal or external injury. If the date of *Deerbrook*'s action is before the passing of the Anatomy Act, the villagers would experience a real fear of Hope after Mrs Rowland's rumour-mongering; if it takes place at a later date, then they are unaware that there is no longer a need for grave-robbing.

Whether they are legitimately afraid or ill-informed, the villagers would place Hope in a quandary. Prejudiced against dissection for whatever reasons, they nonetheless charge Hope with a lack of sufficient knowledge to practise effectively. Miss Nares, one of the village's milliners, tells Lady Hunter the story of Mrs Russell Taylor's nursemaid, who tripped over the string of a kite and broke her arm: 'The gentleman in the corner-house was sent for immediately, to set it. Now they say (you, my lady, know all about it, of course,) that there are two bones in that part of one's arm, below the elbow ... Well, my lady, all the story depends upon that. The gentleman in question did set the bones; but he set them across, you see' (2:257). Miss Nares's story conforms with a general tendency of the time to begrudge medical men the means of acquiring anatomical knowledge and then to threaten them with malpractice suits if they betrayed ignorance in their practice (Arnott 483).[13] The Russell Taylor's nursemaid (who, when beckoning the children, is now said to look as if she were shooing them away) is supposedly sent away to preserve Hope's reputation, but Maria, who breaks her leg, provides a new focus for anomalous and, in this case, demonstrably false charges: 'Do not you know the story they have got up about Miss Young's case. They say Mr. Hope set her limb so badly that he had to break it again twice' (3:42).

In the mob violence to which the villagers' prejudice against anatomy leads, the corner-house is ravaged, providing a tangible counterpart to the Hopes' emotional distance from the domestic ideal.[14] The surgery, 'being the place where the people expected to find the greatest number of dead bodies,' is plundered and its contents brought outdoors to fuel a bonfire greater than 'the famous one at the last election but one' (2:261–2, 295). An effigy of Hope is made and fitted with a knife and a phial from Hope's surgery. After being 'sufficiently insulted,' it is to be thrown on the fire, a plan that identifies Hope with witchcraft and suggests the plural etymology of the term *pharmakos*, meaning healer, wizard, magician, and poisoner.[15] *Pharmakos* also means scapegoat, and there is a clear correspondence between the treatment of Hope's effigy and ancient rites to purge a city of evil.[16] Philip Enderby prevents the villagers from burning the effigy, however, by obtaining Hope's skeleton from the waiting-room, illuminating its eyes and ribs with candles, and bringing it outside to confront Hope's likeness. The people flee, including Sir William Hunter, who has been supervising the proceedings against the Hopes: 'There was something rather piteous in the tone of his appeal: – "I am Sir William Hunter! I am – I am Sir William Hunter!" The spectre disregarding even this information, there was nothing for the baronet to do but to gallop off – his groom for once in advance of him' (2:266–7). The people are frightened away by an instrument of anatomical study.

For modern critics such as Theodora Bosanquet, the catastrophes that befall the Hopes are 'beyond the limit of any moderately critical reader's belief,'[17] and even contemporary reviewers of *Deerbrook* found aspects of the mob's violence difficult to accept. In particular, G.S. Venables felt that the representation of Sir William as virtually a participant in the riot was excessive: 'If Sir William did not care for his duties, or fear the Lord Chancellor's interference with the next commission, he would at least see that proceedings so riotous were in a high degree disrespectful to himself' (Venables 184). That magistrates often participated in the intimidation of electors was, however, an acknowledged fact;[18] and that they were capable of rousing the people to acts of violence against persons suspected of exhuming bodies is made clear by Thomas Southwood Smith:

> ... aversion to this employment may be pardoned: dislike to the persons who engage in it is natural, but to regard them with detestation, to exult in their punishment, to determine for themselves its nature and measure, and to endeavour to assume the power of inflicting it with their own hands, is absurd. Magistrates have too often fostered the prejudices of the people, and afforded them the means of executing their vengeance on the objects of their aversion. (Southwood Smith 83)

The catastrophes that befall the Hopes seem exaggerated only when they are considered ahistorically.[19]

In addition to providing a focus for the villagers' wrath, Hope's anatomical practices also signal a development in the education of medical men in the early part of the nineteenth century. At the start of the century, medical men were commonly defined by their corporate affiliation. Hope is called an 'apothecary,' suggesting a connection with the Apothecaries' Society, which received its royal charter in 1617. Before this time, apothecaries were affiliated with the Grocers' Company of the City of London. Apothecaries kept a shop, compounded and dispensed drugs, and were taught by apprenticeship. As a consequence, they were regarded as tradesmen, yet apothecaries also performed minor surgical operations and in the early part of the eighteenth century obtained the legal right to prescribe drugs. With the Apothecaries' Act of 1815, which was vigorously opposed by the Royal College of Physicians, apothecaries were allowed to practise medicine; the Apothecaries' Society was also allowed to grant a licence (the LSA) required by all medical men who prescribed and dispensed drugs (Peterson 11, 17). Now entrusted with the power of accreditation, the Court of Examiners of the Apothecaries' Society extended courses of study and required candidates to complete a five-year term of apprenticeship and a two-year term of attendance at lectures and hospital practice.[20] In hospitals, apothecaries shared educational duties with physicians and surgeons, and it became recognized that the distinctions among medical men no longer signified in practice (MR 66). By the 1830s, it also became usual for holders of the LSA to obtain a Membership of the Royal College of Surgeons (the MRCS), creating a hybrid class of general practitioners that numbered between 12,000 and 14,000 in England in 1836 (MR 89).[21] Equipped with knowledge of anatomy, which was the prerogative of surgeons in the pre-industrial form of medical stratification, Hope is 'no ordinary case of a village apothecary' (1:52). He is one of the new GPs, representing the efforts of medical men to unite into a single identifiable group and to achieve professional status.[22]

With the attack on his house by the mob and the collapse of his practice, however, Hope's own efforts to secure professional status are not very successful. Compelled by financial necessity to dismiss their servants, the Hopes perform their own household chores: Hope shovels snow from his front steps, and Hester makes beds and toast, for example. In fact, the Hopes effectively lose their middle-class status. What was unacceptable to contemporary reviewers of *Deerbrook* was that the Hopes should enjoy this loss. As I suggested earlier in this chapter, the public and the private spheres are divided by opposed teleologies in the corner-house: the Hopes seem to be happy only when Hope's practice is in ruins. As Hester tells Mrs Grey during their trials: '... we were never so happy in our lives. This may seem rather perverse; but so it is' (3:36).[23] To the extent that happiness in the midst of professional failure and poverty constitutes a significant disruption of middle-class ideological norms, Hester's pronouncement may indeed seem perverse, and contemporary reviewers were eager to explain (away) the incongruity of the Hopes' position. For the reviewer of *Deerbrook* in the *Athenaeum*, the Hopes' happiness was a subject for outrage. 'It is above nature,' he asserts, that the Hopes 'should *welcome* such heavy trials – that, in the exultation of their own spirits, they should positively *enjoy* the household labour, entailed on them by the superstition of their enemies. Serenity and hopefulness may pilot the virtuous through dreary times; but they are exaggerated to a point, we fear, unexampled, if not unattainable.'[24] G.S. Venables shared this sense of an ideological disruption, and went so far in his review as to provide a table of the Hopes' assets and expenditures to prove that if their happiness was not exaggerated, then their poverty was.[25] Venables is surprised that Martineau, 'who understands public and private finance so well,' should embellish the Hopes' penury. If poverty is equated with happiness for Martineau, it may be recalled that the collapse of her father's manufacturing business enabled her to pursue and to enjoy a professional career. For Hester, on the other hand, exaggerated happiness accompanies a process of deindividuation, as I will show.

Poverty in *Deerbrook* does not only befall the Hopes; economic hardship is felt throughout the country as inflation follows upon scarcity.

For Deirdre David, this widespread hardship is another sign of Martineau's failure as a novelist: unlike Elizabeth Gaskell in *North and South* and Charlotte Brontë in *Shirley*, 'Martineau cannot develop an imaginative parallel between the financial difficulties of an individual family and of a nation' (David 81). That Martineau does not develop such a parallel is certainly true, but that does not seem to have been her aim. Instead, the hardship felt by the people, which finds its expression in increased poaching and the overturning of meat-carts, leads to the villagers' susceptibility to a fever epidemic, creating a market for Hope's skills and an opportunity for him to regain his professional reputation. That poverty and malnutrition increase the likelihood of contracting fever was a popular view well before 1839. John Thomson had claimed twenty years earlier that epidemic fever 'has always committed its chief ravages' at junctures of scarcity.[26] He considered that want of fuel and clothing were 'evils of first-rate magnitude,' and that when combined with filth they critically debilitated the poor: 'Can it be wondered at, then, that febrile contagion (which is seldom dormant in large cities) should spread widely in such a mass of apt materials, – or that, when fanned by the sigh of despair on the one hand, and of hunger on the other, it should be blown up into one of the most raging Epidemics that has appeared for many generations?' (Thomson 416–17). Thomson's views are shared by Hope, who thinks the fever is 'a very serious affair, happening as it does in the midst of a scarcity, when the poor are already depressed and sickly' (3:204). In fact, Hope thinks that a place more likely to produce an epidemic is hard to imagine, given 'the extreme poverty of most of the people, and their ignorance, which renders them unfit to take any rational care of themselves' (3:192).

The ignorance Hope alludes to refers to the villagers' faith in the conjurers, fortune-tellers, and quacks who invade Deerbrook to take advantage of the epidemic. The problem of unqualified practice was a serious one for general practitioners in the first half of the century, occupying a prominent place in the agitation for medical reform that began with the passage of the Apothecaries' Act in 1815 and continued until the passage of the Medical Act in 1858. Between 1840 and 1858, seventeen bills were introduced into Parliament aimed at reorganizing education and licensing in England, and in most of these bills the registration of medical men was a primary focus. A register of qualified practitioners was generally seen as desirable, but general practitioners objected to one that preserved hierarchical designation according to corporate affiliation, and corporations objected to one that represented uniformity (Peterson 30, 33).[27] Indeed, the Fellows of Colleges and the Freemen of the Apothecaries' Society were not greatly interested in the issue of qualified practice at all, since it had no immediate bearing on their own privileged concerns and interests: 'Our charters protect monopoly, not science,' Neil Arnott protested.[28] For Arnott, whose ire was provoked by the notorious success of St John Long, it was grievous that the people could estimate the professional credentials of clergymen and of lawyers, and be 'grossly ignorant' about the acquirements and claims of medical men.[29] It was also grievous that professed medical men, unlike lawyers and clergymen, could practise without credentials in the first place.[30] The problem, then, was two-fold: medical practitioners lacked the autonomy to regulate their supposed 'profession,' and the people did not recognize this 'profession' and turned instead to quacks. Quacks take advantage of a place 'where there are enough who are ignorant to make the speculation a good one,' Hope complains, and stalls are set up in the village to sell fumigating powders and pills that are 'an infallible remedy against the fever' (3:193–4, 206). To the extent that Hope's medical skills are seen as superior to rival treatments, *Deerbrook* illustrates the practitioners' struggle for recognition as competent, professional men.

Hope's efforts to cure fever conform with the directions medicine was taking in the nineteenth century. One of these directions involved a concern for public hygiene as a means of prevention.[31] Hope's immediate response on hearing of the fever is 'to consult about some means of cleansing and drying the worst of the houses in the village' (3:192). Therapeutic moderation was consistent with this concern for cleanliness, and fever cases in the village are treated with pragmatic ministrations. Under Hope's surveillance, Margaret nurses a sick family, the Platts, by sponging and drying their fevered limbs, by kindling a small fire, and by depositing their filthy linen outdoors to be cleaned. She also empties a charmed pail of water into a nearby ditch ('the fortune-teller had charmed the pail ... and had promised a new spell in the morning' [3:221]) and conveys 'pailful after pailful of the noisome shavings to the dunghill at the back of the cottage, wondering the while that the inhabitants of the dwelling were not all dead of the fever long ago' (3:223).

Such explicit descriptions of the treatment of fever patients bothered some of *Deerbrook*'s contemporary readers. For the reviewer of the novel in the *Edinburgh Review*, 'the needless obtrusion of the very disagreeable details of Margaret's visit of charity to the infected cottage of the Platts' was one of the novel's defects.[32] The narrative certainly provides a vivid account of the Platts' sickness. Consider the scene that confronts Margaret when she enters the cottage:

> [Mrs Platt] lay moaning on a bedstead spread with shavings only, and she had no covering whatever but a blanket worn into a large hole in the middle. The poor woman's long hair, unconfined by any cap, strayed about her bare and emaciated shoulders, and her shrunken hands picked at the blanket incessantly, everything appearing to her diseased vision covered with black spots. Never before had so squalid an object met Margaret's eyes. The husband sat by the empty grate, stooping and shrinking, and looking at the floor with an idiotic expression of countenance, as appeared through the handkerchief which was tied over his head. He was just sinking into the fever. His boy lay on a heap of rags in the corner, his head also tied up, but the handkerchief stiff with the black blood which was still oozing from his nose, ears, and mouth. (3:220–1)

What is presented to the reader is a case-historical description of the Platts in graphic detail. There is no iatromechanical or theoretical speculation concerning the movement of poison through the blood and no nosological classification of the fever according to the complex network of specifications that prevailed in the eighteenth century.[33] Instead, the fever has a general structure with localized symptoms – impaired vision, bleeding orifices (following F.J.V. Broussais's theory that all fevers begin with a single gastrointestinal irritation, the Platts seem to be suffering from gastroenteritis in its advanced stages: 'there is a reduction in strength, and a blunting of the intellectual powers ... the tongue becomes brown, and the mouth is coated with a blackish substance' [*BC* 190]). In short, what prevails in the passage is a relentless empiricism as the narrative describes with quantitative exactness the objects of Margaret's precise, surface gaze. In fact, what the reviewer in the *Edinburgh Review* objected to was an example of the novel's clinical discourse – a discourse which informs *Deerbrook*'s overall narrative.

So far I have been primarily concerned to relate Hope's status as village apothecary to historical events of the early 1800s. In this context, my purpose may be thought similar to George Levine's aim in *The Realistic Imagination* to show how scientific debates in Victorian society also occupied the attention of such writers as Mary Shelley and George Eliot. Levine's methodology has met with criticism, however, for its reliance on popularized discussions of nineteenth-century controversies. In his recent work, *Vital Signs: Medical Realism in Nineteenth-Century Fiction*, Lawrence Rothfield argues that an understanding of realism as 'rehearsing a popularized philosophy of science' is liable to epistemological inaccuracy (since, even if scientists are writing articles for *Blackwood's*, they may say different things in a popular forum from what they would say in a scientific arena).[34] For Rothfield, this problem is overcome by focusing on writers who deploy a specific scientific vocabulary in their texts or cite specific scientific authorities. For example, George Eliot's *Middlemarch* is ideal for Rothfield's scrutiny since Eliot explicitly refers to such figures as Xavier Bichat in her novel. Balzac and Flaubert, who also use specific vocabularies and cite specific figures, also make excellent subjects. In contrast, Martineau, who had deployed many specific authorities and vocabularies in *Illustrations of Political Economy* and *Society in America*, regarded the opportunity to write a novel as a freedom from such requirements, and since there are no references to historical figures in her novel, it seems reasonable to turn to a popular context for consideration.[35] Martineau is not attempting to make her readers accede to a specialized discourse in *Deerbrook*, as she did in her *Illustrations*. If the novel has an educative role, it is with respect to popular ideas.

Rothfield also believes that Levine's understanding of realism is limited in its scope, and this is an important question. Unlike Levine, Rothfield considers the ways in which a scientific discourse may inhabit a narrative. In other words, he considers how scientific discourse can 'help to shape such formal features as point of view, characterization, description, diegesis, or closure' (Rothfield xiii). Arguing that the history of ideas has provided no satisfactory contextual explanation for nineteenth-century critical realism (Lockean empiricism had provided one for eighteenth-century formal realism, which differs from critical realism in its naïve assumption that representations convey truth),[36] Rothfield suggests that this literature has, in fact, no such counterpart; whereas the emergence of the sciences as rivals to philosophy in the nineteenth century (which offers us limited rather than absolute knowledge) provides an appropriate focus for study of the century's realist novels. Medicine is especially conducive to this approach since it, like the realistic novel, is fundamentally concerned with issues of mimesis and knowledge (Rothfield 8–12). Medical discourse, or, more specifically, clinical discourse, is not only related to *Deerbrook's* thematic preoccupations but inhabits the novel's narrative and shapes its formal features. Martineau, whose family were traditionally physicians, had an enduring interest in clinical methodology and, particularly, in the relation of organic structure to what she termed 'Mental Philosophy.'[37] *Deerbrook* evidently reflects this interest.

The description of Margaret's visit to the Platts' cottage is, as I have suggested, only one example of the clinical discourse that informs the narrative as a whole. From the very beginning of the novel, in the surface description of the Greys' house as seen from a passing stage-coach, the text has been fundamentally concerned with the gaze. It has been engaged in a spatial proliferation of detail, as in the precise rendering of the Hopes' conjugal home. In fact, the entire plot of the novel, which revolves around the arrival of the Ibbotson sisters in Deerbrook and the series of events arising from it, may be termed 'anatomoclinical' in its structure, anatomically situating 'the *figures of localization*' in the Ibbotson sisters, and then clinically tracing 'the *structures of pathological kinship*' in their marriages and relations to the other villagers.[38] It is in the shaping of character, however, that the novel's clinical perspective may be most illuminating. Critics of *Deerbrook* consistently fault the novel's characterization. For David, Martineau's characters lack 'psychological complexity' and function 'more as psychological and moral emblems than as anything else: Hester stands for destructive jealousy, Margaret for noble renunciation, Edward for moral rectitude, Philip for dignified adherence to his own moral code. And Maria Young ... for sequestered detachment' (David 78). For Valerie Pichanick, 'the characters are not flesh and blood creatures but idealized creations ... unlike Brontë or Eliot who succeeded her, she was concerned less with character development than with character delineation' (Pichanick 119). Critics attribute the flatness of Martineau's characters to her limited ability as a novelist, but this 'fault' may also be a necessary effect of the novel's clinical perspective. Foucault maintains in *The Birth of the Clinic* that the clinical gaze 'establishes the individual in his irreducible quality' and that the '*object* of discourse may well be a *subject*.' For Foucault, whose work centres around the constitution of the individual at the end of the eighteenth century, the clinical gaze 'is no longer reductive' but rather heralds the 'accession to the individual.' It opens up 'the concrete individual, for the first time in history, to the language of rationality' (*BC* xiv). But while Foucault insists on the individual's new authority, now signalled by his identification with his own disease, he passes over the necessary objectification of the patient. The clinical gaze searching for signs of disease 'gives absolute epistemological privilege to the *surface gaze*' (*BC* 129). That is, it reduces its objects to surfaces, flattening them out for scrutiny, and also for control.[39] In a feminist reading of *Deerbrook*, the flattening of characters effected by the clinical/realist gaze is especially evident in Hope's use of this gaze to control female characters.

An example of this domination occurs early in the novel. The children are having a tea party for their cousins in the summer-house when it is interrupted by the arrival of Mrs Plumstead, the village scold. The description of 'the virago' is a documentation of madness: 'Her widow's cap was at the back of her head, her hair hanging from beneath it, wet in the rain: her black gown was splashed to the shoulders; her hands were clenched; her face was white as her apron; and her vociferations were dreadful to hear' (1:167). Mr Grey and Mr Rowland try to control the scold, but 'they could not make themselves heard,' and 'she shook her fists at them' (1:168). Mr Enderby fails as well. With Hope's arrival on the scene, however, 'the vixen's' mood changes:

> At the first glimpse of Mr. Hope, her voice sank from being a squall into some resemblance to human utterance. She pulled her cap forward, and a tinge of colour returned to her white lips. Mr. Enderby caught up little Mary and carried her to her mamma, crying bitterly. Mr. Hope might safely be left to finish his conquest of the otherwise unconquerable scold. He stood still till he could make himself heard, looking her full in the face; and it was not long before she would listen to his remonstrance ... (1:169)

This confrontation between Hope and Mrs Plumstead may be termed a clinical experience and can be characterized in terms that Foucault dismisses as 'simple' and 'unconceptualized' (*BC* xiv–xv). It is a confrontation that takes place prior to discourse, that is, rational discourse, or Hope's discourse. It is a confrontation between a gaze and a face – his look, her face. It is a transference of power from her to him. In short, it is a 'conquest,' and Hope 'had the satisfaction of seeing her lock herself into her house alone before he returned to his party.' The narrative's commentary on the action is provided by the response of one of the children: 'It remained to console little Mary, who was still crying, – more from grief for Mrs. Plumstead than from fear, Maria thought, though Mrs. Grey was profuse in assurances to the child that Mrs. Plumstead should not be allowed to frighten her any more' (1:170).

Hope's relation to Hester may also be seen as a conquest, or as a treatment of chronic pathology in a narrative of pathological organi-cism.[40] As stated at the outset of this chapter, Martineau proffers the domestic ideal in the Hopes' marriage only to withdraw it, and Hes-ter's temperament is one of two main problems that disturb relations in the corner-house (the other being Hope's unbrotherly affection for Margaret). I have also suggested that what seems to be Hester's exag-gerated happiness in poverty accompanies the process of her deindi-viduation. I shall now trace that process and Hope's role in it.[41]

The (anatomo)clinical gaze is fundamental to this process. It is a dia-critical gaze that, beginning at the surface, travels vertically from the symptomatic to the tissual, 'in depth, plunging from the manifest to the hidden' (*BC* 135).[42] The gaze lends itself to a translation into psy-chological terms: behaviour and the mind correspond to symptoms and tissues; or, as Rothfield puts it, a pathologically organic self has a conscious and 'rational' self 'able to give formal reasons for his or her actions,' and an impassioned self which might be thought of as 'a Freud-like unconscious' (Rothfield 106–7). In other words, the patho-logically organic character is a double entity. According to Rothfield in his discussion of *Middlemarch*, 'the vicissitudes of Lydgate, Rosamond, and Bulstrode result from their efforts to sustain a coherent image of a unified self, either by suppressing one of these two elements of their being, or by searching for an environment in which a psychic economy ... can be sustained' (Rothfield 107). However, the clinical gaze also involves a transfer of authority from the patient to the doctor, since doctors' expanding knowledge of anatomy renders a patient's account of his own illness extraneous. As Foucault describes it, the new struc-ture is indicated by the decisive change 'whereby the question: "What is the matter with you?", with which the eighteenth-century dialogue between doctor and patient began ... was replaced by that other ques-tion: "Where does it hurt?", in which we recognize the operation of the clinic and the principle of its entire discourse' (*BC* xviii). The clinical gaze, I would argue, requires the effacement by the doctor of the patient's rational, conscious self that is able to account for its own dis-ease or behaviour. In *Deerbrook*, Hope effaces Hester's rational self, flat-tening her out from a double into an apparently single entity subject to scrutiny and control.

Hope's obsession with surfaces is indicated when he first appears in the novel. It is one of Hope's oddities that 'he could never see a piece of paper before him without drawing on it' (1:18). Planning outdoor trips for Hester and Margaret, he draws the spring and the abbey ruin, and the children are disappointed that he has not drawn any faces: 'Are there no faces this time, Fanny? None anywhere? No funny faces this time! I like them the best of Mr. Hope's drawings.' By drawing faces, Hope reduces identities to surface representations. It is a means of securing authority over the object drawn – an authority of which Hope is possessive. When Sophia brings out her music books, which are covered with Hope's faces, she is reminded to put them away: '... you know if Mr. Hope is ever reminded of them, he will be sure to rub them out' (1:19).

It is the same obsession with surfaces that attracts Hope to Margaret. Unlike Hester, Margaret is not a pathologically organic character. She is not a double entity but rather a unified 'type,' lacking the introspective conscious self that explains personal behaviour.[43] It is Hester's beauty and Margaret's 'sincerity and unconsciousness' that strike Hope forcibly when he meets the sisters, and he looks 'at every object in and around the familiar place with the eyes of the strangers, speculating on how the whole would appear to them' (1:76). Writing to his brother Frank, it is again Margaret's lack of a conscious self that captivates Hope: 'She *is*, and there is an end of the matter. Such pure *existence*, without question, without introspection, without hesitation or consciousness, I never saw in any one above eight years old' (1:153). Margaret is a transparent object for Hope's clinical gaze. She is an open and uncomplicated character, and her narrative depends on what Rothfield calls 'physiognomic organicism': like the Garths' plot in *Middlemarch*, her plot involves 'entanglements, mysteries, and vicissitudes that are circumstantial rather than existential, so that time stabilizes rather than destroys or mutilates the self' (Rothfield 104–5). Margaret's separations from Philip Enderby are caused only by Mrs Rowland's lies, and only time is required to expose these falsehoods and to establish her union with Philip.

In contrast with Margaret, Hester suffers in Hope's opinion from 'too close a contemplation of the self,' as reviewers also recognized (1:155). According to Lister, Hester suffers from a 'diseased sensitiveness, which craves with an unhealthy appetite for undue demonstrations' (Lister 497); for Venables, she demonstrates 'the impossibility of a practical faith in the harmonious uniformity of feeling, which she has never realized in herself' (Venables 181). Hester is a pathological character, possessing a jealous temperament and a conscious, rational self capable of accounting for it. It is this second self that makes her ill-suited to Hope's clinical perspective. Instead of allowing Hope to distinguish the signs of her illness, she explains her symptoms herself, and although this may have worked well in an eighteenth-century medical context, it does not fit the nineteenth-century clinical framework that defines Hope. In Foucauldian terms, Hester answers the unasked question 'What is the matter with you?' when Hope only wants to know where it hurts – he wants simply to treat an infirm case 'as a matter of fact,' as he puts it himself (1:84). The assertion of Hester's rational self and Hope's inability or unwillingness to hear her is most evident on the eve of their wedding.[44] Hester's awareness of her own selfhood defines her response to Hope's question, 'There is something on our minds, Hester. Come, what is it?': 'Do not say "our minds,"' Hester insists (1:273). There is something 'that I cannot make you believe,' she tells Hope and begins to give an account of her 'sick heart,' but Hope interrupts her: 'Dismiss it – ' (1:275, 276). Hester, however, is anxious to be heard: '"Oh, hear me!" cried Hester, in great agitation.' She then advances her own case history: 'I vowed to devote myself to my father's happiness, when my mother died; I promised to place the most absolute confidence in him. I failed; I fancied miserable things. I fancied he loved Margaret better; and that I was not necessary to him; and I was too proud ...' (1:276). Hester is complicit, however, in the process of her deindividuation: '... you must cure me,' she entreats Hope (1: 278). Hope immediately starts reading the signs of her illness. He believes that it is 'the weakness of many' to worry about the future; 'I believe that it is yours,' he concludes (1:279).

Hope treats Hester, then, by generalizing her condition. He denies Hester her individuality, insisting that her problems are common ones. We see this again in a later encounter: 'My temper is not to be trusted,' she claims. 'Very few are,' he replies (2:53). Hope would see Hester precisely as a 'type,' or as a single case study of a widespread complaint, but Hester's rational self understands Hope's strategies: '"I understand you," said Hester. "I take the lesson home, I assure you. It is clear to me through your cautious phrase, – the 'we,' and 'all of us,' and 'ourselves.' But remember this, – that people are not made alike"' (2:54). By refuting his quantifying perspective, Hester thwarts Hope's clinical gaze, and Hope moves away from Hester, 'covering his face with his hands.' Hester goes to bed, and Hope tells Margaret that they 'must avoid bringing emotions to a point' (2:57). Margaret, who, as a physiognomically organic character thinks that there 'is something sickly' about self-analysis, sympathizes with Hope, and together they agree that Hester 'requires to be drawn out of herself ... and when it comes to acting, see how she will act!' (2:56, 58). Margaret and Hope agree that Hester needs to be diverted from introspection. Her conscious mind needs to focus on something other than her impassioned self. Only then will she stop offering accounts of her symptoms and be flattened out into a single entity to be read and controlled by the clinical gaze. Hester capitulates to this strategy in the following exchange. Outraged that Hope will not share his brother's letter with her, she denies him access to her inner self, blocking his anatomoclinical vision: 'breathe not upon my conscience – look not into my heart, – for what are they to you? I reclaim from you, as your servant, the power I gave you over my soul, when I supposed I was to be your wife' (2:216–17). Insisting on his new strategy, Hope diverts Hester by recalling her to the woes they are about to undergo with the failure of his practice: 'I see how your spirit rouses itself at the first sound of threatening from without. I knew it would.' '"Are you mocking me?" doubtfully whispered Hester. "No my love," her husband replied, looking calmly in her face' (2:218–19). Reminiscent of Hope's encounter with Mrs Plumstead, this is another confrontation between a gaze and a face. It is another of Hope's conquests. Hereafter, the signs of Hester's impassioned self are implied by the text's clinical perspective: 'Hester started, thereby showing that she was moved' (2:285). Her attempts at self-understanding are constantly silenced: she wonders why she is unworthy '"that such an one as Margaret should love me and my child." "Enough, enough. I only want to show you how I regard the case,"' Hope interjects (3:140). And the index of this slow process of her deindividuation and disarticulation is found in her response to Margaret's reminder that she once told Margaret never to marry: 'Is it possible that I said so? – and of all marriage?' (3:187).

At the end of the novel, the narrative claims that the Hopes live happily ever after. Margaret is aware that Hope 'had permanently established Hester in her highest moods of mind, strengthened her to overcome the one unhappy tendency from which she had suffered through the whole of her life, and dispersed all storms from the dwelling wherein his child was to grow up: but she did not know half the extent of his victory, or the delight of its rewards' (3:299). If this is true, and Hester's deindividuation produces a happy outcome, then the novel is indeed a disappointing one for feminists. In fact, it would be doubly disappointing, since Hester's jealousy has Margaret's friendship with Maria as its chief focus. Hester would herself like to have a primary emotional relationship with her sister, in accordance with a pact they made with each other when they first arrived in Deerbrook. That exchange begins with an intimate image: 'Hester called Margaret to her, put her arm around her waist, and kissed her again and again'; and ends with 'the vision of a friendship which should be unearthly in its depth and freedom' (1:23, 27). Most of Hester's jealousy springs from the frustration of this possibility. Reasons for doubting the narrative's closing statement derive, however, from a recognition of disruptions to the novel's clinical/realist perspective and, as a consequence, to the narrative authority that makes this final pronouncement.

There are two such disruptions that I think are significant. The first occurs when Philip Enderby charges Hope with a mutual attachment to Margaret. Hope adopts the role of the patient in a clinical setting – 'There must be entire silence upon the whole subject of himself' – assuming that there will be insufficient signs for Enderby to diagnose a truth 'which would become untruth by being first admitted now' (3:84). What Hope hears, however, is a vast quantity of evidence – a rehearsing of the novel's entire narrative, in fact – supporting Enderby's false belief:

> There seemed to be no circumstance connected with the sisters and their relation to Mr. Hope, that Mrs. Rowland had not laid hold of. Mrs. Grey's visit to Hope during his convalescence; his subsequent seclusion, and his depression when he reappeared – all these were noted ... [Enderby] now thought he must have been doomed to blindness not to have discerned the truth through all this. – Then there was his own intrusion during the interview which Hope had with Margaret; – their countenances had haunted him ever since. Hope's was full of constraint and anxiety; – he was telling his intentions: – Margaret's face was downcast, and her attitude motionless; she was hearing her doom. (3:87–8)

Enderby's retrospective clinical perspective recalls the signs of Hope's and Margaret's behaviour and diagnoses them incorrectly. The authority of the clinical gaze is undermined. The capacity of detailed description to function as a transparent window on reality is severely qualified.

The second disruption to the text's realism occurs when Margaret recovers a ring. The ring had been stolen by Mr Platt (dressed as a woman), who returns it when Margaret nurses his family.[45] The ring was given to Margaret by Philip, and Margaret interprets its return as an omen that she and Philip will reunite. Gillian Thomas has noted the 'melodrama in such episodes as the theft and restoration of the ring,' and the overdetermination of Philip's and Margaret's reunion may suggest a lack of available resolutions to physiognomically organic plots.[46] What also requires attention, however, is that the insistence on the supernatural significance of the ring's restoration points to a struggle between medical/realist discourse and supernaturalism for the power to determine what counts as truth.[47] In this struggle, not only is supernaturalism given the last word, but Hope loses the power of his clinical gaze:

> 'Dear Margaret!' said Hester. 'She is now drinking in the hue of that turquoise, and blessing it for being unchanged. She regards this recovery of it as a good omen, I see; and far be it from us to mock at such a superstition!' As usual, when she was upon this subject, Hester looked up into her husband's face: and as usual, when she spoke on this subject, he made no reply. (3:267)

In this confrontation between a gaze and a face, Hester's gaze searches Hope's face. Hope loses the authority of the gaze and becomes instead a silent body. In a second discussion of the ring, Hope recovers his anatomoclinical perspective. Hester asserts that Margaret 'carries a prophecy about her on her finger,' to which he responds, 'I should rather say she has carried a prophecy in her heart all these long months ... of which that on her finger is only the symbol.' Once again, however, Hester and supernaturalism are given the last word: 'There is no resisting a prophecy. What is written is written' (3:287). Once again, the authority of the clinical/realist perspective is qualified.[48]

If these disruptions to the authority of the clinical/realist perspective undermine the authority of the narrative voice, which is based on this perspective, then the closing statement about the Hopes' happiness resulting from Hester's deindividuation may be regarded with scepticism. It might be superfluous to add that, for Rothfield, the kind of psychic unity that Hester is said to have at the end of the narrative can be only temporary anyway, 'deferring inevitable strains' (Rothfield 108). However, a third plot in the novel may provide the strongest qualification of Hester's and Hope's supposed bliss. With the plot of Maria Young, the governess, Martineau multiplies her perspectives, providing a developmental alternative to the supression of Hester's rational self.

It is not an exaggeration to say that the problem of the governess has become a commonplace in Victorian studies. With the work of such critics as M. Jeanne Peterson and Mary Poovey, the difficulties and contradictions of the governess's situation have been carefully considered.[49] Moreover, Valerie Sanders has examined extensively Maria Young's role as governess in Martineau's novel. It is not my intention to rehearse these studies here. I will refer to these critics' main points, however, because although I sympathize with Sanders's assessment of Maria's 'archetypal qualities,' my own view of Maria's role in the novel differs from Sanders's view of her status.

Impoverished by the death of her once successful but finally insolvent father, Maria is one of a relatively small number of women compelled to work as governesses in the first half of the nineteenth century.[50] Very few jobs were considered appropriate for middle-class women at the time, and, in addition to teaching, dressmaking and millinery were by far the most common employments among them: as Maria teaches Margaret, 'the tutor, the tailor, and the hatter' are the middle-class woman's chief occupations (3:166).[51] Of these three, governessing was regarded as the most 'genteel' employment because of the proximity of the governess's work to the middle-class female norm. This proximity also created difficulties, however, and despite the small number of women working as private teachers, governesses received a disproportionate amount of attention by mid-century: 'Because the governess was like the middle-class mother in the work she performed, but like both a working-class woman and man in the wages she received, the very figure who theoretically should have defended the naturalness of separate spheres threatened to collapse the difference between them' (Poovey 127). The governess posed ideological problems, and these problems had their counterpart in emotional hardships. Because the governess was 'neither fish nor fowl' – neither a member of the family nor a domestic servant – nobody knew precisely how to act towards her. For instance, she might be invited to join a family event at one moment and required to work at the next. In short, the governess occupied a contradictory place in society and was therefore treated in conflicting ways (Peterson 12).

In keeping with her problematic position, Maria may be thought to exhibit the classic signs of the governess syndrome. Valerie Sanders notes that Maria regards herself early in the novel as 'a wise observer of other people's lives' and adds that 'it was natural enough for the governess to be an observer' (Sanders 61). To see Maria as simply a case study of a general problem, however, reduces her to a type, flattening out a character who may be more complex. It is worth qualifying Sanders's generalization by emphasizing that Maria's inactivity is the result in part of her lameness: watching the party of cowslip gatherers, 'the gazer' wonders 'whether I should have been with the party if I had not been lame' (1:63, 64). Sanders also notes that 'the governess-spectator is always drawn into the love-affairs of the other characters' and that Maria becomes Margaret's *confidante* without telling her anything about her own love for Philip (Sanders 61, 66). For Sanders, it is Maria's love for Philip that makes the novel disappointing for feminist readers. After the publication of her novel, in an article for *Once a Week*, Martineau attacked the Brontës for their representations of lovelorn governesses – '[Governesses] have no gratitude for the Brontës; and will have none for any self-constituted artist, or any champion, who raises a sensation at their expense, or a clamour on their behalf'[52] – but, for Sanders, these attacks came after she had written *Deerbrook* and were probably intended 'to compensate for her own preoccupation with the same problem' (Sanders 63). Love, Maria declares, 'is the grand influence of a woman's life,' and this is a position she appears to hold throughout the novel (1:303).

Maria's characterization is, however, more complicated than critics suggest. Unlike most, Maria is clearly a qualified governess. When we first see her, she has been reading Schiller's *Thirty Years' War* in German; it is later said that she would be called 'philosophical' if she were a man (1:37, 93). Maria has an impassioned self, but she also has a rational, conscious self that explains her behaviour, making her a double entity or complex character who does not undergo a pathological process of deindividuation. She is never forced to display a psychic unity and so is never subject to control by the clinical gaze. Instead, one of her last statements in the novel is an assertion of self and a blocking of Margaret's (and the reader's) anatomoclinical, reductionist perspective:

> Nay, Margaret, why these tears? For their sake I will tell you – and then we shall have talked quite enough about me – that you are no fair judge of my lot. You see me often, generally, in the midst of annoyance, and you do not (because no one can) look with the eye of my mind upon the future. If you could, for one day and night, feel with my feelings, and see through my eyes ... if you could do this, you would know, from henceforth, that there are glimpses of heaven for me in solitude, as for you in love. (3:302)

Maria experiences the problems inherent in the governess's situation without being reduced to those problems. She is, in fact, consistent with Martineau's protest in *Once a Week*: '[Governesses] feel that they have their troubles in life, like everybody else; and that they ought, like other people, to have the privilege of privacy, and of getting over their griefs as they may' (*GHH* 269). Maria is an 'evolutionary' character (Rothfield 118). She takes a moment that would be pathological for a morbid character and insists, instead, that it be regenerating. She does not resolve the disappointment of Hester's submission to Hope, but she provides an alternative ending.[53]

Maria's independence, complexity, and impenetrability are distinguished from Hester's dependent, flat, and dominated profile. Moreover, Maria's self-assertion of happiness contrasts with the happiness Hester is reported to experience by the narrative voice – a voice whose authority in making this final pronouncement is disturbed by disruptions of the text's clinical/realist perspective. For these reasons – both because the novel holds up an educated, double-faceted, and autonomous female character and because Hester's purported happiness is undermined in the novel – *Deerbrook* should be regarded as a feminist text. It is also one of the earliest novels to consider the relation of women to medicine. The novel not only represents popular scientific controversies, but, at the same time, it is inhabited by scientific discourse, creating a tension in the novel between the importance of recognizing medicine's professional status and questioning how women may relate to that profession. The novel promotes professionalism, but not professionalism at any cost: it also harbours an early feminist message about the gaze, surveillance, identity, and power. In chapter 5, Martineau's own uneasy relation to the medical profession will be examined. First, we shall turn to the second and last of Martineau's published novels: *The Hour and the Man: A Historical Romance* (1841).

Chapter Four

History and Romance:
The Hour and the Man (1841)

After the publication of *Deerbrook*, Martineau embarked on a Continental tour. She accompanied an invalid cousin to Switzerland and then travelled through Italy with two other friends. The tour provided Martineau with some favourable opportunities, not the least of which was that of escape from London, where relations with her mother were becoming increasingly difficult. Mrs Martineau was now partially blind and required more attention than her daughter wished or was able to give. The tour also enabled Martineau to visit the fortress of Joux near Besançon in the Juras, where Toussaint L'Ouverture, the black leader of the revolution (1791) and self-proclaimed 'Buonaparte of St. Domingo' (now Haiti), was imprisoned by the French and died in 1803.[1] Martineau had considered writing a novel about Toussaint's life before writing *Deerbrook*, and although she was discouraged from the topic by a friend, she was still fascinated by his history. Finally, the tour was to include topographical studies of Italy for Charles Knight's edition of Shakespeare, supplementing earlier research she had conducted for him in Scotland. Unfortunately, by the time Martineau reached Venice, she was debilitated by gynaecological complications. She returned to England and took up residence at Tynemouth, where she was confined for the next five years. Martineau's illness and recovery are the subject of the next chapter, but I mention them here because it was during her illness that Martineau finally wrote her novel about Toussaint L'Ouverture. *The Hour and the Man: A Historical Romance* (1841) was considered a better novel than *Deerbrook* by her contemporary reviewers, and, although it has received minimal attention from recent critics, the novel raises important questions about historical meaning: problems surrounding the knowledge and representation of history, the alliance of history and romance, the experience of history by the colonized subject, and the relation between history and women are fundamental issues in Martineau's text.[2]

To say that *The Hour and the Man* surpassed *Deerbrook* was not to say that the novel lacked faults, and, like so much of her work, *The Hour and the Man* provoked extreme responses from contemporary readers. Lord Jeffrey wanted to kiss Martineau's hand (and the hem of her dress) for providing such a 'beautiful,' 'touching,' and '*noble*' work; yet, at the same time, he had problems with the novel's black characters: 'I do not at all believe that the worthy people (or any of them) ever spoke or acted as she has so gracefully represented them, and must confess that in all the striking scenes I entirely forgot their complexion, and drove the notion of it from me as often as it occurred.' In Jeffrey's opinion, it was impossible that Toussaint could have been the Scipio-Cato-Fénelon-Washington that she described.[3] Carlyle shared these doubts. He too considered the book 'very beautiful,' but he also ridiculed Martineau's portrait of Toussaint as an intelligent man: 'You saw her *Toussaint L'Ouverture*: how she has made such a beautiful "Black Washington", or "Washington-Christ-Macready", as I have heard some call it, of a rough-handed, hard-headed, semi-articulate gabbling Negro.'[4] In fact, disbelief in Martineau's representation of Toussaint was the prevailing response to the novel, with some variations. The reviewer for the *Spectator* called Toussaint 'a softer edition of the Duke of Wellington' and felt that 'it is contrary to nature that her hero should be the calm, contemplative, comprehensive, philosophising person she paints.'[5] *Tait's* also scorned the idea that 'freed negroes' could have 'imbibed the elevated sentiments, or spoken the pure language put into their lips';[6] and so did the *Athenaeum*: 'The Slave is, and must be, what slavery has made him; and slavery would be a thousand times less hateful, if it did not corrupt and debase mind as well as body. Do the negro justice, we say, by all means; but keep him, for half a century at least, out of our imaginative literature.' If reviewers objected to *Deerbrook*'s middle-class hero, they found a black one even harder to accept, and especially one with 'the African's physiognomy, but the European's tongue.'[7]

The Emancipation Bill had become law in 1834, and so it may not be surprising that, only seven years later, readers regarded *The Hour and the Man* with profound ambivalence. However, more recent critics continue to disparage the novel's black characters. Vera Wheatley describes Toussaint as 'too good to be convincing.'[8] Robert Webb claims that the characters and their conversations are impossible, and, as for Toussaint, he is 'neither a Negro, nor an emancipated slave, but a philosopher and a philanthropic statesman,' as if these were incompatible (Webb 191). Valerie Pichanick thinks the characters 'lack authenticity' and that Martineau's 'urbane, philosophical Toussaint more than slightly resembled Shakespeare's noble Moor' (Pichanick 126). This last remark is interesting because it contradicts an opinion in the *Spectator* that, unfortunately, Toussaint was not at all like Othello. In *Othello*, the reviewer felt, one sees the true 'barbarian traits' of 'the Negro,' such as his 'child-like simplicity,' his 'childish jealousy,' and 'his leaning to swagger.'[9] Such views have dominated the scant criticism of the novel to date.

The issue of characterization is complex, and in order to understand it more fully we need to recognize that the complaints made against Martineau's characters are essentially twofold: it is objected that these black characters speak like Europeans and, further, that they speak like intelligent, educated Europeans. When examining these charges, a consideration of Martineau's previous treatment of the language of blacks is instructive. In 'Demerara,'[10] Martineau resisted portraying 'the language of slaves' because she felt that their 'jargon' would be difficult for both writer and reader if sustained throughout an entire volume.[11] She therefore made her characters speak standard English, believing that this was what they would have spoken if they had been allowed to receive an education. In *Society in America*, she changed her strategy and allowed slaves such as Harry to speak in their own voices. Both 'Demerara' and *Society in America* departed from a tendency in abolitionist writing (and, in particular, in abolitionist writing since 1788) to represent slaves as unnamed and voiceless. The representation of slaves' language in *Society in America* was also an important step in establishing slaves as speaking subjects free from cultural overwriting by dominant social groups. However, the language of slaves in *Society in America* is pidgin English. Pidgin had been used in earlier abolitionist writing, such as Sarah Robinson Scott's *The History of Sir George Ellison* (1776), and, although it gave slaves voices, these voices were simplistic, childish voices that signalled racial and class difference.[12] As a consequence, reviewers of *Society in America* had no objection to the representation of slaves' language in that text. Moreover, if readers objected less to her English-speaking slaves in 'Demerara' than to those in *The Hour and the Man*, it is partly because they were more concerned with Martineau's argument that 'man cannot hold property in man,' and partly because she offered an apology for her use of standard English.[13] *The Hour and the Man* contains no such apology. Unlike her earlier texts, it erodes racial and class difference.

Assuming that Martineau did indeed elevate the language of her characters in her historical romance, the responses of nineteenth-century readers to similar adjustments of language in other historical romances – romances by Maria Edgeworth and Sir Walter Scott – make it clear that they perceived a special threat in the representation of blacks' language in *The Hour and the Man*. For example, one reviewer of Edgeworth's novels in *Fraser's Magazine*, considering the author's portrayal of Irish characters, praised Edgeworth's genius for redeeming and elevating 'the rudest and rankest of created existences above the natural condition in which it finds them.'[14] J.A. Heraud's commendation of Scott was comparable: 'His delineations of rustic or uneducated characters are without coarseness. He appears not to deem it necessary to make them out either by vulgarity or ungrammatical construction.' For Heraud, 'it is better at all times to distinguish individual character by the matter than the manner of discourse,' and this is especially so given 'the repugnance which every polished mind feels in condescending to an acquaintance with cant of any kind, and vulgarity of all degrees.'[15] Heraud's view suggests that readers could recognize alterations to the languages of other classes and, further, that these modifications may have been made for their benefit. As a consequence, elevated diction posed no threat in these contexts since it could be recognized as an artificial adjustment. Since such adjustments have continued to be seen as valid by theorists, it is odd that more recent critics of Martineau's novel, such as Webb, should also find them objectionable. Georg Lukács asks, '... does faithfulness to the past mean a chronicle-like, naturalistic reproduction of the language, mode of thought and feeling of the past? Of course not.' He finds support for this view in Hegel's *Ästhetik*: '... the developed culture in representing and unfolding the substantial necessitates a change in the expression and form of the latter' (see Lukács 61).

The representation of characters' language in *The Hour and the Man* is, however, problematic. Martineau was not simply replacing a lower, or simplistic, form of English, like pidgin English, with standard English, as she did in 'Demerara.' Instead, the languages she would have been departing from were French and Haitian Creole, a patois based on African languages, French, and Spanish. Indeed, Martineau refers to these languages in her novel, as in a conversation between

Thérèse and Jacques Dessalines (later Empress and Emperor of Haiti during 1804–6) in the presence of M. Papalier, a white plantation owner and Thérèse's former master. Jacques is in the process of proposing marriage to Thérèse:

> Here, remembering the presence of a white, Jacques explained to Thérèse in the negro language (which she understood, though she always spoke French), the new hopes which had arisen for the blacks, and his own intention of following Toussaint, to make him a chief. He concluded in good French, smiling maliciously at Papalier as he spoke, 'You will come with me now to the priest, and be my wife.' (1:170–1)

The passage indicates that Jacques's use of the 'negro language' is only noise for Papalier and that Thérèse and Jacques usually speak French. Both of these factors contribute to the identification of blacks and whites that readers have resisted. For the reader, the implied operations of French and Creole are very different from the implicit elevation of 'lower' or variant forms of English: readers, like Heraud, who recognize that a character's language has been elevated from an 'ungrammatical' version of English have a clear sense of alterity, or 'otherness,' since a lack of education, low class status, and an inability to speak 'proper' English are often synonymous.[16] This sense of alterity is absent for readers who, like Papalier, do not know Creole: it is more difficult for these readers to see these characters as different by virtue of class. Racial difference is also challenged when characters who speak Creole also speak 'good French.' Martineau's implied translation from French to English would have been doubly hard to bear for readers who objected to Toussaint's 'European tongue,' despite the fact that the term romance itself derives from *enromancier, romançer,* or *romanz,* meaning to translate or compose in the vernacular.[17] Ultimately, in the absence of a clear sense of class and linguistic difference, the only thing distinguishing blacks from whites is skin colour, or the 'African's physiognomy.' The difficulty in seeing these blacks as otherwise 'other' is summed up, ironically, by Papalier. Thérèse and Jacques go off to get married, and Papalier is left to his musings: "'All alike!" muttered Papalier, as the pair went out. "This is what one may expect from negroes, as the General will learn when he has had enough to do with them. They are all alike"' (1:172). Papalier can only say that blacks who speak Creole and good French and are married by a Catholic priest are all alike. He cannot easily say how they are different from white Europeans.

One final irony which deserves attention is that slaves' knowledge of European languages was deliberately planned from the early days of slavery. Slaves brought to both English and French colonies were intentionally separated from other members of their language groups in order to make rebellions less likely (Ashcroft et al. 146). As a consequence, they were compelled to use the language of European plantation owners. However, so long as slaves remained uneducated, their voices continued to signal their difference from their masters, but, if a slave received instruction, he or she temporarily or permanently entered a privileged class that controlled the means of communication. Admittedly, education of slaves was rare, but there is evidence to suggest that Toussaint was educated. The *Biographie universelle*, one of Martineau's acknowledged sources, states that 'la préciose activitée de son esprit l'affranchit bientôt de l'état de profonde ignorance auquel il semblait condamné; par les soins d'un noir nommé Pierre-Baptiste, il reçut les premiers éléments d'une instruction très commune, mais dont il sut merveilleusement profiter.'[18] Martineau puts the case somewhat differently: in *The Hour and the Man* Toussaint's instruction is facilitated by his owner, M. Bayou, who lends Toussaint his books and allows him to buy others for himself. Of course, these conflicting 'facts' point to the problem of determining the reliability of historical 'evidence.' What is certain is that for readers of *The Hour and the Man*, meaning has not resided in 'evidence,' or even in language itself, but rather in the social and political positions held by those who use it. For these readers, the use of educated, European language by blacks necessitates an identification with blacks from which they have recoiled. The novel's 'fault,' then, is a serious one since the pleasure of a romance depends on the reader's identification with the central characters: 'We are transported. The absurdities of romance are felt when we refuse to inhabit the world offered us and disengage ourselves, bringing to bear our own opinions' (Beer 8). Phrasing the matter in different terms, we can say that 'history' and 'romance' are mutually conflicting in Martineau's novel. As Helen Hughes maintains, '"Realism" allows [a] text to be consumed as surrogate experience, while fantasy gives an opportunity for wish-fulfilling motifs which symbolically represent the hopes and fears of the readership.'[19] For readers of *The Hour and the Man* who fear identifying with blacks, 'realism' is untenable, and surrogate experience is repressed.

These considerations already suggest that *The Hour and the Man* raises important questions about how to represent history – questions about how to represent historical characters and how to represent their language, about determining the nature of historical 'evidence,' and about the relation between romance and history. Moreover, it raises these questions at a time that was supposed to witness the dawn of an objective historical consciousness, and I should like to suspend my analysis of *The Hour and the Man* momentarily to establish a theoretical framework within which to proceed. *The Hour and the Man* was published in the same year that Leopold von Ranke's *Die Römischen Päpiste* (3 vols, 1834–9) was translated into English by Sarah Austin. Ranke's writings were thought to be truthful histories based on sources other than tradition and legends. At the end of the century, Lord Acton commended von Ranke's 'colourless' composition and his style that allowed 'transparency to the facts.'[20] It was also in the nineteenth century (and especially in the first half of the nineteenth century) that Hegel's work was greatly influential and that Carlyle encouraged a concerted effort to 'search more and more into the Past; let all men explore it, as the true fountain of knowledge; by whose light alone, consciously or unconsciously employed, can the Present and the Future be interpreted and guessed at.'[21] Notwithstanding this new historicizing impulse as the basis of an emergent epistemology, many writers in the period recognized that the representation of history was not such a straightforward matter. In *Shadowtime: History and Representation in Hardy, Conrad and George Eliot*, Jim Reilly examines the problems of representing history in novels by these writers. Reilly's study is important and deserves consideration.

Reilly borrows the theoretical premises of his work from Adorno and Foucault. He 'backdates' Adorno's view of the Second World War as lacking conventionally historical elements – 'continuity, history, an "epic" element,' the capacity to leave 'a permanent, unconsciously preserved image in the memory' – to the nineteenth century, when the proliferation of historical discourse counteracts a felt absence of historical continuousness.[22] The argument is also Foucault's, who sees that in the nineteenth century man already 'found himself emptied of history.'[23] In chapter 2 of *The Order of Things* Foucault outlines a history of the decline of reference and representation and develops his influential theory of epistemes. Representations in the medieval episteme mirror a nature envisioned as a divinely decreed set of resemblances, establishing a pattern of self-referential similitude that continues until the publication of *Don Quixote* in 1605. *Don Quixote* heralds the start of a new episteme, in which writing ceases 'to be the prose of the world;

resemblances and signs have dissolved their former alliance; similitudes have become deceptive and verge upon the visionary or madness; things still remain stubbornly within their identity: they are no longer anything but what they are' (*OT* 32). When Don Quixote fights windmills, he thinks they are giants. Signifiers and signifieds are wrenched apart. With the Classical episteme, signifiers are still perceived to be without referents, but are seen to relate synchronically to other signifiers, resulting in a relentless taxonomy both of the natural order and of representations. With the contemporary episteme, emerging between 1775 and 1825, the relation of signs becomes diachronic:

> ... a profound historicity penetrates into the heart of things, isolates and defines them in their own coherence, imposes upon them the forms of order implied by the continuity of time ... above all, language loses its privileged position and becomes, in its turn, a historical form coherent with the density of its own past ... things become increasingly reflexive, seeking the principle of their intelligibility only in their own development, and abandoning the space of representation. (*OT* xxiii)

History and representation become problematized in an 'event' from which we may not yet have emerged.

For Reilly, Foucault's conception of history and representation in the nineteenth century as antagonistic is all-important. Reilly departs from Lukács's conception of history as 'straightforwardly' portrayed in the nineteenth century and instead, armed with Foucault, searches the works of Hardy, Conrad, and Eliot for signs of the interrogation of historical representation and historical meaning, or, for the dramatization of questions such as 'Where is the standing-ground of history? Where does it take place? Literal topographic ground, the frustrating and indeterminate experience of an individual, subsequent journalistic or historical discourse ...?' According to Reilly, the historical event is 'diffused amongst a whole range of ontological categories' (Reilly 12). Reilly's study is also in tune with Foucault's conception of a future 'historicity linked essentially to man himself' (*OT* 369; Reilly 5). Italo Calvino describes what such a future might look like based on shifts that he sees in the 1960s, but which Reilly sees as nineteenth-century developments:

> If we had to give a brief definition of this process, we could say that the notion of man as the subject of history is finished – the antagonist who

has dethroned man must still be called man, but a man very different from what he was before. Which is to say ... the end of economic and ideological Eurocentrism; and the claiming of full rights by the outcasts, the repressed, the forgotten, and the inarticulate. All the parameters, categories, and antitheses that we once used to define, plan, and classify the world have been called into question.[24]

My argument is that these processes which Calvino describes and the dramatization of those questions that Reilly asks are all seen to operate in *The Hour and the Man*. In this view, I wish to depart from Reilly, who deliberately excludes the historical novel from his study. His rationale for this exclusion derives from Adorno, for whom, in Reilly's terms, 'it is in avowedly historical works that history – and more particularly the issues surrounding how historical meaning and representation are now felt to be simultaneously crucial and in crisis – is most conspicuously absent' (Reilly 2). Notwithstanding his considerations of Stendhal's *La Chartreuse de Parme* (1839) and Eliot's *Romola* (1863), Reilly maintains that 'it is precisely when freed from the presuppositions of the historical genres' that writers can explore 'the fraught and unexpected forms historical meaning begins to adopt in the nineteenth century' (Reilly 4).

I wish to argue instead that it is precisely in the genre of the historical romance that the crises surrounding historical representation and historical meaning are most conspicuously played out and, in particular, in Martineau's novel. Indeed, the very term 'historical romance' itself suggests these crises, aligning history both with the themes of romance (adventure and sexual love) and with the motifs of romance (abductions, escapes, rescues, disguises, and charms). When so combined, 'history' and 'romance' can be seen either as mutually enhancing, whereupon the distinctions between them are blurred, and 'history' and 'romance' become indistinguishable; or, mutually contradictory, in which case the reader is offered two distinct and opposed means of conceiving 'truth,' 'order,' and 'reality.' The point might seem too obvious to make were it not that many critics, like Reilly, tend to overlook it. I suspect this is in part a result of their referring not to the 'historical romance' but rather to the 'historical novel,' being influenced, no doubt, by Lukács's study. Of course, Lukács is dedicated to a materialistic treatment of literary history, and so it is not surprising that he might wish to engage in a deliberate misprision of the genre's definition. That other critics who do not profess to share his politics nonetheless reproduce his terminology suggests the extraordinary influence Lukács has had in the (mis)understanding of this genre.

Gillian Beer expertly charts a history of romance that overlaps with Foucault's succession of epistemes in many respects. To paraphrase Beer's arguments, medieval romance mirrors the world around it, which is itself seen as a divinely ordained pattern of similitudes.[25] Shelton's translation of *Don Quixote* in 1612 and 1620 is a watershed in the history of romance and signals a conscious polarity between the ideality of romance and the observable facts of life. *Don Quixote* is followed by the decline of romance and the rise of neo-classical forms. By mid-eighteenth century these have been superseded by the novel of domestic manners in which the sign relates directly to ordinary life. At the same time, appearances of resemblances are illusory: *Clarissa* scarcely deals with events that occur daily in the world (Beer 52). The novel of manners is followed by the Gothic revival, or the rediscovery of the power of sensation and, more importantly, by the Romantic revival. Towards the end of the eighteenth century, writers look back to the Middle Ages, to popular broadsheet and border ballads, to oriental tales, and to the Gothic novel for forces of the imagination which had been repressed and which they sought to emancipate (Beer 59–60). Writers trace the history of romance as the basis for their imaginative representations.

My paraphrase of Beer is clearly oversimplified; nonetheless, it suggests correspondences between the history of romance and Foucault's history of the decay of reference and representation. Furthermore, the relation between the contemporary episteme and the Romantic revival is especially instructive. Overlapping Foucault and Beer, one sees that the proliferation of historical discourses and the conception of representation as inherently problematic coincide with the revival of romance and the surge of imaginative representations. The historical romance is, I would argue, the site where these processes at once combine and where the problems surrounding the representation of history are most distinct. In fact, Beer argues that the 'historical novel' as exemplified in the writings of Scott is separated from the romance tradition by its historical realism (Beer 66). Beer is influenced in this opinion by Lukács, and, like Lukács, she does not explore problems surrounding the representation of history in historical novels.[26]

Martineau did perceive problems with Scott's historical realism, and she outlines them fully in an article for *Tait's* entitled 'The Achievements of the Genius of Scott.'[27] For one thing, she did not think that

Scott's novels represented the lower classes of society. Unlike Lukács, for whom the interactions between 'the "above" and "below" of society create that incomparably truthful, historical atmosphere which in every novel of Scott reawakens a period' (Lukács 48), Martineau laments the fact that the lower classes were secluded from the light of his genius: 'What is there of humble life in his narratives? What did he know of those who live and move in that region? Nothing. There is not a *character* from humble life in all his library of volumes; nor had he any conception that character is to be found there' (AGS 452). Martineau maintains that the Edie Ochiltrees and Dirk Hatteraicks and Caleb Balderstones of Scott's novels are more bound up with aristocratic systems than affiliated with lower-class life and insists that even the character of Jeanie Deans does not derive its interest from her station. For Lukács, Jeanie is a 'Puritan peasant girl'; for Martineau, 'her simplicity is that which might pertain to a secluded young woman of any rank' (Lukács 52, AGS 452). Although Scott portrayed, with 'the nicest acumen,' the characters and the passions of the higher levels of society, which he knew best, he did not know these passions could be found magnified in the humbler ranks, and the consequence of his partial knowledge is 'the obliteration to himself and to his readers, as far as connected with him, of more than half the facts and interests of humanity' (AGS 453). Martineau sees Scott's Toryism as the cause of his partial histories.

Martineau's analysis of social leaders in Scott's novels is consistent with her view of his biases and omissions and, again, stands in direct contrast to Lukács's arguments. For Lukács, part of what separates Scott from Romanticism is his depiction of society's important figures as peripheral to the action of his novels. These figures are not objects of Romantic hero-worship but are rather the somewhat abstracted embodiments of historical movements. They are, in Hegelian terms, 'world-historical individuals' that arise on the broad basis of 'maintaining individuals,' and they unite in themselves 'the salient positive and negative sides of the movement concerned' (Lukács 39, 40). In contrast, for Martineau, the people are not so much represented by these leaders as they are 'slaves' to them, and nobody seems to consider either historical movements or the needs of society:

> None of Scott's personages act and suffer as members and servants of society. Each is for his own; whether it be his family, his chief, his king, or his country, in a warlike sense. The weal or woe of the many, or of all, is

the only consideration which does not occur to them – the only motive to enterprise and endurance, which is not so much as alluded to. There is no talk of freedom, as respects anything but brute force, – no suspicion that one class is in a state of privilege, and another in a state of subjugation, and that these things ought not to be. (AGS 454)

The Hour and the Man attempts to provide a corrective for some of these failings, but before moving on to a further consideration of this novel, it is necessary to add a few more words about Lukács. Lukács's perception of a movement away from hero-worship in Scott does not take into consideration such events as Waverley's response to meeting Charles Edward, 'whose form and manners, as well as the spirit which he displayed in this singular enterprise, answered his ideas of a hero of romance.'[28] In fact, Lukács suppresses all of the romantic elements in these novels. To continue with the example of *Waverley*, the Waverley-Flora plot, the Waverley-Rose plot,[29] Waverley's rescue from the charge of Gilfillan, his disguise as Francis Stanley, the mystical visions by which Fergus foresees his fate, visions of blood on the floor at Waverley-Honour, the novel's narrative device of *entrelacement*, and Scott's Romantic nostalgia for a lost culture (to name a few) are all excluded from Lukács's study, contributing to a myopic emphasis on the novel's historical realism and to a disregard of how history is challenged by romance in these novels.

Martineau's criticism of Scott concludes with a consideration of the work that remains for novelists: 'There is a boundless field open before them; no less than the whole region of moral science, politics, political economy, social rights and duties.' In addition, novels that relate to classes other than the aristocracy have yet to be seen, 'for there has yet been no recorder of the poor' (AGS 458). Impatient with waiting for the appearance of the 'legitimate offspring' of Scott's volumes, Martineau herself assumes responsibility for bringing such 'offspring' into being: *The Hour and the Man*, tracing the rise to power of a black slave and the assumption of political rights by an oppressed people, remedies the perceived omissions in Scott and presents a history of 'the claiming of full rights by the outcasts, the repressed, [and] the forgotten,' to recall Calvino's description of innovations in the 1960s. Toussaint is portrayed as a representative of the blacks and of a historical movement. He is called 'the Spartacus predicted by Raynal, whose destiny it should be to avenge the wrongs of his race' (1:191). Those who serve him do so not because they are 'slaves' but because they are 'free men and fellow-citizens,' and the French err when they do not see 'that a great part of their devotion to Toussaint was loyalty to their race' (3:147).

The French response to Toussaint has been generally problematic. In an Appendix to the novel, Martineau discusses the short and derisive accounts of Toussaint to be found in biographical dictionaries and popular histories of the day. Toussaint is frequently described as possessing an inherent genius for war and government, but also as hypocritical in religious matters and, in all affairs, 'the very prince of dissemblers' (3:247). Martineau explains these accounts by tracing them to reports made by thwarted invaders of St Domingo, from which later accounts were copied without further consideration. Fortunately, Martineau also gathered information about Toussaint from other (differently biased) sources, such as an abolitionist article in the *Quarterly Review* providing a digest of various narratives, and the *Biographie universelle*, referred to above, which furnished her with the dates and details of specific events but with a 'confused impression' of Toussaint's character.[30] In all, Martineau's experience with sources suggests the problems of knowing history through its prior textualizations and addresses the question of whether history is to be found in 'subsequent journalistic or historical discourse' – one of the questions that Reilly considers immaterial to the historical novel. Martineau is aware that histories are constructed by interested parties. Histories are not only thereby aligned with imaginative fictions, but, for Martineau (perhaps with Aristotle's *Poetics* in mind), her fiction represents Toussaint more accurately than 'authoritative' historical texts: 'I have arrived at the conclusion that his character was, in sober truth, such as I have endeavoured to represent it in the foregoing work' (3:248). Her novel is not, as one critic would have it, simply 'a free translation of actual history.'[31]

In contrast to negative portrayals of Toussaint by French historians, Martineau represents her hero as a loyal Frenchman. In the opening pages of her novel, she carefully charts the political climate of St Domingo in 1791, thereby highlighting Toussaint's part within it. On 15 March of that year, the French National Assembly decreed that mulattos were to enjoy the privileges of French citizenship, including enjoyment of suffrage and possession of seats in parochial and colonial legislatures. The decree was brought about largely by the cruel executions of Vincent Ogé and his brother the preceding year for their heading a mulatto uprising in St Domingo: at a time when 'Liberty' and 'Equality' were hailed by the colony's white proprietors, the mulattos 'innocently understood the words according to their commonly received meaning' and, desiring an equal share in political and civil rights, attempted to wrench from the whites those freedoms which they unreasonably withheld (1:2). The cruelties inflicted on the Ogés precipitated lobbying in France, resulting in the decree of 15 March. The whites of the colony resolved to ignore this decree and to establish a new General Colonial Assembly. One hundred and seventy-six deputies were elected and met at Cap Français on 20 August. For several days, they hosted dinner parties for the colony's proprietors, bailiffs, clergy, and magistrates. These events are described in the novel but predate the novel's action, which commences on 22 August 1791. On this day, the blacks, who have been left to themselves for several days, revolt. Toussaint, instead of joining in the insurrection, secures his master's escape on a ship to the United States and then travels to the Spanish part of the island to fight on behalf of the king of France with the king's Spanish allies.

If it seems surprising that, in the midst of a black revolution, Toussaint desires to work for a new 'task-master' instead of enjoying his new freedom (1:67), it must be remembered that, for Martineau, the subservience of slaves was 'the best argument for Negro Emancipation' (AGS 456). Toussaint's degradation is made explicit: '"I am free," said Toussaint, "and I am an oppression to myself. I did not seek freedom. I was at ease, and did not desire it, seeing how men abuse their freedom"' (1:92). As is common among victims of slavery, Toussaint is represented as suffering from an eroded sense of self, caused by a deliberate repression of his cultural identity. To borrow from Adorno, Toussaint experiences himself solely as the object 'of opaque process and, torn between sudden shock and sudden forgetfulness, [is] no longer capable of a sense of temporal continuity.'[32] Reilly argues that such conditions are inoperative in the 'historical novel,' but Martineau's description of Toussaint's crisis of identity and cultural dislocation renders the enslaved subject the exemplary figure of the nineteenth century's problematized historicism. Toussaint feels regret for his own lost youth. It was then that Toussaint had learned to read, and the books he read were Epictetus and Fénelon. He had become a stoic and a quietist:

> ... and, while busied in submitting himself to the pressure of the present, he had turned from the past, and scarcely dreamed of the future. If his imagination glanced back to the court of his royal grandfather, held under

the palm shades, or pursuing the lion-hunt amidst the jungles of Africa, he had hastily withdrawn his mind's eye from scenes which might create impatience with his lot ... It was not till his youth was past that he had learned anything of the revolutions of the world – too late to bring them into his speculations and his hopes. He had read, from year to year, of the conquests of Alexander and of Cæsar: he had studied the wars of France, and drawn the plans of campaigns in the sand before his door till he knew them by heart; but it had not occurred to him that while empires were overthrown in Asia, and Europe was traversed by powers which gave and took its territories, as he saw the negroes barter their cocoa-nuts and plantains on Saturday nights – while such things had happened in another hemisphere, it had not occurred to him that change would ever happen in St. Domingo. (1:120–1)

Toussaint has engaged in a radical forgetting of his own culture and history. He has been 'emptied of history,' to use Foucauldian terms. As a consequence, he has a strong sense that history is the prerogative of whites, which, of course, was largely true; Hegel, for example, defined Africa as 'outside history.' Indeed, Martineau herself felt that Toussaint had been forgotten; hence, her epigraph to the novel: 'Now there was found in it a poor wise man, and he by his wisdom delivered the city; yet no one remembered that same poor man. – ECCLESIASTES, ix. 15.' Furthermore, if history was the exclusive privilege of whites, so were revolutions: 'The mutabilities of human life had seemed to him to be appointed to whites – to be their privilege and their discipline; while he doubted not that the eternal command to blacks was to bear and forbear' (1:121–2). Toussaint's adumbrated perception that historical consciousness is the prerequisite of social change accords with Lukács's view of the importance of history to revolutions: 'propaganda ... has to reveal the social content, the historical presuppositions and circumstances of the struggle, to connect up the war with the entire life and possibilities of the nation's development' (Lukács 23–4).

Immersed as he is in European history, it follows that Toussaint would join the Spanish forces now allied with the king of France. It is equally inevitable that he would teach his sons the history of European wars, rather than their own ancestral history, as he trains them to be soldiers in the Spanish army. In the evenings, Toussaint amuses his sons

by giving them the history of the wars of Asia and Europe, as he had learned it from books, and thoroughly mastered it by reflection. Night after night was the map of Greece traced with his sword's point on the sand behind his tent ... Night after night did the interest of his hearers arouse more and more spirit in himself, till he became aware that his sympathies with the Greeks in their struggles for liberty had hitherto been like those of the poet born blind, who delights in describing natural scenery – thus unconsciously enjoying the stir within him of powers whose appropriate exercise is forbidden. (1:123)

Appropriately, Toussaint's insights are also the cause of his blindness. He is blind not only to his own cultural history, but also to the 'reality' of those wars and struggles that he has only read about and described but never seen or experienced. He feels 'like one lately couched, by whom the order of things was gradually becoming recognised, but who was oppressed by the unwonted light.'[33] Toussaint is both blinded and oppressed by European history, and while he continues tracing with his sword 'how this advance and that retreat had been made above two thousand years ago, he was full of consciousness that the spirit of the history of freedom was received more truly by the youngest of his audience than by himself' (1:124). These considerations again raise the question – Where is history? If it existed in advances and retreats made thousands of years ago, how can it be represented now? In books, in the tracings of a sword through sand (Foucault imagines that when humanist history is finished 'man would be erased, like a face drawn in sand at the edge of the sea' [*OT* 387]), in a 'spirit' that may or may not be received? History and the representation of history are both fundamental and ontologically indeterminate in Martineau's text.

The problem of knowing history is made even more problematic by the fact that even witnesses to events cannot understand what they mean. When Toussaint hears of the decree of the French Convention confirming and proclaiming the liberty of blacks, he leaves the Spanish army and returns to Cap Français. The mulattos, as angered by the new decree as the whites were by that which proclaimed the mulattos' liberty, have imprisoned General Laveaux. It is worth mentioning here that if these white-mulatto-black conflicts remind the reader of antagonisms among English aristocrats, ten-pound voters, and chartists, contemporary readers were also struck by the similarity.[34] In an 1839 article, Archibald Alison noted that the discontent of the working classes had 'at length attracted the notice of Government.'[35] The topic had become a pressing one at the time of Martineau's writing and worried observers: 'Little by little, life is leaving the centre, and is stirring, disordered, fractionary, and unequal at every point of the circumference,' Joseph Mazzini complained, recalling 'the few years that sufficed to crumble into ruins this giant-like labour of ages, and the few months that sufficed to elevate, on these ruins, the formidable, absorbing, and hitherto despised Third Estate which, at the commencement of the Revolution, *was nothing, and longed to be something*.'[36] In contrast to such concerns, Martineau enthusiastically portrays Toussaint's invasion of Cap Français (described earlier in the novel as the colony's 'centre')[37] and his release of General Laveaux. Toussaint is asked to be the colony's lieutenant-governor. He is hailed as 'Toussaint L'Ouverture' because, as the French commissary Poverel says, he 'is making for us an opening everywhere' (1:194). In short, he overturns the social hierarchy, making it clear that political activity is not solely the prerogative of upper classes.

Understanding what all of this means is not, however, easy, not even for the history-maker himself, let alone for witnesses. Toussaint walks in the gardens of Government House alone, trying to comprehend recent events:

> I, whose will is yet unexercised, – I, who shrink ashamed before the knowledge of the meanest white, – I, so lately a slave, – so long dependent that I am an oppression to myself, – am at this hour the ruler over ten thousand wills! The ways of God are dark, or it might seem that he despised his negro children in committing so many of them to so poor a guide. But he despises nothing that he has made. It may be that we are too weak and ignorant to be fit for better guidance in our new state of rights and duties. It may be that a series of teachers is appointed to my colour, of whom I am to be the first, only because I am the lowest; destined to give way to wiser guides when I have taught all that I know, and done all that I can. (1:197–8)

Once again, Toussaint considers himself the object of 'opaque processes,' the series of dashes in the representation of his thoughts signalling a narrative breakdown symptomatic of crisis. Unable to locate himself in 'history,' to find the absent cause of his present circumstances, experienced as 'Necessity,'[38] he projects a future history that will make sense of new status. History, as it is happening, appears disjointed to Toussaint, and it is only by imagining the future that he can impose order on his perplexing circumstances. Once more, the question is 'Where is history?' In the frustrating experiences of the individual, perhaps. Making sense of history is an imaginative act. The problem is recognized not only by Martineau but also by her contemporary theorists:

> ... a Romance writer, if he is to be tolerated at all, must be a poet in feeling and in heart. He can find but to a very small extent the materials of composition in the scenes around him. Even the annals of the past, to which he must revert as his sources, present him with his materials in the rudest, barest, and most disjointed form. The more he penetrates into the minutiae of history, the more he accumulates about him a mass of incoherent particulars. The *callida junctura* must be his own ...[39]

The imagination of the romance writer imposes order on historical materials that are otherwise unrepresentable, or representable only as an antiquarian mosaic: in the historical romance, the problems of understanding and representing history are a primary concern.

These problems continue to surface throughout the novel, as witnesses to events are repeatedly unable, or considered unable, to determine their significance. For example, two of Toussaint's sons, Placide and Isaac, have been sent to France, partly for educational purposes and mostly as a guarantee for the security of whites in St Domingo. They send home reports of Napoleon's kindness, the truth of which Génifrède, one of Toussaint's daughters, is sceptical: '... they speak as they think: not as things really are.' The brothers' perceptions are clouded by their hopes for St Domingo; what appears as 'evidence' is confused with fantasy. Of course, such blurred distinctions call in question the reliability of empirical evidence as a guarantor of truth, a point which concerns Génifrède's sister, Aimée: 'How can you so despise the testimony of those who see what we only hear of?' (1:295). These indeterminacies are never resolved in the text. According to Toussaint, history will conclude what is wrong: 'In the eye of the world [Napoleon] may be great, and I the bandit captain of a despised race. On the page of history he may be magnified, and I derided. But I spurn him for a hero' (3:3). Ultimately, things will be seen 'as they are' only in heaven (3:52), and, as for Toussaint, he insists that his real character will be the absent subject of historical representations: 'If my name live, the goodness of those who name it will be its life; for my true self will not be in it. No one will the more know the real Toussaint' (3:240).

Toussaint's real self cannot be represented, and historical knowledge is more properly the domain of radical phenomenology. As for Martineau, she concludes the Appendix to her novel with both a reproduction of the correspondence between Henri Christophe (later king of Haiti) and General LeClerc (Napoleon's brother-in-law and leader of the French invasion of St Domingo),[40] and a copy of the Declaration of the Independence of the Blacks of St Domingo. Where is history? Martineau suggests that her fiction portrays Toussaint's character accurately, yet she feels compelled to supplement her novel with hard historical 'evidence,' or with 'the letter that kills,' as Heraud calls transcription (Heraud 557). In fact, Martineau frames her novel with such 'evidence,' beginning it with a textbook map of St Domingo. In short, what emerges from her text is conscious confusion about how to represent history: inability to represent historical meaning is both the implicit message of her framing device and an explicit theme within the novel itself.

Martineau's addition of letters to her novel is intended to demonstrate the literacy and education of the blacks she portrays, preempting the charges of implausibility that critics have made nonetheless. According to some theorists, literacy leads to the emergence of historical consciousness, allowing scrutiny of a constant past (Ashcroft et al. 81). As has been seen, the historical consciousness of Toussaint, at any rate, is a consciousness of European history and a repression of his own ancestral origins. Since Toussaint is so dominated by Europe, it is worth considering what other forms this domination takes. Toussaint represses his cultural history because it 'might create impatience with his lot.' This seems to mean that images of Africa might make him fruitlessly wish for their realization. Alternatively, it could be read as signifying Toussaint's displeasure that his cultural background is, in fact, African instead of European. He would rather be white. Certainly there are abundant examples in the text of a perceived white supremacy. When made lieutenant-governor, Toussaint declares that all of his resources shall be directed towards the elevation of his race to a state of 'intellectual and moral equality with the whites' (1:192). Moyse, Toussaint's nephew and prospective son-in-law, maintains that Toussaint 'reveres the whites. He reveres them for their knowledge. He says they are masters of an intellectual kingdom from which we have been shut out, and they alone can let us in' (1:283–4). Toussaint is considered to be 'more eager to gratify the whites than the blacks' (2:142), and he even exhorts blacks in the midst of war to 'save first the creole whites, and next your wives and your children' (2:253). The perceived superiority is also manifest in architectural terms. M. Loisir, a European architect, arrives in St Domingo to build a house for Henri Christophe. General Vincent suggests that he simply 'tell him, or any others of my countrymen, that any building you choose to put up is European, and in good taste, and they will be quite pleased enough' (1:293).

The perceived superiority of Europe causes a mimicry of the unchallenged centre and an immersion in those values that have been imported from abroad. Among those values targeted for adoption are Christian values, notwithstanding that the relation between Christianity and slavery has been sometimes strained. In the treaty signed between England and France at the end of the Napoleonic Wars, for example, the restoration of French colonies to France (excepting the Isle of France, Tobago, and St Lucia) was a restoration of those colonies to the slave trade, which, although recognized as despicable, was nonetheless allowed by England to continue for five years despite the fact that England was in a position to compel her European neighbours to accept abolition if she had chosen to do so. What especially incensed commentators on these matters was that this perpetuation of the slave trade was decreed in an act in the name of the '"*Most Holy and Undivided Trinity*" – the God of Justice, Prince of Peace, and the Spirit of Holiness.'[41] If, in 1840, England had wished to atone for her former sins, she might have either obtained the concurrence of France and America in declaring the slave trade piracy, or she might have repealed the protecting duty on East Indian sugar. At this time, the yearly importation of slaves in Spanish and Portuguese colonies was at least 150 000.[42] Martineau thought her story would 'do a world of good to the slave question' (*HMA* 3:216). She may have had these agendas in mind, along with the abolition of slavery in America.[43]

Christianity and freedom, then, are sometimes at cross purposes. This is also occasionally the case in *The Hour and the Man*. When Toussaint learns of the French decree recognizing the freedom of blacks and decides to leave the Spanish army, he visits Father Laxabon to confess his intentions. Laxabon is surprised at the importance Toussaint attaches to the proclamation and is alarmed by his enthusiasm, not finding in his tone his former 'humility and reliance upon religion' (1:140). Insisting that 'the General does not think so much as you do of this event; nor even does Jean Français' (Jean Français is a black who prefers to be a Spanish noble than a representative of his race), Laxabon deserts Toussaint in his 'hour' of need: 'I dare not so pray for one self-willed and precipitate; nor, till you bring a humble and obedient mind, can I receive your confession. There can be no absolution where there is reservation. Consider, my dear son!' (1:148, 149). As was the case in *Society in America*, Christianity is portrayed here as detached from the principles of justice and liberty. Indeed, Jacques Dessalines's opinion that priests were 'brought in by the whites for a convenience' (1:84) recalls the uses of Christianity by pro-slaverites considered in chapter 2: religion offers consolation for trials suffered on earth, and priests preach eternal punishments in order to frighten slaves into submission.[44] Laxabon tries such intimidation here: 'How will you answer when [God] asks you, "What hast thou done with the rank and the power I put into thy hand? How hast thou used them?" What can you then answer, but "I flung them away, and made myself useless and a reproach"' (1:144).

This interview does not repulse Toussaint from Christianity, so strong it seems is his reverence for European values. Instead, as lieutenant-governor, he holds a levee at which he explains to priests sent from various districts of the colony that they 'are the true rulers of this island and its inhabitants.'[45] Toussaint's charge is 'the soil on which, and the bodies in which, men live'; the priests 'have in charge their souls, in which lies the future of this world and of the next' (1:217). As noted in chapter 2, this distinction between the soul and the body has been used by patriarchal authority in order to exercise greater control over the body. Not all things import well, and Toussaint's strict patriarchal authority is the most disturbing aspect of his character.

Moyse and Génifrède, Toussaint's nephew and daughter, are the most obvious objects of patriarchal abuse. Knowing the pair are in love, Toussaint nonetheless requires Moyse to prove himself worthy before he consents to their marriage. Toussaint has a 'higher duty than that to my family ... Moyse must therefore prove what he can do, before he can marry his love' (1:262). Having sent the incompetent commissary, Hédouville, back to France and the governor of Cap Français to the legislature, he unfairly requires Moyse to protect the Cap until a new governor is appointed. Unlike Toussaint, Moyse hates whites, and he turns a blind eye to the murder of some whites in his district by blacks. Moyse is not a Christian and quarrels with 'none who avenge our centuries of wrong' (2:161). Toussaint, wanting to reassure the whites, resolves that Moyse must die. He is inflexibly just, insists on a single code, 'NO RETALIATION,' and ignores precedent: he had recently forgiven a group of insurgent mulattos. These events are a combination of history and romance: Moyse was Toussaint's nephew and was executed at his command, but he is not known to have been engaged to Toussaint's daughter. History and romance are blurred, and not without significance. Torn between his obligations as a ruler and as a father, Toussaint manifests patriarchy's inherent contradictions. Génifrède, learning the fate of her beloved, flees the family's house in Pongaudin and visits Moyse at the Cap. Moyse knows that he must die and resolves that she must die too: 'I can direct you to one, near at hand, who prepares the red water,[46] and knows me well. I will give you an order for red water enough for us both' (2:163). Génifrède is terrified, not of the red water itself, but of their being separated after death. Nonetheless, she takes a small carved ivory ring from Moyse to No. 9 in the Rue Espagnole, obtains the red water, but is unknowingly given henbane by Thérèse when she returns, causing her to sleep until the execution is over the next morning.

Early historical romances tend to offer conventional images of women. Indeed, one of Martineau's chief objections to Scott was that 'a set of more passionless, frivolous, uninteresting beings was never assembled at morning auction, or evening tea-table, than he has presented us with in his novels' (AGS 456).[47] It was not until the 1920s that women writers of historical romance foregrounded the problematic roles of women in society, and even then, although female characters were allowed to question society's conventions, to a limited extent, they were ultimately forced to conform 'and to enjoy conforming' (Hughes 42). Patriarchy was ultimately fulfilling for women, and protests against male power were essentially blunted. In contrast, in this early novel, the protest against patriarchy is anything but blunted. Unlike her successors about a century later, Génifrède does not internalize a male system of values. Instead, father, law, Christianity, and white/male history form a consolidated authority that she flatly rejects. When the reader first sees Génifrède, she demonstrates a marked irreverence for her father's passionate historicism:

> 'Epictetus was a negro,' said Génifrède, complacently.
>
> 'Not a negro,' said her father, smiling. 'He was a slave; but he was a white.'
>
> 'Is that the reason you read that book so much more than any other?' (1:11)

The exchange emphasizes the often automatic identification of race and slavery, but it also signals Génifrède's rejection of her father's reading and values. Unlike Aimée and Isaac, she does not read her father's books about whites. Now, after the execution of Moyse, her protest is sharpened. Having awakened from her induced sleep, she confronts successively the patriarchal figures of Laxabon and her father:

> 'My daughter ...' said father Laxabon. She came forward, with a docile and wistful look. 'My daughter,' he continued, 'I bring you some comfort.'
> 'Comfort?' she repeated, doubtingly.
> 'Not now, father,' interposed Thérèse. 'Spare her.'
> 'Spare me?' repeated Génifrède, in the same tone.
> 'I bring her comfort,' said the father, turning reprovingly to Madame Dessalines. 'His conflict is over, my daughter,' he continued, advancing to Génifrède. 'His last moments were composed: and, as for his state of mind in confession ...'
> He was stopped by a shriek so appalling, that he recoiled as if shot, and supported himself against the wall. (2:195–6)

Laxabon is left pacing in 'great disturbance, – not with himself, but with the faithless creature of passion he had to deal with' (2:196). In the meantime, Génifrède has headed to a nearby reservoir:

> ... her hands were clasped above her head for the plunge, when a strong hand seized her arm, and drew her irresistibly back. In an ungovernable rage she turned, and saw her father.
> 'They say,' she screamed, 'that every one worships you. Not true now! Never true more! I hate ... I curse ...'
> He held up his right hand with the action of authority which had awed her childhood. It awed her now. Her voice sank into a low shuddering and muttering. (2:196–7)

Toussaint's silencing of his daughter is reminiscent of Edward Hope's silencing of Mrs Plumstead in *Deerbrook*. Unlike the 'scold,' however, Génifrède does not remain silenced for long. Toussaint tells her to go home: '"Home!" she exclaimed, with loathing. "Yes, I must go home," she said, hurriedly. "You love Pongaudin, – you call it paradise. I wish you joy of it now! You have put an evil spirit into it. I wish you joy of your paradise!"' (2:198–9).

What these events immediately suggest is that the exercise of patriarchal authority is synchronous with the disruption of the family, or
that the domestic haven, or 'paradise,' is rendered demonic by the
operations of patriarchal power. Once again, Martineau disrupts contemporary ideology: the family is supposed to maintain and support
male activities in the public sphere. These events also indicate that
women's roles in society are both limited and fatal: as the dutiful
daughter, Génifrède loses her love; as the dutiful lover, she loses her
life, or would if she had not been drugged. How she would have died
is also significant, for the reference to 'red water' signals the latent
presence of African culture in the text. To say that 'red water' is the
poisonous red juice of the sassy-tree, or red-water tree, of West Africa
is to provide the gloss on the term that Martineau withholds; and
because she withholds it, she allows the term to register cultural difference. The meaning of the term is established by its context, not by a
definition that would mean a privileging of her reader's position, or of
the 'receptor' culture (Ashcroft et al. 66). Instead, Martineau allows
Toussaint to gloss the term. Toussaint, now clearly representing both
blacks and whites, stands Janus-like between two cultures, and his
'reading' widens the cross-cultural gap: 'Can it be possible that my
poor child has been wrought upon by such jugglery?' By 'jugglery,'
Toussaint is referring both to the red water and to the ivory ring, which
Thérèse shows him. The ring summons up memories: '"How strange,"
said he, "are old thoughts, long forgotten! This bit of ivory makes me
again a young man and a slave. Do you remember that I once had the
care of the sick at Breda, and administered medicines? ... I began that
study as all of my race have begun it, till of late, – in superstition. With
what awe did I handle charms like this!"' (2:179). Such 'charms' are
part of Toussaint's forgotten past. Again, he has repressed his cultural
origins. This time, he destroys their tokens. Confronting Moyse, just
before dawn and his death, 'Toussaint crushed the ring to dust with
the heel of his boot, and dashed the phial against the ceiling, from
whence the poisonous water sprinkled the floor' (2:184).

Toussaint's behaviour is culturally denigrating: he consciously suppresses African values with a supposedly superior cultural model.[48]
When *The Hour and the Man* was published, abolitionism was the subject of heated controversy. Despite the efforts of England, France, and
Holland to put an end to the slave trade it continued to flourish
(through the efforts of Spain and Portugal), and many thought that
their object would have been better attained if they had concentrated

on 'civilizing' Africa.[49] In many respects, *The Hour and the Man* sustains a dialogue with this controversy, for although Toussaint sets out to 'civilize' St Domingo with European ideology, there is evident concern in the text for the culture that is being erased. In fact, it is reasonable to suggest that *The Hour and the Man* is sympathetic to postcolonial concerns, precisely because it often foregrounds tensions between a vanishing African culture and the values and assumptions of the imperial centre. Moreover, since women's identities in the text are at least partly inscribed by African culture, their roles are also rendered uncertain as a consequence of these tensions.

One indication of this gendered cultural inscription is sartorial. At Toussaint's levee, the most conspicuous effect of Génifrède's and Aimée's dress is that it 'was far from resembling the European fashion of the time. No tight lacing; no casing in whalebone; – nothing like a hoop' (1:211). Instead, they wear 'deep yellow India silk,' violet velvet, and heavy ornaments (1:212). Toussaint and his brother Paul, in contrast, are dressed in French uniforms. Toussaint, in particular, wears 'blue, with scarlet cape and cuffs, richly embroidered. He had white trousers, long Hessian-boots, and, as usual, the Madras handkerchief on his head' (2:215). His dress is predominately European, excepting the headwear. The identification of women with Africa is also linguistic and historicist. At L'Etoile, the home of Charles Bellair, a Congo chief kidnapped in his youth and brought as a slave to the island, and his wife, who now goes by her African name, Deesha ('Would we all knew our African names, as you know hers! Deesha!' Madame L'Ouverture exclaims [1:275]), Madame L'Ouverture recounts the history of her husband's royal descent:

> ... how he was grandson of Gaou Guinou, the king of the African tribe of Arrudos: how this king's second son was taken in battle, and sold, with other prisoners of war, into slavery: how he married an African girl on the Breda estate, and used to talk of home and its wars, and its hunts, and its sunshine idleness, – how he used thus to talk in the evenings, and on Sundays, to the boy upon his knee; so that Toussaint felt, from his infancy, like an African, and the descendant of chiefs.

It will be recalled that these are memories which Toussaint represses and that he focuses instead on the conquests of Alexander and Caesar. Not so for his wife: 'This was a theme which Madame L'Ouverture loved to dwell on' (1:292). Indeed, in the eagerness of her talk with the

Bellairs, 'they were perpetually falling unconsciously into the use of their negro language, and as often recalled by their hearers to that which all could understand' (1:292–3). These hearers include a small party from France and the L'Overture family, excepting Toussaint. Only one member of the party is aloof from the event. He is the character who took the L'Ouverture boys to France, and he is first a Frenchman and second a black: 'Vincent alone, negro as he was, was careless and unmoved. He presently sauntered away, and nobody missed him' (1:293). Vincent's allegiance to the imperial centre extinguishes his interest in African history. For others, black history and language are vitally important, and Vincent is not missed.

The Bellairs suffer a tragic fate. Fighting the French with Toussaint in the mornes, their two boys are killed by Cuban bloodhounds brought to the island by the French army. From that time until their torture and murder by the French, the pair direct their energies exclusively to vengeance. Deesha, in particular, is a relentless soldier: '... the forces of the First Consul had no more vindictive and mischievous enemy than the wife of Charles Bellair' (3:66). Clearly Deesha challenges gender constructions. She is also one of only two women in the novel whose character and history Martineau was able to discover from sources, although she could not learn her name. Thérèse, the first empress of Haiti, is the other. This is not surprising. Public, political, and military activities are traditionally the constituents of history, and since few women have engaged in such activities, most women have been marginalized in historical discourses, or forgotten altogether. Martineau had to invent most of her female characters.[50] Again, this points to the problem of knowing history through its prior textualizations. And, again, it suggests that Martineau's novel aims at providing a history whose subject is not 'man,' but 'the repressed, the forgotten, and the inarticulate,' to recall Calvino.

Notwithstanding the frequent omission of women from written histories, women have played a crucial role in patriarchy's efforts to certify the past through patrilineal genealogy. In other words, women's sexuality, or, more precisely, the control of women's sexuality by men, has been fundamental to patriarchy's certification of history by means of the 'repeating patrimonial.'[51] Consistent with his immersion in European ideology, such concerns are also central to Toussaint. At his levee, he is delighted to learn from the priests that there have been eight thousand marriages celebrated on the island. As a young priest says, 'under the religious rule of your excellency ... enforced by so pure an example of piety, the morals of this colony will be established, and the salvation of its people secured' (1:217). In other words, the colony will be able to establish its visible sanctity by a legitimate line of inheritance. The tracing of an unambiguous and conjugally sanctioned line of descent is an act of historical consciousness; it attempts to authorize and to institutionalize history and historical knowledge.

Promiscuity and illegitimate children endanger these historicizing processes, which are important to Toussaint. The question is, how far will he go to insure that 'morals' are enforced? At the beginning of the novel, Thérèse and her owner, Papalier, have a baby. During the march to the Spanish territory, where Toussaint joins the Spanish army, a group of insurgent blacks approaches Toussaint's party, which includes Thérèse, Papalier, and their child. The party hides in the trees, fearing attack. The baby begins to cry and is taken from Thérèse and killed. Thérèse believes that Papalier has killed her child; however, when she nurses him on his deathbed, he swears that it was not he.[52] Learning that Papalier is not the culprit, Thérèse is 'agonized by suspicions as to whose hand it was by which her child had died. In a moment, she formed a resolve which she never broke, – never again to seek to know that which Papalier now refused to tell' (3:141). Neither Thérèse nor the reader learns the answer to the persistent question in the novel – 'Who killed Thérèse's child?' – but there is something unmistakably ominous in Toussaint's admonishing of Thérèse once she and Jacques have been married:

'Did Jacques say, and say truly, that you are his wife?'
  'He said so, and truly. I have been wretched, for long ...'
  'And sinful. Wretchedness and sin go together.'
  'And I was sinful; but no one told me so. I was ignorant, and weak, and a slave. Now I am a woman and a wife. No more whites, no more sin, no more misery! Will you not let me stay here?'
  'I will ... You will atone, (will you not?) by the purity of your life.'
  (1:184–5)

We never know for certain that Toussaint killed Thérèse's baby, but that his patriarchal authoritarianism could have found a target in the illegitimate child is not refuted by the text either.[53]

The efforts of patriarchy to institutionalize history and knowledge are threatened not only by promiscuity, but also by behaviour and experiences that question the bases of prevailing metaphysics. In this novel, women are repeatedly the foci of events that challenge the increasingly dominant European world-view. One such woman is Mme Ogé, whose sons were killed in the mulatto uprising mentioned at the beginning of this chapter. Mme Ogé is regarded as something of a *mystérieuse* because she always seems to have prior knowledge of misfortunes, and just before the invasion of St Domingo by the French, Mme Ogé visits the convent at Cap Français. Some of the nuns are afraid to receive her, recalling how 'she came to this very house the first day of the meeting of the deputies, in that terrible August of ninety-one. She came a day or two before the rising against Hédouville. She came the night before the great hurricane of ninety-seven – ' (2:225). Mme Ogé's uncanny foreknowledge of events might be linked to Christian prophecy, but instead she is viewed by the nuns as a 'sorceress,' or as an instrument of evil. As a consequence, the abbess finds it necessary to rationalize Mme Ogé's behaviour: she is a 'wretched woman, whose woes have been such as might naturally have shaken her reason, and prostrated her will' (2:226). On the one hand, this explanation of Mme Ogé works positively against the view that well-informed women are witches; on the other hand, it disempowers Mme Ogé and insists on a straightforward explanation of her behaviour, which may, in fact, be misleading. Martineau maintains that Mme Ogé was 'probably very unlike what I have represented' (3:266). She is a figure of romance that challenges the restraints of rationalism. She stands for an alternative way of knowing 'truth' and 'reality,' competing with reason and history for the right to determine what counts as 'meaning' and 'knowledge.'

Génifrède proves to be another such figure. When her family is stationed in the mornes fighting the French army, Génifrède disappears to the top of the mountain:

> She cared neither for heat nor chill while there, and forgot food and rest; and there was sometimes that in her countenance when she returned, and in the tone of her prophesying about the destruction of the enemy, which caused the whisper to go round that she met her [dead] lover there, just under the clouds. M. Pascal, the rational, sagacious M. Pascal, was of the opinion that she believed this herself. (3:43)

Génifrède does indeed believe this. When Toussaint is finally captured and taken to France with the rest of his family, Génifrède opts to stay behind with Paul – her uncle and Moyse's father. She whispers to her father, 'I have seen Moyse, – I have seen him more than once in the Morne; and I cannot leave this place' (3:171). As with Mme Ogé's uncanny foreknowledge and Margaret's view of the supernatural significance of her ring's restoration in *Deerbrook*, Génifrède's visions of Moyse are a foil to logic and empiricism. M. Pascal, the author of the *Provinciales* and hailed by Toussaint as bringing 'the honours of piety, of reason, and of science' to the island, might think Génifrède believes she sees visions on the morne, but he cannot think so himself. Génifrède's visionary experiences undermine epistemological imperialism, disrupt the text's surface historical reality, and challenge the bases of historical knowledge. They may also qualify monocultural thinking: Génifrède's visions of Moyse are consistent with Vodouisants' direct access to the spirit world (Catholicism is less democratic), and Génifrède's belief that she can be sustained by these visions may be aligned with Vodouisants' faith that the spirit world responds to their needs and offers assistance in dealing with the practical matters of life.[54]

Toussaint's capture and transportation to France finally bring him to what has been the centre of his psychic life and historical consciousness. He has worshipped France and idolized Napoleon. Indeed, he has been delighted to hear himself called 'the Napoleon Bonaparte of St. Domingo' and has felt that he and Napoleon are brothers in glory (1:193). Even during his voyage, after Napoleon's betrayal of him, he still dwells on the prospect of meeting Napoleon and, at last, of seeing France. As it happens, 'none of his dreams were verified' (3:186). Obeying the geometrical laws of colonialism, Toussaint has revered the centre, is brought to the centre, but never sees it:

> Nothing did he see of Paris but some of the dimly-lighted streets, as he was conveyed, at night, to the prison of the Temple. During the weeks that he was a prisoner there, he looked in vain for a summons to the presence of the First Consul, or for the First Consul's appearance in his apartment. One of Bonaparte's aides, Caffarelli, came indeed, and brought messages: but these messages were only insulting inquiries about the treasures, – the treasures buried in the mornes; – for ever these treasures! This recurring message, with its answer, was all the communication he had with Bonaparte; and the hum and murmur from the streets were all that he knew of Paris. (3:187)

The interrogation of Toussaint about treasure stems from an incident in the mornes: two French officers overhear Toussaint's war plans and are taken prisoner, but not before they see the spades and pick-axes that Toussaint has been using to build a post in the Plateau. They decide he has buried treasure in the mountains, and France wants it returned. This misunderstanding is described as 'romancing' (3:39) and is documented in historical sources. Romance and history again become blurred, or, indeed, indistinguishable. France, the centre of legal and historical discourse, fails to know and to represent 'history' correctly. As for Toussaint, his pursuit of the centre and of the historic event, or meeting, is forever deferred. France becomes the novel's blind spot. The centre does not confer identity but is instead a black hole that erases and destroys it. Taken to the fortress at Joux, Toussaint and his servant are concealed from the villagers, who would otherwise see their colour: 'It was clear that the complexion of the strangers was not to be seen by the inhabitants' (3:188). In the fortress itself, Toussaint is led down 'a passage, dark, wet, and slippery,' to a dark cell that is 'slippery with wet' (3:196–7). In an inversion of the birth process, he dies in his mother country, the text's anti-colonialist strategies perhaps overlapping with stresses in Martineau's relationship with her own mother. Imprisoned in this cell, Toussaint's thoughts return to St Domingo as he now pretends to read the books he is given. The destabilizing effects of imperial power characterize his final experiences precisely:

> In pushing the colonial world to the margins of experience the 'centre' pushed consciousness beyond the point at which monocentrism in all spheres of thought could be accepted without question. In other words the alienating process which initially served to relegate the post-colonial world to the 'margin' turned upon itself and acted to push that world through a kind of mental barrier into a position from which all experience could be viewed as uncentred, pluralistic, and multifarious. (Ashcroft et al. 12)

Toussaint meditates on his circumstances in related terms: 'It is true that I erred, according to the common estimate of affairs, in not making myself a king, and separating my country from France, as France herself is compelling her to separate at last' (3:238). He now hopes for his country's independence and that blacks might teach whites how to be Christians. His final moments once again confuse 'reality' and romance, or fantasy:

He raised himself but once, – hastily and dizzily in the dawn (dawn to him, but sunrise abroad). His ear had been reached by the song of the young goatherds, as they led their flock abroad into another valley. The prisoner had dreamed that it was his boy Denis, singing in the piazza at Pongaudin. As his dim eye recognized the place, by the flicker of the expiring flambeau, he smiled at his delusion, and sank back to sleep again. (3:242)

The end of the novel is invented because Toussaint's death is not found in historical records: the event and discourse are not always synchronous. The official version is that he died of apoplexy, but most believe he was murdered (again, the official discourse of the centre is directly challenged). The text's pluralities are never reduced. History and romance can be seen as opposed or as indistinguishable, making it impossible to represent accurately historical meaning. The historical romance is not, as Lukács and Reilly believe, immune to the problems surrounding the knowledge and representation of history. Instead, it is precisely in this genre that the 'crisis' of history is most clearly articulated. *The Hour and the Man*, in particular, foregrounds these issues distinctly. It also carries with it a warning to Martineau's own society about the abuses of patriarchy and the dangers of unqualified monocultural thinking.

Chapter Five

Invalidism, Mesmerism, and the Medical Profession:

Life in the Sick-Room (1844) and *Letters on Mesmerism* (1844)

Martineau wrote *The Hour and the Man* during the first part of an illness that was to last five years. She had been travelling through Italy with some of her friends when she was debilitated by gynaecological problems at Venice in 1839. Returning to England, she established herself at Tynemouth, where she was attended by her brother-in-law, Dr Thomas M. Greenhow. As for many Victorians, illness provided Martineau with a reprieve from the stresses of life, but it was not a permanent condition for her. Instead, Martineau believed that she was cured by mesmerism and published an account of her recovery in the *Athenaeum* in 1844, creating a great sensation. Alison Winter has published a superb study of the history of mesmerism in Victorian England, but Martineau's biographers generally condescend to her belief in this popular practice.[1] Robert Webb, for example, describes Martineau's account of her case as 'almost hopeless' and bases his discussion of her condition on the testimony of professional medical men (Webb 193n). In particular, he relies heavily on the *Medical Report of the Case of Miss H– M–*, which Greenhow published in defence of his professional reputation after Martineau's public testimony.[2] Greenhow's *Report* does provide an important historical record of a medical diagnosis that contributes greatly to our understanding of Martineau's case, but Webb's account also reiterates the medical profession's prejudices against mesmerism in the 1830s and 1840s, albeit from a modern standpoint that regards nineteenth-century alternative (if not mainstream) therapeutics as merely naïve. This chapter attempts to situate mesmerism and Martineau's illness in their contemporary cultural and medical milieux. In particular, it examines Greenhow's diagnosis and Martineau's subjective experience of illness, the doctor-patient relationship between Martineau and Greenhow, the identification of mesmerism with hysteria, and the threats posed both to the medical profession and to social organization by perceived displays of extraordinary self-control, deceit, and sexuality by female somnambulists.

When Martineau was overtaken by illness at Venice, she consulted a local physician named Dr Nardo about her condition. Her symptoms were related to Nardo in some detail: an irregular bloodlike vaginal discharge and the protrusion into the vagina of a solid, insensible substance were described in a letter to Nardo by one of Martineau's travelling companions. From these reported symptoms, and without any examination of his own, Nardo concluded that Martineau was suffering from either a prolapsed uterus or a polypus (fibroid) tumour. Martineau was equally straightforward about her illness in letters to Greenhow from Italy. She describes irregular catemenia (menstruation), an irritating discharge, an 'inability to stand or walk, aching and weariness of the back, extending down the legs to the heels,' 'tenderness and pain, on pressure, in the left groin, extending by the hip to the back,' and 'a *membranous substance*, like the end of a little finger' projecting from the mouth of her uterus.[3]

Martineau's explicit account of her symptoms challenges the emergent power dynamic in the nineteenth century between the subject/doctor, whose increasing anatomical knowledge enabled him to determine the seat of an illness by means of clinical examination, and the object/patient, whose articulation of subjectively perceived symptoms, so important to diagnosis in the eighteenth century, was becoming increasingly extraneous.[4] Her account also challenges Webb's opinion that Martineau's account of her own case was 'almost hopeless.' Indeed, one of Martineau's letters from Lucerne dated 6 July 1839 allowed Greenhow to 'fix' the period when uterine retroversion occurred:

> I cannot walk without injury, as I said, and keep my feet laid up, and my knees somewhat raised, as the easiest posture. I began to use the syringe, as you and Dr. Nardo recommended: it was a great relief, but in *three days* there *was no room for it*, and on this account I have never been able to use it since. I discontinued the sponge, finding it irritating, as you say, and it is not now *necessary*. (Greenhow 10–11)

Martineau's letter indicates that both Nardo and Greenhow were able to prescribe for their patient solely on the basis of Martineau's description of her own symptoms, making it easy to characterize the doctor-patient relationship in this instance as one of mutual cooperation.

Following Martineau's public announcement of her recovery by mesmerism, however, the relationship between her and Greenhow soured. Feeling that his professional authority and reputation were at stake, Greenhow published his *Report* as a shilling pamphlet. Martineau had consented to Greenhow's publishing an account of her case but had assumed it would appear in a medical journal. Instead, the pamphlet was 'not even written in Latin, – but open to all the world!' (*HMA* 2:198n). By disclosing the particulars of her gynaecological state to the general public, Greenhow both competed with Martineau's own published account of herself, and thus her professional authority, and subjugated her by turning her into an object of (common) knowledge. 'No man would like it,' Edward Barrett observed, 'much less a woman. They quite turn her inside out.'[5] It seems that after Martineau's apparent mesmeric cure, Greenhow attempted to assert the power of the doctor over his patient, and Martineau, whose indignation at Greenhow recalls the initial resistance of *Deerbrook*'s female characters to Hope's clinical strategies, broke off her relationship with him.

Prior to the *Report*'s publication, however, Martineau was pleased with Greenhow's care. In her first letter on mesmerism to the *Athenaeum*, she refers to him as her 'kind and vigilant medical friend' who did what he could to cure her illness and to alleviate her pain. Her reference in her letter to Greenhow to the uses of a syringe (employed for injecting water into the vagina) and a sponge (used as a pessary) calls attention to the treatment of uterine problems at the time of her illness, and it should be observed that after inspecting her, Greenhow diagnosed Martineau as having an enlarged, prolapsed, and retroverted uterus accompanied by polypus tumours.[6] Greenhow used an array of measures to alleviate Martineau's symptoms, and despite the popular view that doctors' treatment of diseases at the time was largely idiosyncratic,[7] there was a surprising consensus among medical men about the management of cases like Martineau's to which Greenhow's prescriptions conform. The syringe and pessary were customary treatments;[8] ergot of rye, which Greenhow used in an attempt to expel a large polypus suspected within the uterus, had also been used in similar cases;[9] and his use of purgatives to relieve constipation caused by the pressure of the uterine tumour on the bowels was a widely encouraged practice.[10] It was also common to apply leeches to alleviate tenderness; and his use of iodide of iron was suggested to him by the eminent gynaecologist, Sir Charles Clarke.[11]

Unfortunately, most of these remedies were ineffective. The syringe and pessary, as Martineau notes, had to be discontinued, and warm baths and ergot of rye disappointed Greenhow's expectations. Greenhow attributed Martineau's cure to the use of the iodide of iron, but his confidence in this remedy may have been overstated. One critic of the *Report* claimed that Greenhow demonstrated a 'lack of medical skill' in prescribing, for three years, iodine pills in such small doses that they could have no more effect than a very weak tonic.[12] Of course, this critic was an interested party. Writing for *Zoist*, John Elliotson's periodical devoted to mesmerism, he might well be expected to depreciate Greenhow's efforts in favour of mesmeric wonders. At the same time, his opinion accords with Martineau's own statement that both Greenhow and Clarke saw her case as incurable.[13] It is also consistent with the opinion of other medical men that in cases like Martineau's cure was unlikely at best: 'We rarely succeed in cases of *prolapsus uteri*, of long standing, in obtaining a radical cure by any remedies, and it is only by an operation that we are to look for such a result,' Dr Oakley Heming insisted (Heming 672). The operation he refers to was first suggested by Dr Marshall Hall and first performed by himself, and its complexity seems exacerbated by diagnostic misnomers: sutures were to be inserted from the *os uteri* to the *os externum* of the partially expelled and incised 'uterus,' 'tumour,' or 'vagina' (Heming 673). The purpose of this procedure was that when ligatures tying the sutures were tightened, the *os uteri* would be moved and supported upwards.

Heming's apparent uncertainty whether he was dealing with a prolapsed uterus or vagina is understandable, but his description of the uterus as a 'tumour' is also consistent with Hall's understanding of pregnancy as an organic disease of the uterus (Hall 503). Hall lists thirteen other organic uterine diseases, four functional diseases or catemenial irregularities, including amenorrhoea and menorrhagia, four diseases of the ovaria, and seven diseases of the mammae. Women's biological differences from men seemed inherently pathological, and although these disorders legitimated the medical profession's role in overseeing and attending to women's 'complaints,' they also were the cause of diagnostic confusion and professional embarrassment. Slight cases of *prolapsus uteri* were often mistaken for gastric problems and treated as such, without benefit, for weeks (Heming 671). Distinguishing between *prolapsus uteri* and polypus (fibroid) tumours could also be extremely problematic. For example, Dr William MacDonald describes the case of a Mrs A., aged thirty-nine, who suffered from irregular vaginal discharges and abdominal pain. Diagnosing her illness as menorrhagia, he inspected the patient internally for the purpose of inserting a plug, when he detected a tumour in the upper part of the vagina, 'the bulk of this fibrous mass being nearly as large as the foetal head at the full period of utero-gestation.'[14] Uncertain as to whether this 'tumour' was the womb itself or a large polypus, and having consulted Dr James Wilson, formerly lecturer of midwifery at the University of Glasgow (who was equally unable to form a diagnosis), MacDonald and Wilson, acting under a 'conjectural view of the disease ... proceeded to operate' by tying a ligature around the base of the tumour. MacDonald describes the case as interesting 'from the great difficulty which two practitioners experienced in forming a diagnosis' and from

> the analogy of cases in which tumours similarly situated were believed to be polypi, turning out to be the wombs of patients in an inverted state; and in which cases the ligatures were applied, constitutional symptoms followed; the ligatures were not immediately loosened; the majority of the patients died, and the tumours were after death found to be really the wombs in different states and stages of inversion. (MacDonald 577)

Whether Greenhow's diagnosis was more skilful or more fortunate than other doctors' can only be a matter for speculation, but his difficulty in knowing how to cure Martineau's illness is certainly suggested by his view that 'the condition of the uterus in December [was] but the *natural sequel* of progressive improvement begun in, or antecedent to, the month of April' (Greenhow 23; emphasis added). For Spencer T. Hall, who first mesmerized Martineau, the significance of such a admission was unequivocal: Greenhow attributed Martineau's recovery to natural causes since it was beyond the scope of 'ordinary' medical treatment.[15]

The diagnostic and therapeutic difficulties surrounding cases of uterine disease suggest an analogy between these cases and cases of hysteria, whose propensity to baffle and to frustrate the century's most accomplished practitioners has become almost a commonplace in medical histories and cultural criticism. Indeed, Martineau's illness seems classically hysterical in terms of her pathological symptoms considered so far.[16] It is well known that the term 'hysteria' derives from the Greek word *hystera*, meaning uterus (which itself derives from the Sanskrit term for belly), and that the Egyptians and the Greeks attributed behavioural abnormalities in women to the wandering of the uterus – usually upward instead of downward (as in cases of uterine prolapse), but prolapse also appears to be described as an hysterical condition in ancient texts.[17] Moreover, the Greeks elaborated a causal relationship between hysteria and sexuality. Plato attributes the womb's migration to barrenness in the *Timaeus*, and Hippocrates believed that sexual inactivity would incite the uterus to roam through the body in search of fulfilment. Roman authors, such as Galen of Pergamon, seem to have shared these beliefs, identifying virgins, widows, and spinsters as the likeliest candidates for hysteria and recommending fornication as the best remedy.[18] As a single woman who claimed never to have experienced sexual love, Martineau would seem to exemplify ancient beliefs about hysterical disorders, but explanations of hysteria themselves wandered away from these early hypotheses. Although it is impossible to trace fully the history of hysteria here, it is necessary to outline the great paradigm shifts in order to understand the diagnosis of Martineau's case.

The first major shift occurred with the spread of Christianity throughout the Roman Empire, giving rise to an understanding of hysteria as a supernatural disorder caused by demonic possession. This was a conception of the condition that contributed to a contradictory view of female hysterics as both victims and witches. Modes of treatment were aligned with this contradiction, ranging from incantations and exorcisms to torture and murder. Fortunately, in the seventeenth century efforts were made to renaturalize the disease, the most important of which was the development of a neurological model of hysteria based on new understandings of the structure and function of the nervous system. Often combined with humoural pathology and iatromechanical and iatrochemical theorization in the later seventeenth and early eighteenth centuries, these new neurogenic analyses supplanted both the supernatural paradigm and the uterine model, the latter of which had been effectively discredited by autopsies on hysterical patients that showed no signs of uterine abnormalities, let alone movement. The uterine theory re-emerged in the late eighteenth century, however, as physicians became involved in a rigorous classification of diseases, but now hysteria was thought to be caused by sexual excess and was compared to the new disease of nymphomania. Philippe Pinel classified hysteria among the 'Genital Neuroses of Women' at the turn of the century, and by the nineteenth century, a proliferation of theories existed concurrently both in France and in England with no one school at the forefront. Following the discovery of ovulation in the 1840s, an ovarian theory of hysteria emerged; Robert Brudenell Carter's *On the Pathology and Treatment of Hysteria* (1853) emphasized the negative personality traits of hysterics, including eccentricity, deceitfulness, and emotionality; and among gynaecological physicians, hybrid theories were popular whereby organic diseases of the uterus, vagina, and ovaries, and functional irregularities in catemenia and lactation, were considered pathogenic, affecting the rest of the body neurologicaly. Remedies within this last disease model included douches, dilations, intra-uterine injections, and the application of leeches to the cervix and vulva (Micale 20–4). My aim is not retrospective diagnosis, but Martineau's condition and treatment seems to accord with this last diagnostic and therapeutic system.

Martineau's case was never labelled hysterical, however, and it is likely that this absent diagnosis relates both to the proliferation of ideas about hysteria at the time of her illness and, simultaneously, to the attempts of medical practitioners to achieve professional status. It seems beyond coincidence that the multiplicity of ideas about hysteria in the nineteenth century accompanies the emergence of a historical consciousness, considered in chapter 4. Foucault's argument that with the contemporary episteme, emerging between 1775 and 1825, signs become related diachronically, and 'a profound historicity penetrates into the heart of things [that] isolates and defines them in their own coherence'[19] clarifies this profusion of theories of hysteria when it is understood that the history of the disorder was not coherent but multifarious. Although less true of theories based on new discoveries, such as ovulation (and yet even the ovarian theory involved a re-eroticization of the disease), ideas about hysteria at this time were essentially reformulations of historical paradigms: the neuro-uterine model clearly incorporates both the uterine and neurological paradigms; the re-emergence of the demoniacal paradigm is suggested in the deceit and, indeed, wilfulness of the hysteric/enemy and is concretely expressed in conjunction with a new psychogenic understanding of hysteria deriving from mesmerism. These last considerations will be discussed more fully below. What merits attention here is that for medical practitioners intent on professionalization, this proliferation of theories of hysteria, marking the absence of an ontological disease category and stable symptom profile, threatened to rob the doctor of his authority and sought-for status. As a consequence, practitioners attempted to minimize the problem of hysteria as much as possible. Janet Oppenheim observes that hysteria was a 'catch-all classification' for women's nervous disorders, and Carroll Smith-Rosenberg has pointed out that many disorders categorized as hysteria in the nineteenth century 'might today be diagnosed as neurasthenia, hypochondriasis, depression, conversion reaction, and ambulatory schizophrenia.'[20] This is certainly true, but it is also true that many disorders that might have been diagnosed as hysteria in the nineteenth century were not diagnosed as such even then, at least in part because of the confusion and subsequent embarrassment that hysteria caused for medical practitioners seeking increased social and political power.[21] Indeed, a meeting of the Medical Society of London in 1844 was dominated by a discussion of the undesirability of the hysteria diagnosis:

Dr. Clutterbuck complain[ed] that the term was indefinite and unsatisfactory, and, in reference to the case related at the previous meeting, he thought it would be more correct to call it by some other name than 'hysterical' ... Dr. Clutterbuck deprecated the system of naming symptoms hysterical which depended on some local cause which might be ascertained. The President related the case of a woman in whom various hysterical symptoms appeared to be the result of diseased action in the spine ... Dr. Clutterbuck did not call these symptoms hysterical, but spinal.[22]

That such avoidance of the term 'hysteria' could pertain equally to cases of uterine disease is made clear by a review in the *Lancet* of Dr John Lever's *A Practical Treatise on Organic Disease of the Uterus*, which won the Medical Society of London's Fothergillian Gold Medal in 1841.[23] Lever's classification of hysteria as a functional uterine disorder dismays the reviewer, as 'a doctrine certainly untenable in the present state of science,' and leads him to add somewhat ambiguously that 'it is equally certain that in a very large proportion of hysterical cases the uterus is not the primitive or even secondary seat of the disease.'[24] The reviewer also objects to the related word 'hysteritis,' which Lever 'unnecessarily' terms 'chronic inflammation following metritis during pregnancy.'[25]

This unwillingness of medical practitioners to diagnose cases as hysteria that might be better classified in terms of localized organic dysfunction may help to explain why many recent critics and biographers of Martineau incline towards and are frustrated by an understanding of her case as hysteria: the diagnosis was resisted by her contemporary physicians.[26] What makes this resistance seem especially odd is that her case conforms with other cases diagnosed as hysteria later in the century. Post-Darwinian psychiatry facilitated the diagnosis of hysteria in those ambitious women who competed with men and were debilitated in the process. As Elaine Showalter writes:

> At the same time that new opportunities for self-cultivation and self-fulfillment in education and work were offered to women, doctors warned them that pursuit of such opportunities would lead to sickness, sterility, and race suicide. They explicitly linked the epidemic of nervous disorders – anorexia nervosa, hysteria, and neurasthenia – which marked the *fin de siècle* to women's ambition.[27]

Darwin explained in *The Descent of Man* (1871) that man's intellectual and physical superiority to woman was the consequence of natural selection, and for a host of doctors in the 1870s, this premise entailed fixed gender roles that both fulfilled the 'natures' of men and women and furthered the needs of the race. Women who defied their 'nature' to compete with men in the public sphere were susceptible to nervous breakdown, T.S. Clouston argued.[28] For Henry Maudsley, not only were women's minds at risk but so was their reproductive capacity. Mental effort could disrupt or arrest menstruation, cause headaches, insomnia, and lethargy, and, worst of all, result in degeneration of the reproductive system.[29] Martineau, whose arduous work schedule and professional successes were succeeded by organic and functional uterine debilitation, seems to exemplify these warnings, but in the early 1840s there were not enough women like her to constitute a crisis. It was only later in the century that the threat posed to social organization by the New Woman was sufficiently urgent to warrant a sophisticated scientific and medical rationale for women's place in the home[30] – a rationale, moreover, which allowed doctors some control over the understanding and classification of hysterical behaviour. As far as Martineau's illness is concerned, any punitive or retributory dimension it may have involved derives chiefly from her own perceptions of her sickness.

Martineau's gynaecological ailments have been emphasized thus far; however, cultural and emotional factors may also precipitate sickness and appear to have been operative in Martineau's case. Indeed, in her *Autobiography*, Martineau seems almost to insist that her illness was psycho- and sociosomatic: 'A tumour was forming of a kind which usually originates in mental suffering' (*HMA* 2:151); 'It was unquestionably the result of excessive anxiety of mind, – of the extreme tension of nerves under which I had been living for some years, while the three anxious members of my family were, I must say, on my hands – not in regard to money, but to care of a more important kind' (*HMA*: 2:150). The three family members referred to were Martineau's elderly aunt, her brother Henry, who moved in with Martineau in 1838,[31] and her mother, who was aging and losing her sight. According to Martineau, her mother coped with her blindness beautifully, 'but [her] natural irritability found vent in other directions; and especially it was visited upon me' (*HMA* 2:150).

Martineau's relationship with her mother had always been problematic. As a small child, she doubted that her mother loved her.[32] As a young woman, her professional ambition collided with her mother's sense of social propriety. Mrs Martineau had fixed ideas about what constituted appropriate behaviour for women, and Martineau and her sisters were never allowed to be seen 'with pen in hand' in the parlour. Instead, they 'were expected to sit down in the parlour to sew' (*HMA* 1:100). When Martineau began to write in earnest following the collapse of her father's business in 1829, she sewed during the days and stayed up during the nights to write: 'I was writing till two, or even three in the morning' (*HMA* 1:147). Living in Fludyer Street with her mother, she reversed these priorities. Occupied all day with literary work, 'I was not allowed to have a maid, at my own expense, or even to employ a work-woman: and thus, many were the hours after midnight when I ought to have been asleep, when I was sitting up to mend my clothes' (*HMA* 2:150–1). Mrs Martineau's unreasonableness about her daughter's hiring a servant undoubtedly reflected her dissatisfaction with Martineau's choice of career – a choice which Mrs Martineau attempted to thwart altogether in 1829. Martineau, who had then begun to write articles for the *Monthly Repository*, was offered a post in London as a woman of letters: 'But, to my disappointment, – I might almost say, horror, – my mother sent me peremptory orders to go home ... to pursue, – not literature but needlework' (*HMA* 1:149). According to Martineau, her mother 'had no other idea at the moment than that she had been doing her best for my good; and I, for my part, could not trust myself to utter a word of what was swelling in my heart' (*HMA* 1:150). Later, Martineau insisted on her right to pursue a literary career, but it is clear that she felt tremendous guilt about her failure to fulfil the role of dutiful daughter. Finally, she wrote, 'The anxieties of my home were too much for me, and I was by that time wearing down fast. The illness which laid me low for nearly six years at length ensued' (*HMA* 1:250–1). Later, in *Household Education*, Martineau would describe an ideal mother in terms bitterly opposed to her own filial experiences: 'It is a kind of new life to a mother who has kept her mind and heart active and warm amidst her trials and cares, to enter into sympathy with the aspirations and imaginations of her ripening children.'[33]

As it did for so many Victorians, illness provided Martineau with a means of escape from the conflicts of domestic and professional life. In her study of the Victorian sickroom, Miriam Bailin argues for the power of the sickroom 'to register and to appear to reconcile contemporary social conflicts and formal disjunctions within the "natural" domain of bodily process and exigent circumstance' (Bailin 13). For Bailin, the sickroom mediates gaps between personal and social experience, and operates as a kind of 'haven' in providing 'an alternative society and mode of existence' (Bailin 9). This is a theory of illness that conforms with Martineau's own view of her invalidism in her *Autobiography*:

> Here closed the anxious period during which my reputation, and my industry, and my social intercourses were at their height of prosperity; but which was so charged with troubles that when I lay down on my couch of pain in my Tynemouth lodging, for a confinement of nearly six years, I felt myself comparatively happy in my release from responsibility, anxiety, and suspense. (*HMA* 2:146)

However, the *Autobiography* was written in 1855, and Martineau's retrospective view of her sickness at times seems different from her immediate impressions recorded in *Life in the Sick-Room*. When Bailin considers the flight of Victorian women into sickness, she refers to those women whose desire to exceed the 'designated and restrictive social role' is mitigated by 'an internalized injunction to renounce that desire' (Bailin 27). Illness for such women involves imitation of the cultural restraints on women's lives in a manner that achieves some power over them. It is a form of passive resistance that both challenges and conforms to social norms: 'Despite its separation from the more taxing demands of fellowship, the sickroom is still located in the domestic centre of Victorian life' (Bailin 20). Illness allows for the preservation of personal identity that would be profoundly threatened by a rejection of culturally prescribed roles. For Martineau, however, sickness was less of a virtually sanctioned means of rebellion than it was an atonement for a successful professional career.

Looking back at *Life in the Sick-Room* in her *Autobiography*, Martineau was dismayed at the book's morbidity and at its reiteration of 'old traditions' as positive convictions:

> All the facts in the book, and some of the practical doctrine of the sickroom, I could still swear to: but the magnifying of my own experience, the desperate concern as to my own ease and happiness, the moaning undertone running through what many people have called the stoicism, and the total inability to distinguish between the metaphysically apparent and the positively true, make me, to say the truth, heartily despise a considerable part of the book. (*HMA* 2:172)

Martineau's reference to 'the metaphysically apparent' refers to her tendency throughout *Life in the Sick-Room* to regard suffering as divinely ordained. 'Pain,' she writes, 'is the chastisement of a Father,' and despite her protest in the book's dedication that work is also divinely appointed, she appears to believe that her successful career is precisely what she is being chastised for.[34] Martineau cannot bear to hear her past work referred to by friends as a matter for solace: 'O! what words can express the absurdity!' Far from inspiring 'complacency' or 'self-gratulation,' reflection on past industry summons haunting visions

> of duties slighted and opportunities neglected – the horrible apparition of old selfishness and pusillanimities – the disgusting foolery of idiotic vanities; if the consoler could catch a momentary glimpse of this phantasmagoria of the sick-room, he would turn with fear and loathing from the past, and shudder, while the inured invalid smiles, at such a choice of topics for solace. (*LS* 22)

Martineau clearly labours under a strong sense of guilt about her past industry, and that this guilt is related to a sense of filial failure, to a sense of having defied her mother's hopes and expectations for her, and to her unwillingness to have taken adequate care of her blind and aging mother when this would have jeopardized her own productivity, is certainly suggested by the nightmares that tormented Martineau when she first arrived at Tynemouth, and which she herself attributes to 'distress' about her mother's well-being: 'I rarely slept without starting from a dream that my mother had fallen from a precipice, or over the banisters, or from a cathedral spire; and that it was my fault' (*HMA* 2:151). Martineau's life before the sickroom deviated consistently from assigned gender roles, and invalidism meant a thorough re-evaluation of social and moral values and of personal worth: 'It is impossible to deny that the illness under which I lay suffering for five years was induced by flagrant violations of the laws of nature' (*HMA* 2:152). Far from preserving identity, illness threatened to annihilate it for Martineau. Her belief that 'ease may be found in self-forgetfulness' (*LS* 20) is consistent with the fact that *Life in the Sick-Room* was published anonymously, as 'Essays by an Invalid.' Martineau's identity, at least on the title page, was literally reduced to a pathological condition.

The consolations were few. As already mentioned, Martineau found solace in pain because 'every tangible proof' that the invalid 'is under chastening and discipline, conveys to him a sense of his dignity – reassures him, as a child of Providence' (*LS* 132). She also found solace in writing, and to whatever extent sickness, as a form of hyperfemininity, was in itself atonement for her literary career, she seems also to have attempted compensation in her *Playfellow* series, a collection of four stories written for children.[35] Considered biographically, these tales featuring children's heroism and self-reliance in adversity bear meaningful insights about perseverance and endurance. *Settlers at Home*, for example, tells the story of how two Dutch children survive the supposed loss of their parents during floods at the time of the English Civil War. *The Peasant and the Prince* recounts the tragic story of the young dauphin in revolutionary France. But these stories and, in particular, her most famous tale, *The Crofton Boys*, also contain Martineau's most conventional writing. Indeed, it seems at first hard to believe that *The Crofton Boys* was written by her. The plot is straightforward. A young boy named Hugh Procter longs to attend his elder brother's school and is at length admitted, making him the youngest 'Crofton Boy.' He is just beginning to learn to adapt socially and intellectually to his new environment when he falls from a wall during a snowball fight and hurts his foot, which has to be amputated. Hugh learns moral strength during his convalescence and is rewarded by being sent into service in India. Hugh's sister Agnes, meanwhile, nurses her brother through his recovery, feels in the way, and is left at home when Hugh leaves the country. The stories are without irony and are most unlike Martineau's earlier feminism, especially in *Society in America*.[36] Martineau believed, however, that these children's stories and, in particular, *The Crofton Boys*, were to be her 'last word through the press,' adding that 'there are some things in it which I could not have written except under that persuasion' (*HMA* 2:169). As Diana Postlethwaite suggests, this admission offers some important clues for understanding these stories. Postlethwaite persuasively argues that *The Crofton Boys* is informed by autobiographical concerns. Hugh is 'Martineau's idealized childhood self, freed from the constraints of gender to pursue education and travel.'[37] At the same time, Hugh's amputation is 'symbolic castration' or punishment for his aspiring to full inclusion in 'the exclusive men's club of intellectual achievement' (Postlethwaite 599). Martineau's own failure to be fully accepted within this club aligns her also with the tangential Agnes; moreover, like Agnes, Martineau was left behind when her brother James went to college. Postlethwaite argues compellingly that 'in writing *The Crofton Boys* Martineau searched for a way to heal this divided self' (Postlethwaite 600), but for Martineau's contemporary readers unacquainted with, and possibly unconcerned by, the author's personal experiences, the *Playfellow* stories probably functioned as conventional tales. With male heroes and marginalized female characters, the *Playfellow* series upholds conventional gender-role socialization. It appears to me to be an apology for her earlier challenging of social norms.

The forms of solace remaining for Martineau were pessimism and solitude. Martineau found no comfort in being assured of her recovery and was only happy when others conceded the hopelessness of her condition.[38] At the same time, she feared becoming a burden to others in what she believed to be her last days. Although popular representations of illness portrayed the sufferer surrounded by loving friends and relations, she stresses the importance to invalids, 'whose burden is for life,' of living alone, tended by a servant rather than a family member – another manifestation, perhaps, of her guilt in failing to attend to her ailing mother (*LS* 31). The picture Martineau paints of her invalidism is morbid, and one should reject the view that illness was empowering for her. Martineau's sickness was not an expression of rebellion, but rather of defeat. Postlethwaite provides an acute and sensitive account of the emotional factors at work in Martineau's case but insists on the 'visionary' dimension of her illness. She claims that 'Harriet Martineau's sickroom was transformed from a cloistered retreat into a place of visionary perspective,' that this 'breadth of vision is symbolized by the telescope she kept in her sickroom,' and, finally, that 'the powers that Martineau attributed to mesmerism were really those she had found within herself as she lay at Tynemouth' (Postlethwaite 603, 602, 604). It is certainly true that Martineau's observation of the world's activities from her sickroom was important to her. Indeed, she believed her powers of understanding what she observed in the world to have been greatly enhanced by her isolation. However, she attributes this improved understanding to her detachment from what she saw. She had effectively exchanged her share of 'world-building' for 'the privilege of the supposed [Miltonic] seraph.' Martineau may have been content to 'lie on the verge of life and watch' (*LS* 65), but to suggest that this posture could be more empowering than activity within the world seems perniciously misleading, especially when one realizes that what prompted her outward gaze in the first place was relief from morbid introspection. Martineau describes the invalid's state of mind:

... where the spirit has lost its security of innocence, unconsciousness, or self-reliance, and become morbidly sensitive to failures and dangers, – where it has become cowardly in conscience, shrinking from all moral enterprise, and dreading moral injury from every occurrence, the temper of anxiety must spread from the sufferer to all about him ... (*LS* 131)

As to the remedy, Martineau maintains: 'The only advice that even experience can give in such an instance, is to revive healthy old associations, to occupy the morbid powers with objects from without, and to use the happiest rather than the lowest seasons for leading the mind to a consideration of its highest relations' (*LS* 133). When Postlethwaite contends that Martineau's telescope literally 'gave her a broad, detailed, and direct vision of the human world beyond the walls of her sickroom, while metaphorically, it could also be trained on her own soul,' she gets the order of events the wrong way around (Postlethwaite 602). It was precisely to thwart self-contemplation that Martineau took a special interest in worldly affairs. The image of Martineau that emerges most distinctly from *Life in the Sick-Room* is not that of sibylline power, but rather one of a suffering woman, 'sinking in weakness before the bare idea of enterprise, abashed by self-consciousness, [and] smarting under tenderness of conscience' (*LS* 151). It is the image of a woman obsessed with recurring ideas of guilt, unable even to read 'while the enemy is hovering about the page' (*LS* 167). Martineau may boast about her ability to understand fully politics and history from her couch, but she is also subject to self-contempt:

> The retrospect of one's own life, from the stillness of the sick room, is unendurable to any considerate person, except in the light of the deepest religious humility ... When to the pains and misgivings of such perpetual retrospect are added the burdens of a sense of present and permanent uselessness, and of overwhelming gratitude for services received from hour to hour, – there is no self-respect in the world that will, unaided, support cheerfulness and equanimity. (*LS* 130)

Narcissism, fragility, self-loathing, morbid suggestibility, excessive religiosity, and an unnatural desire for solitude: Martineau's subjective experiences of illness resemble what recent historians recognize as hysterical symptoms.[39]

Fortunately, sickness was not an end in itself for Martineau, as it was for many Victorians. According to Bailin, 'the conventional pattern of ordeal and recovery takes on its particularly Victorian emphasis in the location of the desired condition of restored order and stability not in regained health but in a sustained condition of disability and quarantine' (Bailin 6). In contrast, Martineau claimed to have found her optimal condition in recovery through mesmerism, embroiling herself in a heated controversy that has not yet been fully understood. I shall explain this controversy and Martineau's role in it, but a brief history of mesmerism is necessary in order to situate the controversy in its larger historical framework and to clarify ideas and terminology relevant to Martineau's case.

It was not until the 1830s that mesmerism began to attract widespread attention in England, despite the fact that it had been practised with documented successes on the Continent for sixty years. Mesmerism, or animal magnetism, originated with the work of Franz Anton Mesmer, born on 23 May 1734, near the town of Radolfzell, Germany.[40] As a medical student at the University of Vienna, Mesmer first suggested a theory of animal magnetism in his thesis, *Dissertatio physico-medica de planetarum influxu* (1766), defining the influence of celestial bodies on humans as 'animal gravity' and maintaining that disruptions of this influence would cause disease. In 1774, he developed a special interest in mineral magnetism. The Jesuit priest and professor of astronomy at the University of Vienna, Maximillian Hell, had apparently found that an iron magnet could cure abdominal cramps, and inspired by Hell's ideas, Mesmer began using iron magnets to treat a young female patient, Francisca Oesterlin. News of the therapeutic power of magnets spread throughout the German-speaking world, but unfortunately for Mesmer, the credit went to Hell. Mesmer responded by developing a theory and practice different from Hell's. He argued that the most important magnet was not iron but one's own body, and he elaborated a healing technique in which the physician could cure ailments by a simple laying on of hands, thereby using his own body's inherent magnetism to restore the natural harmony of magnetic fluid in the patient's body. At the same time, he argued that healing aids could assist the process: iron rods could direct this magnetic fluid; water could conduct it (Crabtree 5–10).

As reports of Mesmer's techniques spread, so did his fame for effecting marvelous cures. A controversial figure, however, he also attracted numerous opponents, and in 1778 he was compelled to leave Vienna for France, where he hoped for a warmer reception. In Paris, he was flooded with patients and managed to engage the support of Charles D'Eslon, a respected member of the powerful Faculty of Medicine. D'Eslon was removed from the Faculty's list of *docteurs-régents* in 1782 for his commitment to animal magnetism, but two years later he managed to convince the government to form a commission to investigate the status of this new science. The Franklin Commission of 1784 was composed of five members of the Academy of Sciences – Benjamin Franklin, who chaired the commission, J.B. Le Roy, G. de Bory, A.L. Lavoisier, and J.S. Bailly – and four from the Faculty of Medicine – Majault, Sallin, J. D'Arcet, and J.L. Guillotin. Within a month, the king appointed a second commission composed of members of the Royal Society to investigate the therapeutic efficacy of animal magnetism. Both of these commissions reported that there was no proof that magnetic fluid existed and that positive effects witnessed were caused by imagination and imitation. However, Antoine Laurent de Jussieu dissented from the Royal Society commission's report and drafted one of his own: he witnessed positive effects caused by an unknown agent, independent of imagination (Crabtree 23–9).

Jussieu's independent report created an opening for further investigation. Political upheaval and the French Revolution intervened, however, and it was not until 1826 that the Académie Royale de Médecine appointed a permanent commission to study the matter. This commission, which carried on investigations for several years, submitted its report in 1831, and the result was a complete vindication of animal magnetism. It described positive effects of animal magnetism, including accelerated respiration and pulse, convulsions, drowsiness, numbness, and, occasionally, somnambulism. Somnambulism, or magnetic sleep, had been discovered by the Marquis de Puységeur in 1784.[41] Puységeur had also emphasized that the effects of animal magnetism depended more on the operator's will than on direction of a magnetic fluid, and it was in part to examine these new developments in animal magnetism and in part to redress the reports of the earlier commissions, whose methods of examination were considered flawed, that the commission of 1826 was appointed. This commission also investigated paranormal activity accompanying somnambulism, including clairvoyance, intuition, prevision, increased strength, and bodily insensibility. They found evidence of the reality of these new faculties but also noted that somnambulism could be feigned, and that 'charlatans could use this phenomenon to their own advantage' (Crabtree 186).

In 1833 John Campbell Colquhoun published an English translation of this 1831 report by the French Royal Academy of Medicine. This was one of the factors that contributed greatly to the development of interest in animal magnetism, or mesmerism, in England in the 1830s.[42] Another significant factor was the work of John Elliotson, mentioned above as the founder of *Zoist* in 1843. Elliotson conducted experiments in mesmerism at University College Hospital in London, where he was senior physician and professor of the practice of medicine.[43] He engaged the support of Herbert Mayo, professor of comparative anatomy at the Royal College of Surgeons, and continued his work in animal magnetism at the hospital until 1838, when the Council of University College decided to stop all such experiments. Elliotson resigned, founded the London Mesmeric Infirmary and later the *Zoist* (Crabtree 145–7). Elliotson's resignation signalled a decisive rift between proponents of mesmerism and the medical profession.[44] At the same time, popular enthusiasm for mesmerism spread throughout the country, as mesmerists held widely attended stage demonstrations of mesmeric phenomena. It was at one such performance in Sheffield, held by Charles Lafontaine,[45] that Spenser Hall developed an interest in animal magnetism. It was another such performance in Newcastle, held by Hall himself, that prompted Greenhow to try mesmerism in Martineau's case.[46]

Hall and Greenhow visited Martineau on 22 June 1844, and in her letters on mesmerism to the *Athenaeum*, she describes her experiences of Hall's mesmeric treatment:

˙ Something seemed to diffuse itself throughout the atmosphere, – not like smoke, nor steam, nor haze, – but most like a clear twilight, closing in from the windows and down from the ceiling, and in which one object after another melted away, till scarcely anything was left visible before my wide-open eyes ... The other effects produced were, first, heat, oppression and sickness, and, for a few hours after, disordered stomach; followed, in the course of the evening, by a feeling of lightness and relief, in which I thought I could hardly be mistaken.[47]

Hall visited Martineau again the next day, but on the third day he was prevented by illness from treating his new patient, and Martineau asked her maid to imitate Hall's mesmeric passes. Her maid complied; Martineau regained appetite and strength; she obtained a copy of Deleuze's *Instruction pratique sur le magnétisme animal*, and the pair continued treatment, using Deleuze's manual, until 6 September. At this point, the situation reached an impasse. Following Deleuze (who followed Puységeur), Martineau believed in the importance of the magnetizer's will to the mesmeric process,[48] and although her maid's ministrations worked well in the short term, Martineau felt they were becoming ineffective as a result of the 'subordination being in the wrong party.'[49] Martineau's friend, Henry Atkinson, arranged for Mrs Montague Wynward to take over her case. Under Wynward's care, the visions of 'twilight' continued, accompanied by 'exceedingly agreeable' sensations of transparency and lightness: 'At such times, my Mesmerist has struggled not to disturb me by a laugh, when I have murmured, with a serious tone, "Here are my hands, but they have no arms to them": "O dear! what shall I do? here is none of me left!"'[50] Martineau distinguished her experiences from paranormal phenomena and professed never to have experienced somnambulism, or magnetic sleep. Nonetheless, she claimed to have experienced 'the great marvel of restored heath' as a consequence of Wynward's efforts.

Martineau may not have experienced paranormal phenomena associated with mesmerism herself, but she related in her letters to the *Athenaeum* her observations of such phenomena as manifested by Jane Arrowsmith, the niece of her landlady at Tynemouth. Prior to Jane's first mesmeric treatment (administered first by a maid and then by Wynward), Jane had suffered from chronic headaches and recurrent eye inflammations for six years. She had seen several doctors and had visited the Eye Infirmary at Newcastle, but without improvement. Jane's looks and health apparently improved after mesmerism. In fact, when somnambulistic, Jane was able to prescribe useful treatments for her own ailments. Notwithstanding, Martineau maintained that Jane 'herself assigns, in the trance, a structural defect as the cause of her ailments, which will prevent their ever being entirely cured.'[51] This purported ability of somnambulists to discern the conditions of disease and prescribe for themselves and others (Jane also prescribed brandy for Martineau) was a commonly reported phenomenon at the time, but medical clairvoyance was not the least of Jane's wonders. When mesmerized, Jane could tell time accurately without seeing a clock, explain the meanings of words she did not know when awake, and lock her arms with such rigidity that no man's force could separate them. Most spectacular of all, Martineau believed Jane to be capable not only of medical clairvoyance but of general clairvoyance as well. Jane had a cousin who was one of the crew of a ship that was reported to have been wrecked near Hull. Nobody knew who, if anyone, had survived the wreck, but according to Martineau, Jane revealed in a trance that everyone was saved but one boy who fell from the ship's mast before the storm. Jane's revelations were confirmed by reports of the actual circumstances of the wreck, and for both Martineau and Wynward, they were a clear indication of paranormal activity.

Martineau chose to publish her letters on mesmerism in the *Athenaeum* instead of a journal like *Zoist* because she wanted to address an Establishment readership and not just the converted. Initially, this strategy appeared successful: six issues of the periodical ran through three editions.[52] Martineau was dismayed, however, when the editor of the *Athenaeum*, Charles Wentworth Dilke, subsequently published a scathing response to Martineau's account. Dilke attacked Martineau on a number of grounds. First, he denied that Martineau's blurred vision, oppression, sickness, and later experience of relief, which she described as ensuing from mesmeric treatment, were extraordinary phenomena. Instead, he insisted that every member of the College of Physicians would have regarded these experiences as everyday occurrences. This brought Dilke to his second point: Martineau was an incompetent witness. She lacked special knowledge of medicine, and, as a consequence, none of her statements respecting her own health or the means of her recovery, if she did recover, merited respect: 'All that can be thence deduced is, that she was ill – and is well, or thinks so; but there is not one tittle of evidence to lead even to the inference that she was cured (if cured) by "mesmeric means" or that Mesmerism had anything to do with the matter.' Dilke minimized Martineau's case and was far more concerned to discredit Jane's supposed clairvoyance, 'before which [Martineau's] own experiences shrink into utter insignificance.'[53] He established to his own satisfaction that Jane knew the particulars of the shipwreck prior to her trance and insisted in subsequent articles that Martineau was a 'dupe'[54] and that Jane was an impostor:

> The too-famous J. must now descend from her dignified position as a Seer, and henceforth take her place in that numerous band of clever damsels, who, with an admired perversity of spirit, and by the mere strength of mother-wit, have contrived to make their own inventions pass with their elders and betters – with scientific doctors and erudite ladies – as revelations of a power surpassing human.[55]

Dilke charges the whole party with 'misrepresentation, collusion, and fraud.'[56] Indeed, he attacks Martineau's character directly: 'We earnestly hope that Miss Martineau will give fair play to her better judgment, and act ingenuously and fearlessly in a matter which so intimately concerns her honour ... and acknowledge openly and honestly that she has been imposed on.'[57]

Prior to Dilke's attack, Martineau had been aware that somnambulists were often accused of deceit. She had tried to communicate to her readers in the *Athenaeum* that Jane was a woman of good character but knew that her personal confidence in the girl would not be accepted by her readers on the basis of mere assertion. At the same time, she insisted on the impossibility of Jane's flawlessly preserving an assumed role for an extended time: 'I am certain that it is not in human nature to keep up for seven weeks, without slip or trip, a series of deceptions so multifarious.'[58] In her opinion, this was not only true for Jane but generally true of somnambulists, who were 'all, invariably and without concert, found capable of such consummate acting, such command of frame and countenance, and fidelity to nature as were never equalled on the stage.'[59]

The problem Martineau isolates was a serious one since the great majority of somnambulists at this time were women, and to charge women with extraordinary, not to say manly, displays of self-command and wilfulness was, in fact, to challenge prevailing gender constructions. Opponents of mesmerism were caught in a double bind, and the more they protested against mesmeric wonders, the more they underscored a contradictory representation of women. The responses of the *Lancet* to John Elliotson's experiments with the O'Key sisters also illustrate the dilemma well. Elizabeth and Jane O'Key, aged seventeen and sixteen respectively, were both epileptic patients of Elliotson. Elliotson performed numerous demonstrations of the effects of mesmerism with the pair, who exhibited clairvoyance, transposition of the senses, and an ability to detect magnetic influence stored in various substances, such as gold and water. For one reviewer in the *Lancet*, these experiments demonstrated 'the extraordinary firmness, the quickness of perception, and the remarkable powers of acting, possessed by the patients, and the inefficiency of the precautions used against deception.'[60] For Dr John Leeson, they proved 'the most extraordinary cunning and ability of [Elizabeth] O'Key,' despite Leeson's initial perception of Elizabeth as being 'of a stunted and spare stature, her countenance being of a chlorotic sickliness, looking pale and melancholy; her age was stated to be seventeen, notwithstanding which there were no evidences of her having made any approach towards puberty.'[61]

Such incompatible representations of somnambulists were not simply the prerogative of diehard sceptics. Critics of mesmerism who were prepared to admit some of its phenomena in certain cases were perhaps even more liable to self-contradiction. Willing to concede that mesmerism might prevail in 'soft and weak natures, where the nervous system is subject to cataleptic seizures, [and] mental and bodily prostration is frequently almost the normal condition,' they insisted that 'soft and weak' persons were most inclined to deceit: 'these intelligible causes, eked out by a vanity and cunning which are always inherent in natures of an inferior type, are quite sufficient to account for the effects of the mesmeric manipulations on subjects of peculiar softness and pliancy.'[62] Weak individuals, such as Jane Arrowsmith, were apparently best capable of evincing the mental and physical fortitude required for deception. The contradiction, with variations, reverberates throughout texts on mesmerism of the period. For William Benjamin Carpenter, an eminent physiologist with medical training, artificial somnambulism was made possible by the abeyance of the patient's will:

Thus he may be played on, like a musical instrument, by those about him; thinking, feeling, speaking, acting, just as *they will* that he should think, feel, speak, or act; but this, *not*, as has been represented, because his Will has been brought into direct subjection to theirs, but because, his Will being in abeyance, all his mental operations are directed by such *suggestions* as they may choose to impress on his consciousness.[63]

At the same time, Carpenter maintained that 'hysterical females,' being 'the class to which the greater number of the reputedly clairvoyant subjects belong,' possess *'a monomania for deception'* and that many of mesmerism's 'higher mysteries' were explained by intentional deceptions perpetrated by weak, hysterical women (Carpenter 538). Abeyance of will accounted for mesmeric phenomena, except when those phenomena were demonstrated by women who were weak and wilful. The opinion that 'Enfeebled or nervous constitutions, women between the ages of fifteen and forty-five, &c., &c., are readily excited by magnetism'[64] was generally accepted and coupled with a conviction that these women, who were most susceptible to mesmerism, were also impostors. Hence, Jane Arrowsmith, whose enfeebled constitution might have made her an excellent candidate for somnambulism, was consequently charged with fraudulent behaviour; and Martineau herself, whose physical and emotional infirmities when sick might have made her equally susceptible to mesmeric treatment, was also accused of shamming. Dilke was not alone in doubting whether Martineau had really recovered: '... my friends are always writing in alarm (*always given by doctors*) to know *how* ill I am, and why I did not let them know. I think of advertising in the *Times* a promise to issue a circular whenever I *am* ill, on condition of being believed well till then.'[65]

The conviction that mesmeric subjects were impostors inspired brutal strategies to detect their chicanery and, in particular, to detect the counterfeit of supposed bodily insensibility in the mesmerized state. John Leeson's suggestion that Elizabeth O'Key was 'passive to the most active stimulants which could be applied to her body' leaves unstated the violent measures used against her and her sister (Leeson 728). Others were less delicate and described how the O'Keys were pinched, cut, and punched when mesmerized:

When in this state [of somnambulism] her body is deprived of all external sensibility. Her hair may be pulled, her flesh pinched or bruised, the point of a pin or needle may puncture her, without any consciousness of pain being evinced. On one occasion it was thought advisable to insert a seton[66] in the back of her neck, with a view to the relief of her headaches; this was done while delirious without any indication of consciousness on her part ... after she was awakened and restored to her natural state, she immediately felt the wound, and was greatly astonished on being informed of what had been done.[67]

For Lardner and Bulwer, such experiments effectively ruled out the possibility of the artfulness of 'the poor little patient,' but others were not convinced, even when the tortures inflicted on the O'Keys included powerful electric shocks. According to the *Lancet*, 'some stress has been laid on the circumstance that O'Key, in the mesmeric state, withstood the shock of a galvanic battery; but the power of resisting the electrical shock is possessed by some, though not by many persons.'[68] For opponents of mesmerism, a precedent had been established: the female somnambulist was the enemy to be exposed and neutralized, if not actually maimed. Jane Arrowsmith was also attacked. Headlam Greenhow, Thomas Greenhow's nephew, had attended unsuccessfully to Jane's eye complaints, and, when invited to witness her mesmeric treatment, he 'wrenched her arm, and employed usage which would have been cruelly rough in her ordinary state.' Greenhow also tried to scare Jane by shouting that the house was on fire, but 'this brutal assault on her nerves failed entirely.'[69] The motives for this rough treatment of mesmerized women are not difficult to comprehend. If women such as Jane were acting, it was necessary to stop their performances, which were demonstrating that women had more self-command than was commonly supposed. If these women were not acting, then they were also defying gender constructions. Animal, that is physical, insensibility was considered the prerogative of men as a necessary condition for abstract thought. According to John Neal, writing for *Blackwood's*, 'where the intellectual faculties are equal, and other circumstances, (as education, age &c. equal,) he who has the *least* bodily sensibility, will be able to think *most* abstractedly and steadily; [whereas] he, who has *most* bodily sensibility, will be *least* able to think, either abstractedly or steadily.'[70] Neal maintains that 'women have more animal sensibility,' which explains their inability to think like men (Neal 394). It was, perhaps, safer to believe that female somnambulists were acting. Of course, this too challenged the ideal of the angel in the house: '"You must rather believe," said an anti-mesmeric lecturer, "that all your wives and sisters and children are false, than think any of these cases true."'[71] It might have been safest of all to concede the truth of mesmeric phenomena, and the unwillingness to do so requires explanation.

A connection between mesmerism and hysteria has already been suggested by the opinion that hysterical women were most susceptible to mesmerism. In addition, the brutal measures used by anti-mesmerists against female somnambulists were similar to those used against hysterical women by doctors who felt threatened professionally and who, in addition, regarded hysterical women as rejecting male authority. Hysterical women both challenged their doctors' medical expertise and escaped from their domestic responsibilities, and for doctors, this made the treatment of such cases a battle of wills: 'Doctors frequently recommended suffocating hysterical women until their fits stopped, beating them across the face and body with wet towels, ridiculing and exposing them in front of family and friends, showering them with icy water' (Smith-Rosenberg 211). The severity used against both hysterics and mesmerized women recalls the torturing of witches/hysterics in the Middle Ages. Indeed, certain members of the Church explicitly revived the demoniacal paradigm to explain mesmerism. The Rev. Hugh M'Neile preached a sermon in Liverpool denouncing mesmerism as satanic: mesmerists were to be regarded as witches, and patients as possessed.[72]

The identification of hysteria and mesmerism may at first seem peculiar. Mesmerism was supposed to treat hysterical disorders, not to be equated with them.[73] However, the effects of mesmerism looked like hysteria. Martineau's inability to feel her arms, for example, suggests an hysterical anaesthesia. To state the matter in more general terms, the symptoms of the magnetized state included 'increase of temperature, heaviness, loss of speech, and increased sensibility; convulsions, "catalepsy," and loss of sensibility; second consciousness and somnambulism; clairvoyance, knowledge of past events, the gift of prophecy and heavenly felicity.'[74] The 'more grotesque' symptoms of hysteria, according to Oppenheim, included 'temporary convulsions, palsies, motor and sensory impairments, respiratory obstructions, and speech disorders' (Oppenheim 181).[75] These symptoms clearly resemble the early stages of the magnetized state. Moreover, mesmerism seemed to share hysteria's mimetic capacity, emphasized by Thomas Sydenham.[76] Jane Arrowsmith, it will be recalled, could rigidly lock her arms in what appeared to be a cataleptic state. Elliotson's experiments with Elizabeth O'Key also produced effects resembling symptoms of disease. In particular, O'Key's response to magnetized nickel imitated one of the cardinal signs of tetanus, opisthotonos, in which the victim's back is arched like a bow:

Her face changed colour, and dilated visibly; she panted violently, and every limb was convulsed; if the Sybil had the advantage in immortal voice, O'Key was never surpassed in the agony of opisthotonos, the intense squint of the eyes, the contortions of the countenance; the face was filled with blood, and dilated by holding the breath, or panting rapidly – *anhelum pectus*. The performance afforded a clear insight into the impositions of ancient priestcraft.[77]

O'Key imitates not only tetanus, but also a full hysterical seizure: limbs contorted, eyes distorted, body writhing and rigid. Indeed, she seems an early precursor of Jean-Martin Charcot's *grandes hystériques*.[78] For medical practitioners seeking professional status, the similarity between hysterical and mesmerized women must have been rather horrific. As we have seen, doctors, whose medical authority was threatened by their inability to define and to treat hysteria, endeavoured to minimize the problem as much as possible. To find hysterical symptoms surfacing as mesmeric phenomena could have only compounded doctors' distress. Janet Oppenheim suggests that doctors' limited interest in mesmerism was caused in part by their suspicion that mesmerism was itself a pathological condition, that it 'would prove exceedingly harmful to the very people who were likeliest to be exposed to it' (Oppenheim 302). I should like to argue, rather, not that doctors were uninterested in mesmerism because it was ineffective, or in itself pathological, but because its phenomena closely resembled hysteria when doctors were being regularly mocked for their bafflement by that disorder: 'Imagination, like hysteria, is a convenient word employed by doctors to cover over what they can't explain; because, on their own confession, they are "quite in the dark" with regard to nervous complaints, they vote them into the regions of imagination, and decree that their cure must come from the same locality' (Nelson 190). Doctors did not understand hysteria, and mesmeric phenomena, in their replication of hysteria, drew further and very widespread attention to apparent medical incompetence. George Sandby expressed the doctors' dilemma well:

... it is now said, that all these [mesmeric] states are the effect of hysteria. Hysteria includes every thing. Whatever may be the condition of the human body, – be it unusual repose or unusual excitement, – be it exquisite sensibility to pain, or an utter unconsciousness of its presence,

hysteria is the cause. Be it so. And how much nearer are we now to resolv-
ing the difficulty? For again I ask, *what is hysteria?* Do the medical men
know themselves? Can they explain it? Can they say what are its causes,
proximate or remote? Are they not confessedly in the dark on the subject?
To explain Mesmerism, therefore, by hysteria, is but to exchange one difficulty for another.[79]

Mesmeric phenomena and hysteria both, in their similarity, defied
doctors' diagnostic categories and challenged, as a consequence, the
medical community's claims to professional competence.

The embarrassment that mesmerism occasioned for doctors was
sometimes directly addressed. One writer in the *Lancet* openly be-
wailed 'the extremely humiliating fact' that 'the information of the
medical profession, generally, on matters of natural science, was very
little greater than that of the people at large.' Doctors were demoral-
ized by 'a vile system of medical legislation' that required them to
occupy their time 'with keeping up a certain establishment and expenditure' and left no time for 'acquiring that scientific improvement
which would render [them] additionally respectable in the eyes of sensible men.'[80] As things were, doctors were ill-equipped to guide the
public mind on such popular subjects as mesmerism, and so they
attempted either to minimize or to attack it: 'When we continually see
patients labouring under hysteria, and analogous forms of nervous
disease, falling suddenly into various states of stupor, trance, and con-
vulsion, without any assignable cause, why should we wonder at similar states being induced by so slight a cause as the pawing of a
mesmeriser?'[81] This reference to 'the pawing of the mesmeriser' calls
attention to a still more serious threat that mesmerism posed for
doctors – one relating to the highly charged eroticism of women's
behaviour in the magnetized state. Elizabeth O'Key's response to magnetized nickel not only imitates a cardinal sign of tetanus and an hysterical seizure, but it also resembles a woman's orgasm. Moreover,
whereas the eroticism of the hysterical fit occurred spontaneously in
the hysterical patient, in mesmerism it was caused directly by the
'pawing,' or magnetic 'passes,' of the operator.

The sexuality inherent in the magnetic process had always been conspicuous. Robert Ferguson, writing for the *Quarterly Review*, describes
the scene in 1784 in Mesmer's treatment rooms in Paris. The desire
to vary 'the worn-out stimulants of this sensual capital' compelled

throngs of people to flood Mesmer's salons, filling his halls 'with the youth, the beauty, and the fashion of the day.' Youths displaying 'manly symmetry' were Mesmer's chosen assistants:

> ... they were employed in making tractions on the body, and for hours together, in compressing and kneading the *hypogastre* with the open hand – delicious airs were poured forth from the harmonica, and everything was resorted to which could excite the senses and the nerves ... Screams, shrieks, faintings, and contortions were heard and seen on every side – extravagant bursts of sympathy between persons hitherto unknown to each other seemed to threaten to level the wholesome distinctions of society. (Ferguson 276–7)

To prevent patients from hurting themselves, Mesmer had a cushioned *salle de crises* where they could convulse in comfort; he could also calm those 'in "crisis" by a touch of his rod' (Ferguson 277).

The Marquis de Puységeur did not believe that 'crises' were essential to the healing process, and he substituted magnetic sleep for them after discovering the phenomenon with Victor Race. However, Puységeur also believed that magnetic sleep was accompanied by a special 'rapport' between the patient and the operator. He thought this rapport aided treatment, but he also worried about the emotional dependency it created for the female patient on the magnetizer. The problem was also recognized by the Franklin commission, referred to earlier. In addition to its public report on animal magnetism (1786), the commission made a secret report to the king of France in which it pointed out that the operator stimulates 'sweet emotions' that are 'missed afterwards' and sought again, creating a morally reprehensible habit.[82] The commission also feared that women in magnetic sleep could be sexually abused (Crabtree 94).

Opponents of mesmerism in England included this potential for sexual abuse as part of their objections to mesmerism. Thomas Wakley, for example, declared in the *Lancet*:

> It is time that the obscenities of mesmerism should engage the attention of the heads of families, and all persons who uphold the character of English society for its purity and morality. The statements which are occasionally sent to us are descriptive of scenes which are highly disgusting. Why do not its medical advocates transfer the practice to the hands of females,

since in nineteen cases out of twenty, the patient, alias the victim, alias the particeps criminis, is a female.[83]

Wakley calls for female mesmerists as a means of stopping abuse and 'obscenities,' but it is clear from an article in the *Lancet* on Martineau's mesmeric experiences that neither an absence of abuse nor a woman magnetizer was grounds for accepting mesmeric phenomena. The writer is concerned exclusively with the apparent sexuality of Martineau's experiences, despite the fact that the major experience he refers to was produced by Mrs Wynward, the widow of a clergyman and a woman of 'mental and moral' power.[84] The larger extract he provides from Martineau's first letter to the *Athenaeum* is worth quoting:

'As the muscular power oozes away under the mesmeric influence, a strange inexplicable feeling ensues of the frame becoming transparent and ductile ... Then begins the moaning, of which so much has been made, as an indication of pain. I have often moaned, and much oftener have been disposed to do so, when the sensations have been the most tranquil and agreeable ... Between this condition and the mesmeric sleep there is a state, transient and rare, of which I have had experience, but of which I intend to give no account ... The ideas that I have snatched from it, and now retain, are, of all ideas which ever visited me, the most lucid and impressive. *It may well be that they are incommunicable* – partly from their *nature* and *relations*, and partly from their *unfitness for translation into mere words* ... no re-action followed, no excitement but that which is natural to every one who finds himself (query, *herself*) in possession of *a great new idea*.'[85]

The writer does not elaborate the implications of Martineau's experiences, but his portrait of Martineau as 'an aged maiden lady' makes it clear that, for him, the *'great new idea'* pertained to sex. Elizabeth Barrett could not understand the writer's motives for such an imputation: 'But she was magnetized by *a woman*,' she wrote to Mary Russell Mitford; 'I thought of what you tell me – I know that such things are attributed ... which is one of the minor causes, by the way, of my repulsions, ... – but she was magnetized by a woman; & her statement makes it clear. How dared they say it then?'[86]

The reason for such imputations was that mesmerism posed a specific professional problem for doctors that constituted a significant part of their violent opposition to it: the sexual displays that were perceived to characterize women's behaviour in the magnetic state were directly caused by the operations of the magnetizer, and husbands and fathers would have no confidence in doctors whatsoever if they saw that doctors were responsible for causing such behaviour in their wives and daughters. Repeatedly, doctors were called on to take charge of the practice of mesmerism so that unprincipled or uneducated operators would not be in control of mesmeric treatment. Martineau herself made such an appeal: 'At present, the knowledge of Mesmerism, superficial and scanty as it is, is out of the professional pale. When it is excelled by that which issues from within the professional pale, the remedial and authoritative power will reside where it ought; and not till then.'[87] But doctors almost unanimously refused to take up the challenge. Medical practitioners were, at this time, intent on securing professional status, and their efforts would have been severely jeopardized if they were perceived as intimate partners in women's sexual desires and behaviour. Doctors insisted that mesmerism was hazardous to 'the reputation of the sciences of medicine in this country.'[88] It was not just the woman who was the potential victim of mesmerism; it was also the doctor. Dr Francis Hawkins, responding to Elliotson's delivery of the Harveian Oration on 25 June 1846, made the point in explicit terms:

> Among quacks, the IMPOSTERS, called MESMERISTS, are in my opinion the especial FAVOURITES of those, both male and female, in whom the SEXUAL PASSIONS BURN STRONGLY, either in secret or notoriously. DECENCY FORBIDS ME TO BE MORE EXPLICIT. From these and similar ARTIFICES, the physician should be carefully removed and guarded.[89]

Some proponents of mesmerism endeavoured to meet the problem of women's sexual displays directly. George Sandby acknowledged the objection that 'even in the presence of a third party the process is one, *qui blesse les convenances*; and that the treatment is what a father or brother would feel a pain in witnessing,' but his counter-argument that a 'Mesmeriser of character' would guarantee fastidiousness was not sufficient to allay the fears of doctors, as indeed Martineau's own case testifies.[90] Like the use of chloroform in childbirth, mesmerism was seen to cause sexual displays by women in which doctors participated directly, and such displays threatened not only the doctor but the Victorian social order. Mary Poovey describes this last in the chloroform debate, with reference to women who appeared to experience sexual orgasms during anaesthetized labour:

> If women were not simply moral but also sexual creatures, that is, or if the morality considered 'proper' to the female was rendered problematic by the same kind of sexual desires that men represented as natural in themselves, then difference could less easily be *fixed* between men and women ... and women's social subordination could less easily be defended against those women (and men) who questioned the inequality of political and economic rights and the social division of labour. (Poovey 49)

Sexual displays by female somnambulists also crossed sexual boundaries between men and women and threatened crucial distinctions in Victorian society. Indeed, supplementary to Poovey's discussion of chloroform, it should be noted that women who were mesmerized during childbirth also seemed to experience unusual, and possibly sexual, side effects. J.P. Lynell, writing for *Zoist*, describes a mesmerized woman in labour:

> *This state of perfect insensibility lasted about an hour and a half, during which time the action of labour was going on almost continually,* some of the throes being *very violent,* so much so as, in one case, to rupture one of the membranes. After this time, sensibility began gradually to manifest itself, the patient at first feeling the pains very slightly, afterwards more acutely, but never so acutely as in the waking state. Although the insensibility was less, the sleep-waking state still continued; the patient however begged me to awaken her, but on being asked why she wished to be awoke, and whether she should suffer less pain when awake than as she then was, she replied that, on the contrary, she should suffer more pain, but that she wished to be awake, – she could not tell why.[91]

After James Braid introduced hypnotism in the 1840s and 1850s, the medical community's response to altered-consciousness phenomena began to relax.[92] The direct role of the operator in producing altered psychological and physiological states was replaced by emphasis on the patient, whose concentration of attention was the factor that made the phenomena of hypnotism possible. As William Carpenter maintained, 'the obstacles which beset the inquiry, whilst Mesmerism alone was in question, have been overcome by the introduction of methods, in which a large number of the phenomena can be developed, without even the semblance of that exertion of power by one person over another, which was always the most suspicious feature in the Mesmeric system' (Carpenter 502–3). Furthermore, the ability of doctors to relate the theories behind hypnotism – the exhaustion of the optic and motor nerves of the eye caused by a fixed stare, dominant ideas, and suggestion – to 'laws fully recognized by every scientific physiologist' enabled them to gain cultural ascendancy in knowledge and power.

Martineau's confidence in the medical profession (excepting Greenhow) was not greatly disturbed by the unwillingness of doctors to treat her claims about mesmerism seriously. She attributed their dismissal of mesmerism to their lack of knowledge, which she believed would be corrected in time, when mesmeric marvels would be established beyond reasonable doubt. Her faith in the clergy, however, was severely shaken, not by their denouncing of mesmerism, but by their sanctioning of illness. Looking back at *Life in the Sick-Room* in her *Autobiography*, Martineau was shocked by its rationalization of pain on religious grounds:

> The Christian superstition, now at last giving way before science, of the contemptible nature of the body, and its antagonism to the soul, has shockingly perverted our morals, as well as injured the health of Christendom: and every book, tract, and narrative which sets forth a sick-room as a condition of honour, blessing and moral safety, helps to sustain a delusion and corruption which have already cost the world too dear. (*HMA* 2:148)

Martineau's renewed health proved to her that her illness was not a necessary and irreversible punishment for violation of God's laws, and she rejected Christian dogma that degraded the health of the body. She had rejected such dogma before in *Society in America*, but anxieties about her own social role seem to have caused her to reconsider her beliefs and values. Martineau's illness was, whatever else, also a crisis of faith. It might be overstating the case to say that Martineau emerged from her sickroom an atheist, but when she recovered her health, she embarked on a project to consider critically Christian doctrine. In particular, she explored the historical origins of Christianity in Egyptian mythology and thereby undermined the authority of Scripture.

Chapter Six

History and Religious Faith:

Eastern Life, Present and Past (1848)

At the same time that mesmerism's opponents harboured lingering doubts about her renewed health, Martineau embarked on a six-month journey to Egypt and the Holy Land, where, despite her recent illness, she proved a surprisingly hardy traveller. She scaled the Great Pyramid and Mount Sinai, bathed in the Jordan and the Dead Sea, and trekked through the desert on camel and on foot. Even more surprising to her contemporaries, however, was the apparent atheism of *Eastern Life, Present and Past*, published in 1848 after her travels.[1] Martineau's personal experience of sickness, described in *Life in the Sick-Room* (1844), was characterized by a profound religiosity, and *Eastern Life* constituted a significant and, to many, a distressing shift in her thought. Scarcely had the brouhaha surrounding her proclaimed recovery by mesmerism abated when Martineau was again embroiled in controversy. As its full title only partly suggests, *Eastern Life, Present and Past* has two overriding objectives: an evaluation of Egyptian society in the late 1840s and, to the dismay and outrage of many of her first readers, an understanding of the implications of ancient Egyptian history for Christianity. Indeed, the public outcry that was generated is an important index of the Victorians' ambivalent attitudes to history.

Although the formation of historical consciousness in nineteenth-century England has received much attention in recent studies, these studies have shared an assumption that historical inquiry was embraced without exception.[2] As Rosemary Jann argues, the historical was 'the common coin of the nineteenth century' (Jann ix). If, indeed, the historical was 'common coin,' it had limits on its circulation and value. Totalizing conceptions of the status of history in the nineteenth century gloss over what were often perceived to be necessary restrictions on historical enterprise. The outraged response to parts of *Eastern Life* arose from the work's historical analysis of the origins of Christian beliefs, and Martineau's critics objected as much to her methodology as to the conclusions she reached. *Eastern Life* participated in a theological dispute that was already in progress at the time of her travels. It was, however, the first popular text by an English author to bring into sharp focus contradictory views of the value of history: if history constituted a primary discipline for Victorians, historicizing activities in religious domains were inevitably controversial. This chapter investigates these issues, as well as the frustrations and difficulties Martineau experienced in her efforts to recover the past. I shall begin, however, with her assessment of the condition of Egypt during her travels. Martineau's visit to Egypt was her second major voyage. Her first had been to the New World during 1834–6; now she was visiting the Old, where, as in America, she was appalled by the institution of slavery and the degraded status of women.

Martineau's decision to visit the East was partly the result of chance. In the autumn of 1846, she went to Liverpool to visit her younger sister, and while there she was invited by Mr and Mrs Richard Vaughan Yates to accompany them on an Eastern tour. After some hesitation – Martineau had recently built a house in Ambleside and was eager to return to her housekeeping – she accepted their invitation and Yates's offer to finance her travel expenses. The party were joined en route by Mr Joseph C. Ewart, the member of Parliament for Liverpool, and they obtained their first view of the African coast on 20 November 1846. Having arrived at Alexandria, the group proceeded to Cairo by steamer and then sailed up the Nile through Nubia as far as the Second Cataract. They inspected the temples, monuments, and pyramids of ancient Egypt during their return to Cairo, and from Cairo they travelled on camels, donkeys, and horses through the desert to Suez, Mount Sinai, Petra, Palestine, and Syria, departing Beirut for home in May 1847. It was a fashionable tour in the 1840s. The Peninsular and Oriental Steamship Company had been permitted access to Suez in 1841, and by 1842 regular P & O service was established on both sides of the isthmus.[3] Egypt had become the highroad to India, and the Turkish ruler, Mohammed Ali, was careful to ensure the safety of European travellers in his dominion – travellers who ranged from civil and military officers of the Indian government making slight detours in their routes to visit ancient monuments, to English tourists who had become bored with the Continent and sought novelty in the Orient.

Notwithstanding the government's care for these travellers, the political climate of Egypt at the time was unstable. The English government had ejected the Turkish Pasha from his newly conquered Syria and had imposed 'agreements' on Egypt to thwart its economic and political development. Martineau was naturally interested in such affairs, but uncharacteristically, and in contrast to her direct engagement with political issues in *Society in America*, she refused to comment on Euro-Egyptian politics in *Eastern Life*, offering instead a disclaimer:

> I have my own impressions, of course, about the political prospects of Egypt, and the character of its alliance with various European powers; but while every word said by anybody is caught up and made food for jealousy, and a plea for speculation on the future, the interests of peace and good-will require silence from the passing traveller, whose opinions could hardly, at the best, be worth the rancour which would be excited by the expression of them. (*EL* 1:16)

Martineau maintained that international politics was too sensitive a subject for commentary at that time. Domestic politics, on the other hand, did not necessarily warrant the same reserve, and Martineau freely expressed her views on what she considered the despotism of the Pasha's local rule. She reasoned that a population which resorted to horrific practices of self-mutilation to evade conscription in the Pasha's army, factories, and schools must have legitimate grounds for its fear, and she cites the twenty-three thousand deaths that occurred during the construction of the Mahmoudieh Canal as an example of what those grounds might be. Consistent with her early writings on political economy, she laments the Pasha's indifference to security of property and other rights: 'He appears never to have learned that national welfare can arise from no reliable national industry where no man is sure of receiving the rewards of his labour.' As things were, labourers on public works had to be 'caught like game,' monitored by soldiers, and paid at the Pasha's pleasure, if they had not been killed off by his inadequate provision of food or inadequate machinery (*EL* 2:170). Parents maimed or concealed their children to prevent their being chosen for attendance at schools. And tax-paying subjects fled to the hills at the mention of an approaching tax-collector. These conditions, combined with a decreasing population and an increasing area of uncultivated land, led Martineau to scorn the Pasha's boast of advancing civilization. However, they did not lead her to justify a British annexation of Egypt to secure the overland route, which was an issue in the minds of most English travellers to the East at that time. In accordance with her disclaimer, Martineau avoids explicit recommendations, but by calling attention to widespread grief at the loss of an Egyptian ruler, she suggests that an Egyptian government might best remedy widespread discontent:

> ... everywhere we found the people lamenting the substitution of Turkish for Egyptian rule. The Turks, it is true, like the lightness of their present taxation, which is pretty much what it pleases them to make it: and everybody knows that the rulers of Egypt impose high taxes: but the religious toleration which existed under Ibraheem Pasha, and his many public works, cause him to be fervently regretted; – chiefly by the Christians, but also by many others. (EL 3:304)

Martineau's avoidance of a strong imperialist stance conforms with the postcolonial directions of *The Hour and the Man*.[4]

When expressing her own regret at Egypt's present condition, Martineau describes the Pasha's labourers at public works as 'virtually slaves' (EL 2:175); nonetheless, she is careful not to deflect attention from the institution of actual slavery in Egypt. As in *Society in America*, she identifies slavery in Egypt with the status of women, and again the identification is not simply a blurring of two kinds of oppression. In *Society in America*, Martineau unravelled the metaphor that characterized women as slaves and left unstated the atrocities of racism and the ownership of human beings. In *Eastern Life*, she emphasizes a literal connection between slavery and the institution of polygamy: female slaves were made concubines and attendants in harems; males were made the harem's guards. For Martineau, these practices gave rise to a doubly nefarious institution: 'These two hellish practices, slavery and polygamy, which, as practices, can clearly never be separated, are here avowedly connected; and, in that connexion, are exalted into a double institution, whose working is such as to make one almost wish that the Nile would rise to cover the tops of the hills, and sweep away the whole abomination' (EL 2:159). Martineau had also wished for a calamitous solution to the evils of slavery in *Society in America*. On the whole, however, her condemnation of the institution is less severe in *Eastern Life*, partly because Egyptian slaves suffered less from racism, being most frequently of the same race as their owners. Martineau also felt that polygamy, rather than slavery, was the worse of the two evils because the former entailed the latter: 'Neither the Pasha nor any other human power can abolish slavery while polygamy is an institution of the country' (*EL* 2:160). As a consequence, her relatively lenient stance on slavery is supplemented by a virulent attack on polygamy and, in particular, on the status of women in the East.

Martineau's opinions on the condition of Eastern women were informed chiefly by visits to two harems. Of course, she was not the first Englishwoman to visit a harem. For example, Sophia Poole had preceded her by several years and formed long-term friendships with many of the women she met.[5] Martineau differed from Poole, however, by denouncing the harem overtly. Whereas Poole could describe harem women as courteous, gentle, adept at needlework, and generally lively and cheerful, Martineau was exasperated by their idleness and vacuity: 'There is nothing about which the inmates of hareems seem to be so utterly stupid as about women having anything to do' (*EL* 2:166). Martineau attributes these women's vacuity to their preoccupation with sex, but rather than stigmatize Eastern women as exotically other, she recognizes correspondences with home:

All the younger ones were dull, soulless, brutish, or peevish. How should it be otherwise, when the only idea of their whole lives is that which, with all our interests and engagements, we consider too prominent with us? There cannot be a woman of them all who is not dwarfed and withered in mind and soul by being kept wholly engrossed with that one interest, – detained at that stage in existence which, though most important in its place, is so as a means to ulterior ends. The ignorance is fearful enough: but the grossness is revolting. (*EL* 2:155)

Martineau maintains that the difference between the East and England is more of degree than kind and thereby departs from an established tendency in the West to regard the harem as both appealing and threatening because it seemed an alternative to the Western model of sexuality.[6] As Jill Matus observes in her fine article, 'in the travel writing of Victorian Englishwomen who visited the East, the harem functions frequently as a site that provokes the visitor's anxieties and questions about English domestic life and the position of women.'[7] Martineau found the harem neither appealing nor fundamentally different from certain attitudes at home. It is a suggestion that also emerges in her remarks on infants born in harems. Martineau believed that because births were so infrequent in harems, children were idolized and often 'killed with kindness,' and she compares this situation with 'the houses at home which morally most resemble these hareems (though little enough externally).'[8] Martineau insists that in both contexts, children are 'murdered' by an excessive 'outbreak of feminine instinct' (*EL* 2:151). Given Martineau's feelings of filial guilt and resentment discussed in the previous chapter, it is tempting to read these statements as self-reflexive and to see Martineau's projecting onto these children her own sense of victimization. In more general terms, the effect of these comparisons between the East and England is to narrow the gap of cultural difference and to bring the problem of women's degradation closer to home. In *Society in America*, Martineau responded with alarm to the statement that the American South was always 'advancing towards orientalism.' In *Eastern Life*, she suggests that England may not be too far behind. Like Eastern women, women at home have insufficient interests to distract them from a 'too prominent' interest in sexuality; and in both cultures children are harmed by women's 'gratification of their feminine instincts' (*EL* 2:151). Not only were prescribed gender roles similar in both societies, but women's adherence to these norms both dwarfed their minds and occasioned inadvertent infanticide.[9] Martineau at once demystifies the harem and challenges the Victorian domestic ideal.

In addition to those shared gender experiences that Martineau acknowledges explicitly, others are suggested by her experiences of travel. One of Martineau's chief objections to the harem is its 'spy system,' or the constant surveillance of the women by the harem's guards. These women regarded such monitoring as a token of their value, and Martineau notes that they 'pitied us European women heartily, that we had to go about travelling, and appearing in the streets without being properly taken care of, – that is, watched' (*EL* 2:154). Martineau's bemusement must have been coupled with a sense of irony: she complains of being watched continually in the East. It is in Asyoot that Martineau first feels 'the misery which every Frank woman has to endure in the provincial towns of the East – the being stared at by all eyes.' She believed that this staring was incited primarily by her uncovered face, considered indecent for a woman, and 'felt it throughout to be the greatest penalty of my Eastern travel' (*EL* 1:54). Martineau had other unpleasant experiences. At Philae, a man, a woman, and a boy surrounded her and tried to steal her gold pencil-case (*EL* 1:259). During a religious festival in Cairo, she was slapped in the face with millet stalks (*EL* 2:133). Riding along the Lebanese coast near Tripoli, she was seized by two men with spears, 'one of them shaking his weapon in my face' (*EL* 3:330). But Martineau was undaunted by these assaults, partly because she knew that the penalties for attacking Europeans were often severe. Her response to the last incident was especially bold: 'I twitched my rein out of their hands, laughed in their faces, and rode away' (*EL* 3:331). The continual staring in conjunction with these insults, however, was understandably difficult to endure. Her public exposure in Greenhow's shilling pamphlet was a fairly recent distress and had been undermining both professionally and personally. Eastern travel offered her an opportunity to re-establish her credentials: she was a published authority on the observation of morals and manners, which was a significant part of her present objective. To find herself the most 'observ'd of all observers' threatened the power dynamic she sought to restore, and however much she objected to the harem's 'spy system,' she herself adopted strategies of surveillance and attempted to reverse the operations of the objectifying gaze. At anchor on the Nile near Asyoot, a canvas on the landward side of her boat was lowered 'so that the people on shore could not pry.' Martineau finds it 'pleasant, however, to play the spy upon them' and describes the activities of the boat-builders and artisans she watches (*EL* 1:52). Whenever 'many people were gathered together,' her 'chief interest' is in 'observing their faces,' including the women's when they are not veiled (*EL* 2:130).[10] Her own authority and identity at issue, Martineau rejects a veil for herself, feeling that it is better for a woman 'to appear as she is, at any cost, rather than to attempt any degree of imposture' (*EL* 1:55).[11] Nonetheless, she evades the gaze when possible. On her way to Mount Sinai, she explores a water-course 'till the sight of some strange Arabs, looking at me from behind the trees turned me back' (*EL* 2:232). The gaze is subjugating, threatening, and sometimes violent. At Akaba, where her party arranged to be escorted to Petra by Sheikh Hussein, Martineau hides behind an umbrella to read Laborde and is startled to discover the Sheikh negotiating with a Council nearby: 'At the first piercing look he fixed upon me, I felt that it was a face which would haunt me for life.' Martineau reverses the process of objectification, describing the Sheikh's appearance: 'He sat with his back against the wall, pouring out incessant clouds of smoke, and attended by his son, his pipe-bearer, and other vassals' (*EL* 2:305).

For Martineau's readers, such descriptions of people and places were the main attraction of *Eastern Life*. In the midst of a proliferation of travel books on the East, Martineau 'sees much that has escaped others, and presents it with more vividness,' her reviewer in the *Spectator* asserted, and he attributed her superiority to her 'searching and trained observation.'[12] J.J. Tayler agreed and believed there was 'an unanimous concession' on the excellence of Martineau's descriptions.[13] What marred the book for her readers were the speculations which accompanied these details. Tayler maintained that

> had [Martineau] been content to appeal to the eye alone, and filled her pages with beautiful pictures, and merely garnished them with such extracts from learned works, as sufficed to throw an air of antiquarian and historical interest over her narrative – she might, with her unquestioned ability in this kind of writing, have produced a work of the highest popularity and won golden opinions from all sides. (Tayler 525)

Tayler would have preferred a work more in the manner of Lady Eastlake, for whom the charm of ladies' travel writing derived from its sheer purposelessness.[14] Certainly there were precedents for superficial Eastern narratives, such as Sophia Poole's *The Englishwoman in Egypt*, described by Eastlake as 'an humble helpmate to [William Lane's] well-known "Modern Egyptians"' (Eastlake 108). Indeed, Poole claimed to have borrowed the scholarship in her book from her brother.[15]

Martineau was never content to amass the details, or symptoms, of social life without also diagnosing their causes. In *Society in America*, she had compared the existing state of American society with its founding principles in the Declaration of Independence. It was unlikely that she would be satisfied with a surface description of life in the East. Since Euro-Egyptian politics were best undiscussed and the people's fear of the government made it difficult for Martineau to know 'anything of the modern Egyptian polity but the significant fact that nothing can be known,' she embraced the opportunity which travel presented for historical research (*EL* 2:180).[16] Indeed, for some, history and tourism constituted a natural association:

> The effect of historical reading is analogous, in many respects, to that produced by foreign travel. The student, like the tourist, is transported into a new state of society. He sees new fashions. He hears new modes of expression. His mind is enlarged by contemplating the wide diversities of laws, of morals, and of manners. But men may travel far, and return with minds as contracted as if they had never stirred from their own market-town.[17]

Not only were tourism and history considered analogous, but both could be intellectually unprofitable if the tourist or student confined his researches to a superficial survey of sites or dates. Martineau laments the 'ignorance and levity' that propelled tourists to Egypt: 'A man who goes to shoot crocodiles and flog Arabs, and eat ostrich's eggs, looks upon the monuments as so many strange old stone-heaps, and comes back "bored with the Nile"; as we were told we should be' (*EL* 2:85). Travel books were seen to reflect this superficiality. Advances in navigation and communication meant that the planet's 'most remote scenes' had been 'explored over and over again.'[18] As a consequence, travellers to the East knew exactly what to expect, and Francis Ainsworth complained that they 'patronise the Pyramids, [and] are on terms of familiarity with the whole family of deserts.'[19] If travel literature was becoming increasingly vapid, however, it required more than 'extracts from learned works,' as Tayler thought, to invest them with interest. These too had become excessively familiar. The Chevalier Bunsen may have displayed greater learning and critical acumen in his researches on Egypt than any Egyptologist before him, but for his reviewer in *Fraser's* his work was nonetheless likely to 'fall still-born from the press'; he reckoned that no other subject had inspired 'such fatiguing monotony, such nauseating repetition, such fallacious arrogation of new discovery, and such faithless or careless plagiarism at the expense of predecessors and contemporaries.'[20] Martineau, who devoted a lengthy section of *Eastern Life* to the '*vexata quaesito* of the Shepherd Kings,' might have been no less susceptible to this reviewer's censure. However, her speculations went beyond the ordering of ancient chronologies of Egypt's rulers. *Eastern Life* included an historical investigation of the origins of Christianity, and if it failed to contribute a welcome interest to a worn-out genre, it was because an historical inquiry into religious doctrine was seen by many to challenge the grounds of religious faith.

Martineau knew before it was published that *Eastern Life* would be controversial. Indeed, as with so many of her works, publication itself was not a straightforward business. Martineau had initially agreed to publish the book with Murray, the leading publisher of travel literature on the East, but he reneged on the agreement after receiving the manuscripts of the first two volumes: 'The story goes that Mr. Murray was alarmed by being told, – what he then gave forth as his plea for breach of contract, – that the book was a "conspiracy against Moses"' (*HMA* 2:295). Martineau supposed that Murray's clerical clients urged him to abandon the book's publication, and she offered the book to Moxon, who accepted on the usual terms.[21] To the extent that Murray's concerns had some basis, however, *Eastern Life* marked an important stage in the development of Martineau's religious beliefs. Martineau's literary career began with her prize-winning essays for the Unitarians. These and her numerous articles and reviews for the *Monthly Repository* demonstrated a commitment to organized religion, but shortly after she moved away from doctrinal speculations and towards the private, individualized religious philosophy of the German Romantic, Gotthold Ephraim Lessing.[22] At the same time, she retained her commitment to necessarianism (unlike her brother James), resulting in an uneasy coalition of materialist and spiritualist perspectives.[23] Following the success of her *Illustrations of Political Economy*, however, her faith diminished as her independence increased. In America, her horror at Christian ministers' condoning of slavery reinforced a long-felt anti-clericalism, consistent with her Unitarian background. At the same time, her idea of religion became increasingly abstract:

> Religion is, in its widest sense, 'the tendency of human nature to the Infinite'; and its principle is manifested in the pursuit of perfection in any direction whatever. It is in this widest sense that some speculative atheists have been religious men; religious in their efforts after self-perfection; though unable to personify their conception of the Infinite. In a somewhat narrower sense, religion is the relation which the highest human sentiments bear towards an infinitely perfect Being. (*SA* 3:224–5)

As Valerie Pichanick has observed, Martineau was 'moving gradually toward a renunciation of Christianity' (Pichanick 175).

With illness, she suffered a relapse. *The Hour and the Man* expressed ambivalence about Christianity. *Life in the Sick-Room* expressed her most morbidly religious views, inspired by her belief that her illness was divine retribution for her transgressing gender roles, or for her 'flagrant violations of the laws of nature' (*HMA* 2:152).[24] Moreover, her sense that she deserved this 'chastening and discipline' and that pain 'reassures' the invalid that she is 'a child of Providence' (*LS* 132) contradicts Webb's opinion that Martineau's ultimate loss of faith has its intellectual origins during her Tynemouth period, when her own sickness and the deaths of some friends 'reinforced her old contempt for the orthodox solution of ascribing justice to God and mercy to Christ' (Webb 287). On the contrary, it seems that Martineau's recovery caused her to question God's justice by demonstrating that sickness was not a metaphysical state, or an irrevocable and rightful punishment for her professional achievements.

Other critics have also seen continuities between Martineau's experience of sickness and her speculations in *Eastern Life*. For Maria Frawley, when Martineau visited the East, she 'took with her enormous confidence in the interpretive skills with which sickness had empowered her' (Frawley 53). Frawley sees the East as a 'second sickroom' for Martineau, and Valerie Sanders shares the view that 'the privileges of tourist and invalid, in her experience, were surprisingly alike' (Sanders 127). In accordance with my own view that sickness was anything but empowering for Martineau, I wish to resist the idea that passively watching the world 'from the verge of life' and travelling in the East were comparable experiences (*LS* 65). Valerie Pichanick contends that *Life in the Sick-Room* and the *Playfellow* series both reflected 'outer conformity rather than inner faith,' but although this assessment seems true for her children's tales, it does not seem to be a valid interpretation of her experience of sickness. Martineau's illness was characterized by excessive religiosity deriving from a strong sense of personal guilt at having violated prescribed gender roles.

Mesmerism appears to have played a significant role in dispelling this guilt and its attendant religious fervour. Her sensation of a 'clear twilight, closing in from the windows and down from the ceiling, and in which one object after another melted away, till scarcely anything was left visible before my wide-open eyes' accompanied a 'melting away' of social norms, or her rejection of their constraints. Another of her mesmeric experiences, described in a letter to Richard Monckton Milnes from Birmingham after Martineau had left her Tynemouth couch, comprised a perception that the great faiths of the world shared an underlying unity:

> I *saw* the march of the whole human race, past, present & to come, through existence, & their finding the Source of Life. Another time, I *saw* all the Idolatries of the earth coming up to worship at the ascending series of Life-fountains, while I discovered these to be all connected, – each flowing down unseen to fill the next, – so that all the worshippers were seen by me to be verily adoring the Source.[25]

Whatever one may think of Martineau's mesmeric visions, they at least suggest an intellectual connection between Martineau's period of recovery and her historical speculations in *Eastern Life*.

The historical investigations in *Eastern Life* can be summarized. Having travelled through Egypt, Sinai, and Palestine (and insisting on the order of this route to future travellers who might wish to engage in a comparable study), Martineau concluded that Christianity was no more than a transitional phase in an evolution of religious faiths. Christianity and Judaism had common roots in the faith of ancient Egypt, and she stressed this teleology explicitly: 'The ground gained by the human mind was never lost; for out of this Valley of the Nile issued Judaism: and out of Judaism issued, in due time, Christianity' (*EL* 1:336). An understanding of Martineau's argument in more specific terms is best gained by following her circuit through the East. It is in Egypt that Martineau first describes correspondences between the Egyptian religion and Christian doctrine. Martineau believed that the faith of the ancient Egyptians was essentially monotheistic; that is, the higher Egyptian priesthood had arrived at a monotheism but had deluded the people by deifying the attributes of the Supreme Being, Amun Ra, who was not to be named but 'adored in silence' (*EL* 1:205). Lesser deities, deriving from the attributes of this one God, but conceived by the general Egyptian mind as actual personages, included Ra, the god of visible creation, Kneph, or Egypt, Isis, and Osiris. It was the last of these that most forcibly suggested associations with Christianity. Sacred above all other gods, Osiris was the incarnation of the Goodness of the Supreme God. He left his heavenly abode, assumed a human form without becoming a human being, died in a battle against forces of evil, rose again to spread blessings over the people and the earth, and was appointed Judge of the Dead and Lord of Heaven. Martineau argued, originally, that it was 'impossible not to perceive that Osiris was to the old Egyptians what the Messiah is to be to the Jews; and what Another has been to the Christians' (*EL* 1:247).[26] Various solutions had been postulated to account for this striking coincidence, but for Martineau, who believed that 'ideas are the highest subject of human cognisance, the history of Ideas the only true history, and a common holding of Ideas the only real relation of human beings to each other,' it followed that 'this great constellation of Ideas is one and the same to all these different peoples; was sacred to them all in turn' (*EL* 1:248).[27] Further researches corroborated this view. Martineau's exploration of the tomb of Osirei, father of Rameses the Great, revealed to her that the two accounts of creation in the Book of Genesis were also derived from ancient Egypt: the serpent, the tree of life, the moving spirit of the Creator, the original spread of water and its separation from the land, the sudden appearance of vegetation and, subsequently, of animals were all to be found in ancient Egyptian representations of creation.[28] Martineau was convinced that ideas were passed from one system of thought to another, and this belief not only explained correspondences between the ancient Egyptian and Christian faiths, but also correspondences between the faiths of Egypt and Moses.

In accordance with her belief that the Egyptian priesthood subscribed to a monotheism, Martineau maintained that Moses derived his monotheism from them and imparted their ideas to the Hebrews:

> He saw that they [the Hebrews] must be first removed, and then educated, before they could be established. In following out this course of speculation, he was led to perceive a mighty truth, which appears to have been known to no man before him; – a truth so holy and so vast that even yet mankind seem scarcely able fully to apprehend it; – the truth that all ideas are the common heritage of all men, and that none are too precious to be communicated to every human mind. (*EL* 2:202)

Moses had a singular appreciation of the 'spiritual rights of man.' This, combined with his perception of the degrading effects of a mistaken polytheism, led him to direct his people to an unmediated knowledge of a single God and to reject ideas inconsistent with this end, such as the belief that evil originated with a malevolent spiritual being.[29] For Martineau, Moses' democratization of monotheism made him 'the greatest of men, and the eternal benefactor of the world,' notwithstanding her perception that many of his expectations for his people were frustrated by their degradation (*EL* 2:202). To be able to relate to God, the Hebrews needed to name him and to conceive of Jehovah as a national God who protected the children of Abraham and was an enemy to the Egyptians and Caananites. In order for the public good to be served, Moses substituted temporal reward and punishment for reward and punishment in a future life, which reduced virtue to a matter of obedience and disregarded the spiritual welfare of the individual. According to Martineau, these were 'politic' limitations of the Mosaic system. She maintains that Moses' greatest disappointment was the Hebrews' need for ritual. The Hebrews were unable to receive a faith without forms, and Martineau describes how, 'after a long and terrible conflict, [Moses] surrendered his highest hopes for the people and pursued a lower aim. – He gave them a ritual, Egyptian in its forms and seasons and associations, but with Jehovah alone for its object' (*EL* 2:282).[30] The Hebrew Tabernacle was devised like an Egyptian temple; Hebrew sacrifices replicated Egyptian sacrifices; and practices of divination followed Egyptian practices and beliefs. Martineau contends that these concessions stifled the people's cry to be returned to Egypt and secured their consent to be led to the Promised Land. Moses may have 'rejoiced that every step removed them further from Egypt' (*EL* 2:291), but for centuries after their arrival in Palestine, the Hebrews were subject to popular Egyptian superstition. When the Hebrew prophets gave place to a Levitical priesthood, the Egyptian and Hebrew faiths and philosophies were scarcely distinguishable. The Hebrews now had ritual to distract them and a hereditary, priestly caste to oversee their religious concerns: 'From this time till Christ arose to free it from its trammels, and revive its life, the religious sentiment of the nation wasted away under the bondage of the Law, the formality of the priesthood, and the sectarianism which inevitably springs up where the administration of religion is appropriated by any body of men' (*EL* 3:92).

When Martineau arrived in Palestine, she evaluated the historical context of Christ's beliefs and teachings. She reasoned that of the sectarian bodies that had arisen, the doctrine of the Essenes was central to Christ's thought. Whereas the Pharisaic sect was concerned with adding a tradition of arbitrary meanings to the original structure of the Mosaic system, and the Sadducees were committed to preserving the simplicity of that structure, the Essenes were preoccupied with the moral significance of the Mosaic law. They were egalitarians, held their goods in common, and denounced slavery and servitude in all their manifestations. Insisting on obedience to civil authority, they themselves abstained from political action, inculcating an agenda of non-resistance and limitless forgiveness of injuries. Because of the striking coincidences between the Essenes' doctrine and that of Jesus, combined with Jesus' unwillingness to denounce the Essenes when he rebuked the other two sects, Martineau concluded that Jesus had received his training from them. She insisted on Jesus' role as a man and a teacher and blamed the schools of Simon Magus for corrupting Christianity with the Egyptian belief 'that the Divine Idea of the Universe, – sometimes called Wisdom, sometimes the Word, sometimes the Creative Power, – is manifested to men in human form' (*EL* 3:186–7). When Christians adhered to this ancient belief, they obstructed the gospel's moral operations (*EL* 3:189). The Scriptures were 'records, and not oracles' (*EL* 3:174). Jesus' failure to predict accurately the time when a spiritual kingdom would be established was evidence enough of that.[31] According to Martineau, Jesus' followers 'wrote his history for the information of the world,' and it was a mistake to regard those scriptural narratives as the Word of God (*EL* 3:172–3). Instead, Martineau argues that 'the history of man is truly the Word of God: and that the reason why the gospel is especially called so is because those Glad Tidings are the most important event in the history of man' (*EL* 3:72). For Martineau, the Word is history, and the Bible an event whereby Christ assessed old faiths and sectarian tenets and presented them 'anew, purified, and expanded' (*EL* 3:73).

Notwithstanding the inherent limitations of any paraphrased argument, the above summary of Martineau's speculations should indicate that *Eastern Life* made some bold assertions, not the least of which was Martineau's explicit denial of the divine authority of Scripture. Martineau not only rejected the belief that biblical narratives were oracles, she condemned the 'worship of the Letter of the Bible, to the sacrifice of its Spirit' as a gross superstition (*EL* 3:69). She agreed with Coleridge that idolatry had been succeeded by 'bibliolatry' and further suggested that the error of bibliolatry was more gratuitous than its antecedent: idolatry, whether Christian or pagan, had some true idea associated with it, however wrongly conceived; of bibliolatry, it could only 'truly be said that "the letter killeth, but the spirit maketh alive"' (*EL* 3:70, 69). In *Society in America*, Martineau had argued against an extralinguistic origin and guarantor of constitutional principles. In *Eastern Life*, she makes a cognate argument about the meaning of Scripture. Not only was it superstitious to mistake the records of Judaism and Christianity 'for the messages themselves,' but there was no indication in the Bible that this was even an appropriate interpretive strategy:

> There is no declaration in the Records themselves that they are anything more than records: and if the writers could have foreknown that the hearts and minds which ought to be occupied with the history and the doctrine would be enslaved by a timid and superstitious regard to the wording of the records, they would have been as much shocked at the anticipation as any of us can be at the sight of it. (*EL* 3:70)

For Martineau, biblical records had no divine referent. Instead, they existed solely as historical records, and it was only by examining them historically that their meaning, or spirit, might be ascertained. As Martineau describes it, the problem surrounding biblical meaning anticipates Foucauldian concerns: it is another function of the contemporary episteme. Biblical language participates in the decay of representation: it too 'loses its privileged position and becomes, in its turn, a historical form coherent with the density of its own past,' to state the matter in Foucault's terms.[32] In Martineau's terms, the timid must abandon their superstition for 'the broad light of historical and philosophical knowledge, which would reveal to them the origin and sympathy and intermingling of the faiths of men, so that each may go some way in the interpretation of the rest' (EL 3:71).

The importance that Martineau attaches to historical investigation of religious beliefs seems consistent with the status of history at the time. Cultural critics and historians confidently assert that the modern study of history was a nineteenth-century innovation, since it was in the 1840s that organizations committed to historical researches gave the impetus for government projects such as the establishment of a central records office and the implementation of university reforms awarding history academic recognition as a discipline.[33] As Stephen Bann argues, 'every historian knows, or thinks he knows, that in the 19th century the pioneers of the modern study of history emancipated themselves from the cloying embrace of literature, and developed a critical method which would make it possible to elicit the truth of the archives.'[34] These developments have been referred to in chapter 4; what I wish to consider here, leaving aside for the moment the burdens and frustrations of historical recovery, is the fraught association of history and religious faith.

Recent studies of professional historiography in the Victorian period tend to share an assumption that history enjoyed epistemological hegemony. History is described as one of the 'dominant intellectual resources which shaped Victorian culture,' but there has been an inadequate consideration of the prohibitions against historical investigation in specific areas, especially religion (Levine 1). Or perhaps it is more correct to recognize that in the nineteenth century a contest was waged over the right to determine what constituted appropriate historical inquiry in religious matters. High-Church Tractarians, allied in spirit and principle with Roman Catholicism, appealed to the traditions and records of the Church as the repository of religious authority. In other words, ecclesiastical history was seen as paramount, not only by the Catholic Church but increasingly by ultra-orthodox Protestant sects. Most other denominations of Protestantism, such as the Low-Church Evangelists, or Scripturalists, also appealed to the authority of Church traditions, but since they attached greater significance to the divine status of the Bible as the revealed Word of God, there could be 'no comparison in any respect, between it and any other supposed source of true doctrine,' according to Baden Powell at any rate.[35] At the very least, the authority of historical records was to be combined with biblical study in Christian instruction; at most, it supplanted Scripture altogether.[36] At the same time, there were inherent limits to the scope of historical material included in Church traditions. Traditional records of apostolic doctrine and institutions were referred to in the earliest periods after the apostles and constituted the body of records after the New Testament that had been preserved by the Church and that had multiplied in the interpretative traditions of the church fathers. When independent researchers such as Martineau went beyond these limits, investigating the ideas and beliefs of ancient Egypt, they threatened Church authority and undermined Christian doctrine. The ecclesiastical tradition was not, perhaps, historical enough; alternatively, antiquarian researches exceeded the limits of acceptable religio-historical study.

In her study of nineteenth-century historiography and its separation into the distinct pursuits of antiquarianism, archaeology, and history proper, Philippa Levine maintains that Egyptological researches corroborated Christian doctrine. She argues that archaeological excavations in ancient biblical lands authenticated biblical narratives and that it 'was the archeological work closer to home which was challenging the fundamentals of time and of religious belief' (Levine 5).[37] Specifically, Levine refers to geological discoveries in the south of England and in France which refuted the idea that the universe was six thousand years old and which conflicted with the Mosaic accounts of creation.[38] The conflict between prehistory and Christian orthodoxy was certainly fundamental; however, it was by no means the sole threat posed to Christianity by the new historiography. Indeed, for Martineau, historical investigations of Christianity could be seen as distinct from geological researches and were less likely to obtain a public hearing: 'It is difficult now for philosophers to make known, – in England, for the incubus presses chiefly there, – what can be proved to be scientifically true in geology and some other directions; and it is much more difficult for philosophers and scholars to make known what can be proved to be historically true or false' (*EL* 3:70–1). Martineau attributes this difficulty to the enslavement of Christians 'under the bondage of the Law or Letter,' and her assessment accords with the relatively minor impact that 'higher criticism' had on Victorian thought prior to the publication of *Eastern Life* (*EL* 3:71).

'Higher criticism' had originated in the work of German biblical scholars and was concerned with establishing the dates, origins, forms, and hermeneutics of scriptural writings. Enormously influential in Germany, it had fewer proponents in England.[39] George Eliot translated David Friedrich Strauss's *Das Leben Jesu* (1835) in 1846, but many readers quailed at its three ponderous volumes (although reviews of the text in the periodical press provided a succinct rendering of its main arguments). Strauss had endeavoured to arrive at an understanding of Jesus as a man and a teacher upon whom Messianic ideas were projected. Charles Hennell made a comparable argument in *An Inquiry Concerning the Origin of Christianity* (1838), which was also less provocative in England than in Germany, where it was published with a preface by Strauss. James Anthony Froude's *The Nemesis of Faith*, a biography of a religious sceptic, did provoke an outcry in England, but, published in 1849, it succeeds Martineau's *Eastern Life*. *Eastern Life* may be legitimately described as the first popular text by an English author to bring to the fore uncomfortable correspondences between Christian doctrine and the religious beliefs of ancient Egypt, and it had a wide circulation because of its official designation as a travel narrative.

My view of the significance of *Eastern Life* differs from Valerie Sanders's argument that Martineau's theological speculations in this text 'retain little lasting importance.' Sanders contends that since *Eastern Life* was published after Eliot's translation of Strauss, Hennell's *Inquiry*, and Charles Bray's *Philosophy of Necessity* (1845), which depersonalized God in accordance with necessarian principles, it 'had not even the advantage of originality' (Sanders 127).[40] It is certainly true that *Eastern Life* participated in a theological dispute that was well established when Martineau left England for Egypt. Indeed, Martineau had read Strauss and was likely acquainted with the texts of Bray and Hennell (Pichanick 178). *Eastern Life* was significant, however, for its effect on a wide audience who read the text as a travel book and found theological arguments thrust upon them. Reviewers complained that Martineau had confused her genres. According to J.J. Tayler, *Eastern Life* had a 'threefold aspect': it was a 'descriptive work,' a 'summary of learned research,' and 'a frank utterance of the writer's own thoughts' (Tayler 524). For Martineau's reviewer in *Fraser's Magazine*, this generic confusion was tantamount to fraud. *Eastern Life* was 'as mischievous and detestable a work as could have crept into a book-club, – with this additional odium attached to it, that it has crept in under false colours. Who looks for all this jargon of English Deists and German Rationalists in a book purporting to relate Eastern Travels?' This reviewer insists that if Martineau 'dares to attack the great points of the faith of the country she lives in, she should have given her book the title which would have announced the impious and offensive contents.'[41] Orthodox Christianity had more to fear than the disruption of its theories about the age of the earth by archaeological researches, as Levine suggests. Martineau reveals that its most basic tenets shared the mythological status of its creationist theories, and it was this revelation that made her book so 'detestable' to readers who sought light entertainment in a travel narrative.

Creationist theories were not refuted by geological investigations alone, after all. At Thebes, Martineau examined a series of 345 colossal wooden statues of successive priests, descending in order from father to son, which had been noted by priests of Amun five hundred years before Christ and which suggested that men had been living in an organized state for at least twenty thousand years. Even more significant, because harder to discredit, were the correspondences Martineau observed between biblical and Egyptian creation accounts, as noted above, which suggested that biblical creationist theories were borrowed from earlier faiths. Such correspondences had the devastating effect of reducing those theories to legendary status, and they were not restricted to accounts of creation. They also had a direct bearing on the nature and role of Jesus. When Martineau blamed Simon Magus for corrupting Christianity with the Egyptian idea of a human manifestation of God, she lamented that the simple teachings of Jesus had been overlaid with 'mysteries and allegories and fables' (*EL* 3:189). Indeed, at Jerusalem, mysteries, allegories, and fables borrowed from other faiths saturated every aspect of Christian doctrine:

> Here we have, in these Christian churches, the wrathful 'jealous God' of the old Hebrews, together with the propitiating Osiris, the malignant Typho, the Hades, the Purgatory, and the incarnations of the Egyptians and their disciple Pythagoras; the Logos of the Platonists, the incompatible resurrection and immortality of opposing schools, all mingled together, and profanely named after Him who came to teach, not 'cunningly devised fables,' but that men should love their Father in Heaven with all their hearts and minds, and their neighbour as themselves. (*EL* 3:127)

Christianity was a curious admixture of historical truth and popular legend, and the two required distinguishing: 'It is the business of the philosophical historian to separate the true ideas from their environment of fiction, and to mark the time when the narrative, from being mythical, becomes historically true; – to classify the two orders of ancient historians, – both inestimable in their way – the Poets who perpetuate national Ideas, and Historians who perpetuate national Facts' (*EL* 1:147).

It might have been supposed a reasonable objective. Victorians had supposedly freed themselves from 'the cloying embrace of literature,' as Bann describes it, and were keen to recount 'what actually happened,' after the fashion of Leopold von Ranke. Moreover, Christianity seemed positively to invite such a study. It claimed to be historically true. It boasted of traceable origins in historical facts and tangible events. It was inherent in the very notion of revelation that a definite meaning should be assigned to 'what actually happened.' That it was considered unnecessary, or even irreverent, to inquire into these revealed grounds of Christian faith at best indicated confusion at the heart of Christianity's claims to historical authenticity. For Baden Powell, the injunction against such inquiries itself had the effect of reducing Christianity to the status of myth:

> Such a view, in fact, directly divests the Christian religion of the attributes of reality; it confounds truth and fable; and makes it idle and dangerous to attempt to separate them, or to unravel the perplexing distinctions between history and tradition, – between fact and fiction. It removes all the landmarks of historical testimony, and reduces the Gospel to a mystical legend. (Powell 205)

Prohibitions against historical inquiries – whether mandated by the Catholic Church, which assumed for itself the prerogative of research into all evidence, or by Protestant sects, which shrouded Scripture in mystery – had the consequence of rendering 'faith no better than fiction; Christianity a fable; its history a legend, – of no better authority than the chimaeras of Paganism' (Powell 207).

Paradoxically, historical inquiries such as Martineau's made precisely these same reductions. Martineau did not maintain that history and legend were indistinguishable, but her insistence that they had been blended in Scripture and required disentangling met with sharp rebuke: '... if Miss Martineau must work at myths, let her attempt to detach fable from truth in the history of Mother Hubbard's dog,' the reviewer for *Fraser's* advised, attributing the tip to Murray.[42] *Eastern Life* effectively transformed the Bible into an historical romance, and reviewers were not slow to object to this new, profane generic designation. As the reviewer for *Tait's* complained, when particularly incensed by Martineau's assent to the opinion that the first four books of the Pentateuch were compiled, rather than copied, from existing documents during the reign of Josiah, 'all our knowledge of Joseph is derived from the Pentateuch. If these books be incredible, Joseph's existence is disestablished. He is no more to us than Waverley or Guy Mannering. Moses may be a myth, and Aaron a mistake, if this belief of the learned be worthy of any attention.'[43] I have argued in chapter 4 that crises surrounding historical representations and historical meaning were most conspicuously played out in the genre of historical romance; in Martineau's analysis, the Bible was no less a site for fraught historical forms. In her opinion, the Bible not only documented historical evidence, it reflected the world of romance, portraying the external circumstances of a past age and, especially, its ideals, which were themselves borrowed from earlier societies. Those who believed in the integrity of Scripture had no conscious awareness of an opposition between the ideality of Christian doctrines and the observable facts of life. Like Don Quixote, who believed that windmills were giants, the devout mistook natural births for annunciations and miracles:

> ... it has been a great misfortune to the average Christian world for many ages, that the old allegories of Egypt, – the old images of miraculous birth, and the annunciation of it from heaven, – should have been laid hold of and repeated from age to age, however the character of the theology might change, till at last, repeated without explanation, it came to be taken, with other mythic stories, for historical truth, and is to this day profanely and literally held by multitudes who should have been trained to a truer reverence. (*EL* 3:223)

The decay of reference and representation which Foucault describes as inaugurating the contemporary episteme excluded the Bible, at least for faithful Christians. Martineau argues that the ancient Egyptian priests, from whom these mythic stories were inherited, understood these ideals as allegories, or as lacking inherent referents. They too told a story of an annunciation, of the appearance of the heavenly messenger, Thoth, to Tmanhemva, Queen of Thotmes IV, to announce that she should bear the son of Amun Ra, the Supreme God. Martineau felt that it was 'harmless and interesting' to trace 'the form of allegory in which the priests presented the concealed doctrine to the people,' and she maintained that the use of such mythologies was 'appropriate to the people and the time' (*EL* 3:222, 223). Unlike Christians, the Egyptian priests did not present their stories as true and essential doctrines:

> ... how much less irreverence attached to the Egyptian doctrines, in their early age: and I think no one can doubt what indignation would be expressed against the blasphemous indecency of Egyptian superstition, if we knew that they had presented to the people, as literal truth, such a story about the birth of the most distinguished of Egyptian men as our poor and ignorant fellow men are told in our Christian churches, through the mistake of an ancient allegory for modern history. (*EL* 3:223–4)

For Martineau, Christians' failure to grasp the limits of representation explained why Christianity failed to win converts from 'multitudes,' who rather 'jested' at their mistaking allegory for historical fact. Moreover, her insistence that ancient Egyptians had a greater appreciation of representational limitations, or the arbitrariness of allegory, disrupted the assumption that progress had led to the uncontested primacy of Victorian England.[44] Philippa Levine maintains that for 'all its damaging and potentially secular implications regarding the antiquity of the human race,' historical research nonetheless serviced 'the presumptions of progress and superiority so fundamental to the maintenance of the Victorian *status quo*' (Levine 98). Martineau, however, stands opposed to this supposed superiority. At Thebes, she wondered why succeeding ages had been led 'to imagine men in those early times childish or barbarous, – to suppose science and civilisation reserved for us of these later ages, when here are works in whose presence it is a task for the imagination to overtake the eyesight!' (*EL* 1:292). At Palestine, she added literary sophistication to Egypt's architectural, scientific, and philosophical dominance. Not only was it understandable that 'multitudes' had resisted conversion to Christianity, but Martineau questioned the rationale of Christian missionary efforts. The Christian Mission at Jerusalem, for example, was flawed in its very conception and not likely to endure:

> It is no light matter to subvert a man's habits of mind and life, to isolate him in the midst of his own city and race, and render him wholly depen-

dent on his religious teachers. It should be well considered whether the loss of the faith of his fathers, and the radical shaking of his own; the exclusion from family, society, and employment; the loss of tranquillity, and the great moral dangers of such an uprooting as none but a Jew can ever experience, are really compensated for by anything that the Mission at Jerusalem has hitherto found itself able to impart. (*EL* 3:112–13)

It was a provocative statement,[45] perhaps originating in the religious and cultural tensions of *The Hour and the Man* described above in chapter 4. According to Martineau, Jews already had 'a noble faith of their own.'

Given the numerous ideological disruptions posed by *Eastern Life* – disruptions of the historical truth of Christianity, of the epistemological value of historiography, and of the supremacy of Victorian culture, especially as 'proved' by studies of the past which were supposedly 'institutionally and individually wedded to that power structure'[46] – it is not surprising that it provoked a violent outcry. According to J.J. Tayler, *Eastern Life* was widely regarded as a poisonous book, and Martineau was thought to have an 'evil tendency' that had caused her to sin against religion and morality. Tayler was even told of a pious clergyman 'who as he read the book took each sheet in succession and committed it to the flames,' watching with 'holy satisfaction' the conflagration of 'so much pestiferous error' (Tayler 526–7). The book required more than burning, however; it required refutation, and reviewers ascribed to Martineau the same predilection to romance that she had ascribed to the Bible. In particular, they attacked Martineau's pretended capacity to act as a witness to events of the past and to access the minds of historical figures. Martineau's speculations on the objectives and character of Moses, for example, were seen as inconsistent with the facts of history. Her fabricated narrative describing how Moses sat under a palm tree, considered the condition of the Hebrews in Egypt, and was led to perceive the 'mighty truth' that 'ideas are the common heritage of all men' bypassed the problem of divine revelation (hence Martineau's confidence in advancing her narrative), but it had no historical basis: 'Of all these meditations not an iota is mentioned in the Scriptures,' George Croly objected, and he reminded his readers that Moses, 'so far from meditating in the desert,' was merely an instrument of God.[47] Martineau was merely 'manufacturing a romance' (Croly 188), and reviewers maintained that *Eastern Life* abounded in such romances. In addition to her fictional representation of Moses, Martineau described ancient Thebes by allegedly seeing it 'with the eyes of three thousand years ago' (*EL* 1:305). Having ascended a peak overlooking the Valley of the Tombs and the Theban plain, Martineau acts as an historical go-between, describing in the present tense activities 'seen' below:

> Here is a multitude below me, too. The women are exchanging their goods in the areas of the streets, – bargaining slowly, it seems, because, having no coin, they have to settle the worth of their valuables before they can agree on that of their produce. And those men, – how they are toiling about that sledge, – advancing it by hairs'-breadths under its load of granite; a mass as large as any merchant's house in the city! What a team of harnessed men, straining at the load! (*EL* 1:307)

It was a recreation that included the auditory as well as the visual, and Martineau also describes 'the hum and buzz' from the crowd, the 'shock of the mallet,' 'the blast of a distant trumpet, and some shrill pipe tones.' Martineau acts as a witness figure, mediating between the reader and the represented historical scene. At the same time, the recreation is a rhetorical conjuring trick posturing as an authentic moment in history, and for reviewers who wished to discredit Martineau's theological speculations, this 'rather vulgar habit of calling up historical fancies when she comes to a remarkable place' undermined her authority and the book's pretensions. Martineau may have conveyed a 'lively idea' of the ancient Egyptian people, but 'whether that interpretation be a true and general account of the ideas suggested by the remains themselves, or peculiar to her imagination, may be doubted.'[48]

Martineau's recreations of past scenes raise an important question about the status of history itself – a question about the ontological duplicity of history both as an event and as a narrative, or discourse, predicated on an event. Hegel supposed that historical narrations 'appeared contemporaneously with historical deeds and events,' but Martineau's recreations rather point to an absent past, just as the linguistic sign itself may be thought always to indicate an absent signified.[49] The question is an important one, since it was the perceived inauthenticity of Martineau's narrations, or their dissociation from knowable events, that caused her reviewers to challenge the authority of her historical speculations and, in particular, her rendering of biblical history. Martineau maintained that the Bible, as a supposed narration of history, had no inherent relation to actual past experience;

Martineau's reviewers countered that her own historical discourse was in reality an imaginative surge.[50] At least two opposed historical narrations – Martineau's text and the Bible – asserted a necessary connection to past events. Moreover, the proliferation of historical signs increases with Martineau's belief that biblical signs could be traced in an abundance of Egyptian inscriptions. Historical events were diffused among a range of competing historical discourses, and in addition to advancing its own version of 'what actually happened,' *Eastern Life* traces the frustrations and burdens of historical recovery. Like *The Hour and the Man*, *Eastern Life* belies the formulation that history in the nineteenth century was 'superbly, straightforwardly and pregnantly portrayed.'[51]

The importance that Martineau attached to Egyptian history and, in particular, to Egyptian inscriptions was a significant cause of her frustrations. If history was both experience and communication of experience, Egyptian communications were scarcely legible to her. Champollion had used the Rosetta stone (found in 1799) to decipher Egyptian hieroglyphics, and the Chevalier Bunsen had prepared a lexicon of the Egyptian language by comparing above four hundred words with known Coptic, but Martineau was unable to learn Egyptian signs beyond the most common symbols.[52] As a consequence, she relied heavily on secondary sources, especially Wilkinson's *Modern Egypt and Thebes* (1843), for an understanding of ancient Egypt. To a considerable extent, then, Martineau's frustrations with Egyptian inscriptions were the result of her limited training. There was also a more serious problem: many Egyptian relics had been defaced. Consistent with the eradicatory agenda of triumphalist history, Christians had plastered over the walls and sculptures of Egyptian temples, covering the symbols of the ancient religion with their own – a literal example of cultural overwriting. At Philae, 'they had put a yellow halo over the lotus-glory; and the dove over the hawk; and St. Peter with his keys of heaven over Phthah with his key of life; and angels with their palm-branches over the Assessors of the dead with their feather symbols of Integrity' (*EL* 1:254). Fortunately, many of these representations could be restored, but Martineau despaired that early Christians had also destroyed Egyptian records. The Emperor Severus had buried the writings relating to the mysteries of the Egyptian priests in the tomb of Alexander. Diocletian had ordered the destruction of all Egyptian books on alchemy.[53] Modern tourists contributed to the destruction and plundering of Egypt's history: 'And what shall we say to a traveller (Mrs Romer), who coolly reports, without any apparent shame, that she has brought away from Benee Hasan the head and shoulders of a figure which she does not doubt to be that of a Jewish captive; her dragoman having cleverly detached from the wall this interesting specimen of antiquity!' (*EL* 2:38).[54] Martineau was outraged by these thefts and was no less concerned by the practices of 'scientific anti-quarians' who sawed through tablets, knocked down pillars, and carted them away, destroying the integrity of a 'repository where everything has its place, and is in its place' (*EL* 2:39). These monu-ments were all that remained of Egypt's records, these and the inscrip-tions which covered their surfaces – inscriptions so staggering in their profusion that they reminded Martineau 'more of the labours of the coral insect than of those of men' (*EL* 1:46). Martineau was over-whelmed by these inscriptions: '... it is indescribable, – unremember-able, – incredible anywhere but on the spot. I have already said all that language can say on this point: and I will leave it' (*EL* 1:279).

Martineau's impression of ancient inscriptions recalls Carlyle's defi-nition of history – 'that complex Manuscript, covered over with form-less inextricably-entangled unknown characters'[55] – and contributes to her oppression by her labours of historical research. There was a super-abundance of historical records in Egypt, where 'the very rocks by the wayside offer indisputable materials of history to you as you pass by!' (*EL* 1:239–40). The standing ground of history was everywhere, and the fulfilment of the historicizing ambition was endlessly deferred. Whole cities were buried beneath the sand of the desert. Martineau insists that her choice of a 'fairy gift' would be

> a great winnowing fan, such as would, without injury to human eyes and lungs, blow away the sand which buries the monuments of Egypt. What a scene would be laid open then! ... Who knows but that the greater part of old Memphis, and of other glorious cities, lies almost unharmed under the sand! Who can say what armies of sphinxes, what sentinels of colossi, might start up on the banks of the river, or come forth from the hill-sides of the interior, when the cloud of sand had been wafted away! (*EL* 1:60–1)

Martineau's hopes for the exhumation of a lost totality immediately give way to anxiety. The recovery of history would be endlessly deferred, nonetheless: 'But it is better as it is. If we could once blow away the sand, to discover the temples and palaces, we should next want to rend the rocks, to lay open the tombs: and Heaven knows what this would set us wishing further. It is best as it is.' Martineau's fan would merely expose an unending signifying chain, and historical meaning would remain absent: 'The minds of scholars are preparing for an intelligent interpretation of what a future age may find ... We are not worthy yet of this great unveiling' (*EL* 1:61).

The quantity and the nature of those monuments that were available for study were themselves sufficient to overpower Martineau. At Thebes, she notes the sinking of her powers of observation.[56] At Philae, she finds the view of the temples 'oppressive' (*EL* 1:118). Having wished for a winnowing fan, she wishes that Manetho, an Egyptian priest in the reign of Ptolemy II, would appear to explain to her the Egyptian language and the condition of ancient Egypt: 'He is the very man we want, – to stand on the ridge of time, and tell us who are below, what was doing in the depths of the old ages. He did so stand; and he did fully tell what he saw: but his words are gone to the four winds' (*EL* 1:189). When the day arrived for Martineau to inspect the Great Pyramids, she 'dreaded' the prospect. The pyramids and the Sphinx were the central event of her Egyptological researches, and she feared failure. Her anxieties about her health, her professional authority, her social role, and her family were all foregrounded in anticipation of her visit:

> Since arriving at Thebes, I had not been well; and I had no reason for confidence in my strength, in a place and enterprise so new. I had made up my mind not to be disconcerted if I should have to return without having been either up or into the Pyramid: but I was sorry to open my eyes upon the sunrise of that morning. I went over in my mind all the stories I knew of persons who had failed, and felt that I had no better title to success than they. My comfort was in the Sphinx. I should see that, at all events. – It did not mend the matter that I found that a messenger was sent to Cairo for our letters ... never, I think was I so anxious about letters from home, or so afraid to receive them. (*EL* 2:62–3)

For Martineau, the pyramids and, especially, the Sphinx were central to Egyptian history and the focus for her anxieties about her historicist ambitions. Her visit to this site would be her central engagement with the ancient Egyptian world; it represented her desire to access history and her fear that historical meaning was utterly oblique.

When Martineau saw the pyramids, she was 'disappointed' in them. Instead of getting larger as she approached, they appeared 'less and less wonderful' (*EL* 2:63). Nonetheless, she ascended the Great Pyramid, explored its interior, and was sufficiently absorbed by the process to forget that she had left her ear-trumpet with an Arab, hearing perfectly well without it.[57] If the pyramids were disappointing, however, the Sphinx represented an especially baffling, frustrating, and deferred encounter with history. When Martineau passed the Sphinx, she failed to see it: 'One of our party said, on our arrival, "When we were passing the Sphinx −" "O! the Sphinx!" cried I. "You don't mean that you have seen the Sphinx!" − To be sure they had: and they insisted on it that I had too; − that I must have seen it, − could not have missed it. I was utterly bewildered' (EL 2:64). If the Sphinx was the centre of Egyptian history, then for Martineau it was also a monumental absence. It was the vanishing point of the ancient world and the blind spot of Martineau's historicist enterprise: '... not to have seen it was inexplicable.' Reminiscent of Stendhal's Fabrizio del Dongo, whose historical engagement with the battle of Waterloo is rendered endlessly problematic by his failure to be sure that he ever finds it,[58] Martineau's encounter with the Sphinx is characterized by its teasing refusal of representation. Later in the day, when Martineau did see the Sphinx, she realized that she had seen it before but had supposed it 'a capriciously-formed rock.' Martineau had understood the Sphinx to be a sacred symbol of the union of physical and intellectual strength. When she finally confronts the Sphinx itself, she sees it as a 'nightmare':

> Now I was half afraid of it. The full serene gaze of its round face, rendered ugly by the loss of the nose, which was a very handsome feature of the old Egyptian face; − this full gaze, and the stony calm of its attitude, almost turn one to stone. So life-like, − so huge, − so monstrous, − it is really a fearful spectacle. I saw a man sitting in a fold of the neck, − as a fly might settle on a horse's mane. In that crease he reposed, while far over his head extended the vast penthouse of the jaw; and above that the dressed hair on either side the face, − each bunch a mass of stone which might crush a dwelling-house. (EL 2:82)

Martineau also describes the Sphinx as 'a record of the Egyptian complexion' resembling 'the Berber countenance.' She believed that the ancient Egyptians were black, and for John Barrell, Martineau's fear of the Sphinx derives from 'an intense anxiety about the boundaries of western self and eastern other.'[59] My own focus is elsewhere. It is with the threatening gaze of the Sphinx, with 'those eyes, − so full of meaning, though so fixed!' Those 'well-opened eyes' had 'gazed unwinking into vacancy' when Martineau had passed the Sphinx and had failed to see it. Martineau had complained of the 'misery' of being continually stared at in the East and had endeavoured to reverse the operations of objectification. Confronted with the Sphinx, that process breaks down. The Medusoid Sphinx threatens to reduce, to objectify, to 'almost turn one to stone.' It challenges Martineau's identity, and it challenges her professional authority. The Sphinx represents the vastness of history. Macaulay reminds us of Bishop Watson's comparison of the geologist to 'a gnat mounted on an elephant, and laying down theories as to the whole internal structure of the vast animal, from the phenomena of the hide' (Macaulay 363). In Martineau's description, the historian compares with the man sitting in the fold of the Sphinx's neck. The Sphinx stands for the oppressive limitlessness of the historicist project. It represents the burden, if not the riddle, of ancient Egypt and the endless deferral of historical meaning.

Martineau's sense of frustration with her project never abated during her travels: 'I verily thought, the whole journey through, and especially at Cairo, that I was losing my observing faculties' (*EL* 2:118–19). Furthermore, when her powers of observation were keen, she was often faced with an inauthentic historical archive. At the Church of the Holy Sepulchre in Jerusalem, for example, she was shown 'the stone on which the announcing angel stood; the place of the cross, – Mount Calvary being a staircase of twenty-two steps, – and about a dozen sacred places, curiously disposed in an exact circle, a few feet distant from each other,' which were all purported to be genuine relics (*EL* 3:163). Martineau dismissed the monks' superstitions, but by the end of her journey she could no longer determine whether anything was 'abstractedly and absolutely true' (*EL* 3:334). As she watched the sunset from the Syrian shore, she laboured under a sense of responsibility to impart what she had learned during her travels: 'Such a function, once recognized, is not to be declined by any one because his powers are humble, his knowledge partial, and his influence insignificant in his own eyes' (*EL* 3:333).

Martineau here furnishes a rationale for publishing a book that she knew would be controversial. At the same time, she acknowledges the inherent limitations of her study. Martineau claimed in her *Autobiography* that the 'result of the whole, when reconsidered in the quiet of my study, was that I obtained clearness as to the historical nature and moral value of all theology whatever' (*HMA* 2:279), but *Eastern Life* reveals crises surrounding historical meaning and historical representations, suggesting that the lost Ur-myth can never be wholly recovered.[60] In Martineau's work, the mummy serves as a metonymy for the otherness of history. It can never be brought back to effulgent life; rather, Martineau had once watched as her dragoman clasped a mummy and 'coolly wrenched off the head, the throat giving way like a fold of rotten leather' (*EL* 2:42). The decapitated mummy suggests the dismembered Osiris and the fragmentation of a heterogeneous past. When *Eastern Life* was finished, Martineau turned her attention to the organic structure of living man. Her *Letters on the Laws of Man's Nature and Development* would be, arguably, the most controversial text of her professional career.

Chapter Seven

Shaking the Faith:

Letters on the Laws of Man's Nature and Development (1851)

In February 1848, prior to the publication of *Eastern Life, Present and Past*, Martineau wrote to Henry Atkinson expressing her concerns about the book's reception: 'The book once out, I am in for it, and must and will bear every thing.' For Martineau, *Eastern Life* was her boldest text to date: 'Some people would think the Population number of my Political Economy, and the Women and Marriage and Property chapters in my American books, and the Mesmerism affair, bolder feats: but I know that they were not.' Martineau had been sustained in these earlier ventures by a belief in a 'Protector who ordered me to do that work.' Following her Eastern travels, that support disappeared: Martineau's religious faith had been eroded by her recognition of the mythological basis of Christianity's central tenets, and *Eastern Life* required, as a consequence, 'the greatest effort of courage I ever made' (quoted in *HMA* 2:345). Three years later, Martineau initiated another courageous literary project. She published her correspondence with Atkinson. *Letters on the Laws of Man's Nature and Development* (1851) is an epistolary exchange on man's nature and place in the universe, and for recent critics it remains problematic.[1] Described as 'one of the strangest books to carry the name of a reputable writer' (Webb 293) and as 'simply one of the many oddities of nineteenth-century publishing' (Thomas 25–6), *Letters* has been regarded not as 'intrinsically important,' but as 'significant for what it tells us, and for what it told her contemporaries, about Harriet Martineau' (Pichanick 187). As Shelagh Hunter maintains, 'the *Letters* are significant in Martineau's emerging autobiographical story, not for their overt promotion of a short-lived and controversial science, but for the ways in which her own contribution requires her to show her thought processes, so that we see her returning to the origins of her moralism in Romantic radicalism' (Hunter 102).

The chief focus of this chapter is that which critics are inclined to dismiss as irrelevant – Martineau's promotion in the *Letters* of a 'controversial science.' Phrenology, which constitutes the basis of Martineau's and Atkinson's study of man, was a physiological study of the brain that removed psychology from the realm of metaphysics and raised religious, social, and political questions of a potentially revolutionary nature. Although it was jointly authored, Martineau herself assumed responsibility for the book's production,[2] and, again, prior to publication she anticipated that her work would destroy her career: 'I might never be asked, or allowed, to utter myself again. I had, on four previous occasions of my life, supposed the same thing, and found myself mistaken; but the "audacity," (as a scientific reader called my practice of plain avowal) was so much greater in appearance (though not in reality) in the present case than ever before, that I anticipated excommunication from the world of literature, if not from society' (*HMA* 2:343). Martineau's concerns were legitimate, for *Letters* provoked a furious outcry. Not only did the text challenge her society's religious beliefs and social institutions, but it was seen to threaten scientific rationalism, that is, the foundations of emergent secular power.

With its overriding concern to advance phrenology, *Letters* participated in a popularization of ideas already topical in Martineau's society. Phrenology, or 'cerebral physiology,' as its founder called it,[3] originated in the work of Franz Joseph Gall, a Viennese physician who believed that bases of human character were empirically discernible, and who based this belief on the following premises: that the mind is the product of the brain's action; that the brain is an assemblage of discreet structures, or organs; that these organs are localized topographically; that the size of an organ is equivalent to its power; and that craniological features indicate the strength of mental faculties since the skull molds itself around the contours of the brain (*LLMND* 16–23; cf. Cooter 3). Gall's ideas were first popularized by Johann Gaspar Spurzheim, a former student of Gall's who came to Britain in 1813. Spurzheim was chiefly interested in the application of phrenology to morals and social reform, and developed the ethical implications of Gall's doctrines in his *Elementary Principles of Education Founded on the Study of the Nature of Man* (1821) and *A Sketch of the Natural Laws of Man* (1825). Arguing that no mental faculty was inherently bad, Spurzheim nonetheless distinguished between animal propensities, or personal survival instincts, and higher faculties essential for the well-being of society – a hierarchical arrangement in which man's higher faculties were supposed to control his animalistic tendencies. Spurzheim initiated phrenology's transformation from a cerebral theory into a vehicle for personal improvement, but it was not until George Combe published *Of the Constitution of Man in Relation to External Objects* (1828) that this transformation was completed and that phrenology became current in England. Inspired by Spurzheim's *Sketch of the Natural Laws of Man*, the *Constitution of Man* is as much a conduct book based on mental organization as an assessment of man and his relation to his environment, and it met with almost unprecedented commercial success, reaching all classes of Victorian society. According to Martineau, the circulation of the *Constitution of Man* approached that of the Bible, *Pilgrim's Progress*, and *Robinson Crusoe*.[4] By 1847, it had sold over 80,500 copies in England (Cooter 120).

Given the immense popularity of Combe's work when *Letters on the Laws of Man's Nature and Development* was published, the fact that neither he nor the *Constitution of Man* is mentioned in *Letters* surprised readers.[5] In part, an explanation for this absence derives from the circumstances of Martineau's own attraction to phrenology, which had nothing to do with Combe and which were in themselves complex. Most conspicuously, Martineau was drawn to phrenology after her proclaimed cure by mesmerism (see above, chapter 5). Mrs Montague Wynward, Martineau's mesmerist, had been recommended to her by Henry Atkinson, and when Martineau finally met Atkinson in 1845, she was naturally interested in his researches, which included phrenology as well as mesmerism. Their friendship (and lifelong exchange of ideas) was not, however, solely responsible for her 'conversion' to the science. Another explanation for Martineau's interest is found in phrenology's apparent empiricism. In between her publicized recovery and the production of *Letters*, Martineau had turned her attention to historical projects, first with *Eastern Life, Present and Past* and then with *The History of England during the Thirty Years' Peace 1816–1846*, written at the request of Charles Knight and published in 1849 and 1850.[6] Martineau's frustrations with her Eastern researches have been considered (see above, chapter 6), and her anxiety when commencing the *History of the Peace* is suggested in the *Autobiography*:

When I had laid out my plan for the History, and begun upon the first portion, I sank into a state of dismay. I should hardly say 'sank'; for I never thought of giving up or stopping; but I doubt whether, at any point of my career, I ever felt so oppressed by what I had undertaken as during the first two or three weeks after I had begun the History ... the quantity and variety of details fairly overpowered my spirits, in that hot month of August. (*HMA* 2:318)

Once again, Martineau had felt oppressed by the burdens of historiography, although the burden in this case was somewhat lightened by the fact that the *History of the Peace* chronicled Martineau's own times. On the other hand, it was precisely this contemporaneity that made the work objectionable to some of its readers. For example, D.T. Coulton, who reviewed the *History of the Peace* together with John Roebuck's *History of the Whig Ministry of 1830 to the Passing of the Reform Bill* (1852), complained that both texts represented the worst of contemporary history: 'They share in its partisanship, its errors, its animosities, but not in its clear and decisive knowledge.'[7]

For Martineau, phrenology obviated such pitfalls. As a 'real science' based on Baconian induction, it offered a means of knowing phenomena objectively and the 'scientific basis' she felt was lacking in her earlier work (*LLMND* 1, 2). Moreover, from a Foucauldian perspective, Martineau's interest in phrenology meant not 'giving up' historical research. For Foucault, the analysis of organic structures in the nineteenth century supersedes the search for taxonomic characteristics, sharing the 'profound historicity' of the contemporary episteme by seeking to define organisms 'in their own coherence' (*OT* xxiii).[8] Indeed, phrenology serves as a bridge between the nineteenth century and the Classical age. Foucault describes the study of organic structures in terms that relate directly to phrenological preoccupations: 'In one sense, there has been a return to the old theory of signatures or marks, which supposed that each being bore the sign of what was most essential in it upon the most visible point of its surface.' At the same time, character is not 'established by a relation of the visible to itself; it is nothing in itself but the visible point of a complex and hierarchized structure in which function plays an essential governing and determining role' (*OT* 228). Phrenology, which maintained that human character was most visible in the shape of the cranium and that cranial features related to cerebral structures, each with its specialized function, participates exactly in the principle of nineteenth-century classification. Foucault maintains:

To classify, therefore, will no longer mean to refer the visible back to itself, while allotting one of its elements the task of representing the others; it will mean, in a movement that makes analysis pivot on its axis, to relate the visible to the invisible, to its deeper cause, as it were, then to rise upwards once more from that hidden architecture towards the more obvious signs displayed on the surface of bodies. (*OT* 229)

Foucault's description of classification in the contemporary episteme also recalls the anatomoclinical gaze considered in relation to *Deerbrook* in chapter 3, suggesting that the relation between visible phenomena, or behaviour, and underlying structures, or causes, was of enduring interest to Martineau. Indeed, notwithstanding Foucault's insistence on the importance of the principle of organic structure to nineteenth-century thought, Martineau perceived that this principle had been dissociated from psychological investigations, and, as we have seen, characterization in *Deerbrook* addresses their association. In *Letters*, Martineau explains that 'the course of physical inquiry' had been established as an appropriate methodology in the field of natural philosophy since the time of Bacon but was deemed unsuitable for the study of mental phenomena, creating a schism between the sciences:

I am sure I do not wonder at scientific men sneering at metaphysics, if the case be at all as I suppose it: – that Natural Philosophy and Mental Philosophy are arbitrarily separated; – that the one is in a regenerate state (thanks to Bacon), and the other in an unregenerate state; – and that we can no more get on in Mental Philosophy without an ascertainment of the true method of inquiry, than the men of the middle ages could get on with Natural Philosophy (except in the departments of detail), till a man rose up to give us a *Novum Organon Scientiarum*. (*LLMND* 2)

Independently of Auguste Comte, whose *Cours de philosophie positive* she would later translate and abridge, Martineau perceived that the sciences were interrelated, and she attributed their division to the persistence of belief in 'spiritual agencies' that made the two departments of science seem so unalike as to require distinct principles of inquiry.[9] 'My wonder is,' she wrote to Atkinson, '– not that there are few so-called Mental philosophers who use or even advocate any experimental method of inquiry into the science of mind; but that there seem to me to be none' (*LLMND* 3).

Of course, there were advocates for physical inquiry into mental phenomena, as Martineau well knew. The most important in her own background was Joseph Priestley.[10] Priestley (1733–1804) may be best remembered today for his discovery of oxygen, but his abridged version of David Hartley's *Observations on Man*, entitled *Hartley's Theory of the Human Mind on the Principle of Association of Ideas* (1775), contributed significantly to association psychology and was once studied by Martineau with 'a fervour and perseverance': 'I am bound to avow, (and enjoy the avowal) that I owe to Hartley the strongest and best stimulus and discipline of the highest affections and most important habits that it is perhaps possible, (or was possible for me) to derive from any book' (*HMA* 1:104, 105). In *Letters*, Martineau disparages her early enthusiasm for Hartley: 'It is astonishing to me now that I could admit without question his supposition that Man has two primary powers which are enough to account for every thing: the capacity for pleasure and pain, and the principal of association' (*LLMND* 118). Phrenology, which sought to localize sensation according to cerebral structures, now seemed more satisfactory. But Priestley's own views on the nature of the mind, although largely in agreement with Hartley's theory of pleasure and pain,[11] also shared basic premises of phrenology. In the second edition of his *Disquisitions Relating to Matter and Spirit* (1782), Priestley announces that his 'principal object is, to prove the uniform composition of man, or that what we call *mind*, or the principle of perception and thought, is not a substance distinct from the body, but the result of corporeal organization.'[12] Priestley's materialism logically entailed a necessarian doctrine, and he published *The Doctrine of Philosophical Necessity Illustrated* (1777) as an 'appendix' to *Matter and Spirit*: '... the doctrine of *necessity*, maintained in the Appendix, is the immediate result of the doctrine of the materiality of man; for mechanism is the undoubted consequence of materialism ... the pretended *self-determining power* is altogether imaginary and impossible' (Priestley v). Priestley had once been a hero of Martineau's, but by the time she produced *Letters*, she was fundamentally opposed to Priestley on religious matters, although she continued to believe in necessarianism. For Priestley, whose scientific achievements bolstered his role as a leader of Unitarianism, physiological psychology and the Scriptures were mutually enlightening, and he advised that the two be studied concurrently by 'rational Christians.'[13] For Martineau, the Bible was an historical romance, and continued belief in 'spiritual agencies,' as noted above, was responsible for the separation of mental from natural philosophy. In opposition to Priestley, and to George

Combe, who also believed in the compatibility of faith in God and a science of mind, *Letters* made a bold statement of atheism.

Phrenology and religion had always seemed incompatible. When Gall reduced mental phenomena to cerebral functions, he was seen to undermine the Cartesian dichotomy between mind and matter and thereby, indirectly, the existence of God. For Descartes, thought and consciousness proved that the mind was animated by an immaterial principle, which mechanical philosophy attributed to God as his unique gift to man. To deny this principle was to deny God's gift and, by extension, God himself. In fact, Gall was not an atheist. He was born a Catholic, educated by priests, and had once been inclined to the priesthood himself. Nonetheless, the emperor of Austria stopped Gall's public lectures in Vienna on the grounds of their evident atheism, and Gall died with his books on the Index (Cooter 5, 40). It was a legacy that George Combe tried to revoke. Fully aware that atheism was widely perceived as dangerous, he publicly affirmed deism and explained atheism as a pathological condition caused by the malfunction or developmental retardation of the faculty of Veneration (Cooter 127). Combe was, however, also keen to dismantle the institutionalized Calvinism that had tormented his youth, and by denying the hereafter and attacking Scriptures, he distressed his religious readers.[14]

When *Letters on the Laws of Man's Nature and Development* was published, it seemed to many that their worst fears about phrenology had been fully realized. Arguing from the premise that supernatural causes of natural phenomena were only required by the absence of sufficient natural causes, Atkinson maintains that 'philosophy finds no God in nature; no personal being or creator, nor sees the want of any' and that theists, who imagined an extra Cause of the world and stopped there, were themselves no more than atheists 'at one remove' (*LLMND* 173, 171). It was true, he conceded, that man inclined naturally to belief in the supernatural, and, like Combe, Atkinson located a cerebral organ of 'reverence, awe, respect, [or] deference.' Unlike Combe, however, he denies that the proper object of this faculty is God:

> Its highest object seems to be, a sense of the infinite and abstract power, – the inherent force and principle of nature. It seems to convey a sense of our dependence on the mysterious force and rule of nature, – of that which is beyond the experience of sense. It causes us from its situation to look up, and speak of high things, – to sink upon the knee, and to bend before the semblance of power and majesty. Uninformed and misdirected,

we personify, humanize, materialize, the object of this sense; and thus we find that the highest feelings, as well as those which we call the lowest, have lived through periods of misdirection and idol worship. (*LLMND* 79)

Atkinson denied the existence of the Judeo-Christian God, and Martineau not only concurred, maintaining that 'there is no theory of a God, of an author of Nature, of an origin of the universe, which is not utterly repugnant to my faculties,' she challenged Atkinson directly when he carelessly referred to God in one of his letters: 'Pray tell me, too, whether, in this last letter, you do not, in speaking of God, use merely another name for law?' (*LLMND* 217, 164). Atkinson conceded his mistake, and, together, the correspondents launched an unequivocal attack on orthodox religion. Recalling Martineau's assertion in *Eastern Life* that the central tenets of Christianity were so many inherited fables, Atkinson compares religious belief to his childhood belief 'in spirits and goblins, – in Jack the Giant Killer; and afterwards in Robinson Crusoe and his man Friday, and in Don Quixote,' with the distinction that religion was 'the greatest romance of all' (*LLMND* 233, 234). For Atkinson, as for Martineau, religious doctrine participated in the decay of reference and representation which Foucault describes as characterizing the contemporary episteme.[15] It was impossible to know anything of a 'motive power' of the universe, and 'no form of words could convey any knowledge of it' (*LLMND* 246). In short, Christianity was 'no better than an old wife's fable'; the belief in a God resembling man was 'universal insanity'; and, put together, Christian dogmas were 'intellectually most absurd and monstrous, and morally vicious and most barbarous' (*LLMND* 239, 174, 205–6). It is perhaps not surprising that in her last letter, Martineau disavows her earlier faith with considerable embarrassment.[16]

Letters appalled its readers, and for a time Martineau experienced the ostracism she had expected before the book's publication. Neighbours in the Lake District avoided her. Friends who had not attended fully to the religious heterodoxy of *Eastern Life* found that in *Letters* 'the full truth burst upon them,' and they ended their relationships with her, sometimes permanently (*HMA* 2:352). Charlotte Brontë, who had visited Martineau at her Ambleside home just prior to the publication of *Letters*, was distressed: 'It is the first exposition of avowed atheism ... the first unequivocal declaration of disbelief in the existence of God or a future life I have ever seen. In judging of such exposition and declaration, one would wish entirely to put aside the sort of instinctive horror they awaken, and to consider them in an impartial spirit and collected mood. This I find difficult to do.'[17] Reviews in the periodical press were less tolerant. In *Blackwood's*, John Eagles described *Letters* as the most 'thoroughly degrading' book ever to be published and blamed Martineau for the text's evident atheism: 'It professes to be a joint work by herself and a Mr Atkinson, one of the clique of infidel phrenological mesmerisers; but it is manifestly the *doing* of Miss Martineau herself. If Mr Atkinson had any hand in the production, the female atheist ("and here a female atheist talks you dead") must have manufactured and cooked much of his philosophy, as of his grammar and diction.'[18] Others blamed Atkinson and puzzled over the 'infantine simplicity' with which Martineau accepted his views as a 'curious physiological problem.'[19] The title of J. Stevenson Bushnan's lengthy review, *Miss Martineau and Her Master*, suggested that Atkinson had mesmerized Martineau and perverted her judgment, and, in what was surely the most devastating review for Martineau personally, her brother James concurred. *Letters* repudiated everything that James believed, and he savagely attacked Atkinson as the 'hierophant of the new Atheism' and the champion of bad prose. As for his sister, he lamented the corruption of her intellect:

> With grief we must say that we remember nothing in literary history more melancholy than that Harriet Martineau should be prostrated at the feet of such a master; should lay down at his bidding her early faith in moral obligation, in the living God, in the immortal sanctities; should glory in the infection of his blind arrogance and scorn, mistaking them for wisdom and pity; and meekly undertake to teach him grammar in return. Surely this humiliating inversion of the natural order of nobleness cannot last. If this be a specimen of mesmeric victories, such a conquest is more damaging than a thousand defeats.[20]

After James's review, Martineau never saw or wrote to her brother again, but almost without exception, such protests reverberated throughout the periodical press. Even the liberal-minded *Westminster Review*, which published two reviews of the book, had difficulty with its arguments.[21] There were, however, exceptions to the chorus of opposition. A working man wrote to the *Leader* praising *Letters*; George Holyoake's *Reasoner* reviewed the book favourably; and Martineau wrote to Holyoake to say that two copies of *Letters* in a Birmingham library were borrowed by 'thinking men & women of the *lower middle,* & working classes, [and] were always out, & read with extreme eager- ness & thoughtfulness.'[22] Reactions to *Letters* such as these invite a closer inspection of the text's ideological operations, especially the socio-political implications of atheism.

By mid-century, religious authority in Victorian society faced severe threats. Not only was it challenged by geological discoveries and by German higher criticism, but disputes between Church factions chal- lenged its capacity to act as a socially cohesive force. James Anthony Froude, whose religious scepticism in *Nemesis of Faith* was superseded by a return to orthodoxy in his review of *Letters* for *Fraser's*, main- tained: 'What with millions upon millions of wretched children grow- ing up in savage ignorance, because the religious bodies cannot settle their differences, or cannot, or will not find common basis of agree- ment – what with these terrible social questions ... we can at least understand the feeling which drives earnest men in despair from reli- gion.' For Froude, *Letters* was symptomatic of a growing exasperation, of a view of religion as 'empty words' or barren signification.[23] How- ever, the erosion of Church power notwithstanding, attacks on religion were nonetheless commonly seen as subversive. After the publication of *Letters*, Martineau received considerable correspondence from per- sons whom she called 'censors,' who were scandalized at her 'shaking the faith' of others (*HMA* 2:360).

But Martineau did more than shake people's religious faith; she rocked the chief ideological superstructure which that faith continued to support: the Victorian middle-class home: 'It were ill indeed for us if there were not still many a home sanctuary which is hallowed and made beautiful by real genuine faith,' Froude asserted. It was an ideal that Martineau endangered. She argued that Christ had offered no teaching in regard to domestic institutions and, further, that it was a meaningless omission since 'these, and all groupings into households by the rule of marriage and blood relationship, may be easily con- ceived to be a matter of rule and arrangement, and therefore of limited duration.' Indeed, the human passions of which these institutions were but the 'temporary form' were a matter for phrenology, not for religion (*LLMND* 245). The Christian might look up to a Father in heaven to thank for his home, his health, and his maintenance, but Martineau saw nothing there, as Froude put it, but a 'deep black glaring bottom- less eye-socket' (Froude 430).

It was a metaphor that might have suited Martineau well, given her anxiety and fear of objectification,[24] but for others the absence of an Almighty Overseer not only desecrated the private sphere but augured civil anarchy. According to the anonymous author of *Materialistic Views of Professor Tyndall and Miss Harriet Martineau Criticized,*

> atheism is, in truth, the creed of the murderer, and the abiding stimulus and final consolation of the criminal classes (the proofs are extant); and the cause is not far to seek, for the man who disbelieves in a God, the soul, and a future state, has naturally the less respect for the life, and less still for the death (especially of others); and he who denies any future retribution has, doubtless, lost one main restraint on his present actions.[25]

Fear of God and of punishment in an afterlife was a basic mechanism of social control, but Martineau had expressed her dissent from the use of such threats early in her career in *Society in America*. In *Letters*, reminded of her travels in the West, she again protests against the future consolations and retributions promised by the clergy, used as a means of restraint: 'What an insult it is to our best moral faculties to hold over us the promises and threats of heaven and hell, as if there were nothing in us higher than selfish hope and fear' (*LLMND* 246–7). True moral health was achieved by rejecting these superstitions and by studying one's own nature, recognizing that after death the materials of life are simply transformed into new organisms in a cycle of change with no beginning or end: '... deeper and deeper down in the abysses of time, farther and farther away in the vistas of the ages, all was still what we see it now, – a system of ever-working forces, producing forms, uniform in certain lines and largely various in the whole, and all under the operation of immutable Law!' (*LLMND* 219).

Martineau's concept of the eternity of matter troubled her readers. In the Malthusian numbers of her *Illustrations of Political Economy*, she had distressed the public by provoking them to consider an unforeseeable future, when the means of subsistence would be outstripped by the requirements of overpopulation. Now she compelled their contemplation of an endless future and an infinite past in which matter underwent ceaseless transmutations, and which precluded the possibility of life after death since life (thoughts, feelings, or the human mind) was strictly the manifestation of matter (or the brain) in action. The argument solved the problem of creation from nothing, but it also overtaxed the Victorian imagination. Bushnan recoiled from the proposition. In a chapter of his pamphlet entitled 'The Limits within

Which Man Can Contemplate the Universe,' he objected that the idea
of eternity failed 'to satisfy any standard of truth with which the
human mind is conversant' (Bushnan 30). For the idea to be rendered
intelligible, it was necessary that it be shown to be compatible with an
intelligent First Cause. It was a paradoxical requirement, but Bushnan
insisted that if matter underwent ceaseless transformations in the universe, it was a 'natural craving of the mind of man' to believe that an
exercise of power accompanied those changes (Bushnan 35). W.E.
Hickson shared this view, arguing that it was inherent in the very concept of Martineau's 'immutable Law' that it be ascribed to an intelligent Being, 'since laws are *rules*; rules of action implying actions
foreseen and designed' (Hickson 208). For Hickson, God had become a
displaced Signifier:

> The only objection to the substitution of the words 'Matter' and 'Nature'
> for 'God' is this, that the words are more commonly used both by atheists
> and other people in a quite a contrary sense, namely to express that which
> *cannot* design and foresee ... We may take any term we please and affix to
> it whatever signification we please, but when we have defined its signifi-
> cation we should keep to it. The terms *'wisdom* of Nature,' *'plans* of
> Nature,' *'laws* of Nature,' when used by a writer who denies the existence
> of a Divine Intelligence, merely show that he has not made up his mind as
> to his own meaning. (Hickson 209)

A Supreme Intelligence admitted, the legitimacy of belief in an afterlife
followed as answering to man's understanding of design and as 'worthy of a beneficent Being' (Hickson 226). The argument might have
been supposed circular in its reasoning, but it provided more incen-
tives and consolations than the horrors of personal extinction that Martineau offered: 'It is to be hoped that there are few so void of true light
as to follow Miss Martineau into the dark abyss to which she would
lead them – where peace, and hope, and joy are sunk and utterly abolished, and where all a man can look forward to is nothing more cheerful for himself than foulest corruption, or to be, at best, *a mummy.*'[26]
The importance attached to the coexistence of laws of nature and a
Being responsible for those laws recurs frequently in reviews of *Letters*
and suggests the ways in which theology served to justify governmental authority. For many, the notion of all-pervading laws of matter
operating apart from a divine Legislator was unthinkable: Hickson's
suggestion that signification was arbitrary was not generally sub-

scribed to, and Martineau's use of the term 'Law' was, as a consequence, challenged as a misnomer. As one reviewer jeered, Martineau's and Atkinson's 'Law' was 'a sort of universal Act of Parliament, passed by nobody, and for no object.'[27] The *British and Foreign Medico-Chirurgical Review,* which assessed *Letters* together with Bushnan's *Miss Martineau and Her Master,* echoed the objection. A 'law of nature' stripped from association with a 'Governor of the Universe' was no more than a generalized expression of phenomena: 'A law can possess no *coercive* character, can do nothing, nor make anything or anybody else do anything, except it be the expression of a *power,* such as that of a Government or Legislator.'[28] The sustained metaphor in these arguments' rhetoric is instructive. On the one hand, God as Legislator defined the terms for conceptualizing legislative authority in the secular realm, mystifying, and thereby mediating, governmental power. At the same time, the metaphor also meant that the existing secular order had been enacted by God himself, obviating the possibility, or even the desirability, of social change. As Froude maintained, 'what religion craves for, is the sense that, whatever becomes of man, all is well – all is well, because God is, and He has willed it all' (Froude 431). In contrast, Martineau's 'immutable Law,' dictating the infinite transformations of phenomena, suggested that change was natural and, indeed, inevitable. As Atkinson argued, 'all is action, change, and growth' (*LLMND* 132). Flux characterized the universe, and it was for this reason that Atkinson also concluded that 'whatever is, is right, and essential to the whole, and could not be otherwise than as it is' (*LLMND* 133). Everything was the necessary, but temporary, manifestation of natural laws dictating change.

As much as Martineau's and Atkinson's views on God, an afterlife, and natural laws were considered subversive, it is important to recollect that their advocacy of phrenology was also seen as an expression of dissent from laws, institutions, and social order. It has already been suggested that this perception was owing, at least in part, to the association of their phrenological views with their evident atheism: their assertion that the faculty of Veneration had no proper object, but only the sense of one, combined with their argument that mind, as a product of brain, could have no continued existence after death, meant that phrenology, in particular, was seen as opposed to orthodox religion. But phrenology was also seen as a threat to other societal norms, and it is important to consider further how phrenology, as Martineau and Atkinson understood and advanced it, operated to challenge accepted thought. In particular, their promotion of phrenology deployed a rhetoric of egalitarianism with the potential to revolutionize all social systems, and in order to understand the operations of this rhetoric, it is necessary to examine the metaphors that constituted the basis of phrenological knowledge.

Roger Cooter reminds us that phrenology was a doctrine concerning the head: '... elevated in the body hierarchy was the seat of the intellect, not the signifiers of human labour, love, emotion, or soul' (Cooter 110). For Cooter, the dominance of the head symbolized not only the exaltation of reason over past superstitions but also 'the struggle to establish the dominance of mental over manual labour.' Moreover, phrenology's representation of the cerebral interior, exemplifying order, classification, and a hierarchy of functions, both reflected the workings of the Victorian middle-class home and functioned analogously to the division of labour in the mechanized factory (Cooter 111). Cooter also considers the metaphor of the body in phrenological imagery, or the description of the brain as the 'organ' or 'body of the mind': the 'body' supported the concept of free will, implicitly denied in views of man as a sophisticated machine, and 'allowed everyone to participate in understanding the "laws of organization"' (Cooter 112). In total, Cooter suggests that the rhetoric of phrenology upheld class hierarchy in Victorian society, which degraded manual labour (although phrenology also challenged privileged social status based on inheritance rather than on intellect), and biologized the social relations of industrial capitalism: '... phrenology naturalized the emergent structures and relations of industrial capitalism by casting them into the descriptive and explanatory language of mental organization and mental function' (Cooter 113). Cooter argues that phrenology was an important vehicle of bourgeois liberalism and that this explains why George Combe was attracted to the science, why Combe's books were immensely popular, and why Martineau placed Combe beside Von Humboldt in her *Biographical Sketches*: 'To her, as to others involved in retailing bourgeois ideology and political economy to working people, Combe was envied as "the agent, if not the author, of a great revolution in popular views"' (Cooter 120).[29]

My own argument does not concur with Cooter in seeing Martineau merely as a retailer of bourgeois ideology, envious of Combe's singular success in that market. Indeed, Cooter's quotation from *Biographical Sketches* forms part of Martineau's critique of Combe, who is said not to have advanced phrenology, but rather to have 'hindered its development by his own philosophical incapacity' (*BS* 276). In particular, Martineau laments, as a great misfortune to the world, Combe's 'passion for "the practical"':

He, and [his brother] Andrew also, thought it was 'practical' to say that such and such a faculty was too strong for some other – (as if it required phrenology to say that); and that they considered that they had 'explained' a case when they had stated that No. 16 was out of proportion to No. 6; and that No. 20 had no chance under the predominance of No. 5. They supposed that they thus 'accounted for' the character of people's minds. (*BS* 269)

Combe had endorsed Spurzheim's view of the superiority of man's intellectual and moral faculties, and he believed that maximum happiness required the predominance of those faculties over man's animal desires. Of course, since too little of that predominance was manifested in the labouring classes, whom Combe depicted as concerned chiefly to gratify their baser inclinations, Combe's hierarchy of faculties also naturalized the exploitation of workers by the supposedly intellectually and morally advanced bourgeoisie.[30] According to Martineau, because Combe 'took [phrenology] up as Spurzheim gave it him in his young days,' he mistakenly perceived the human brain as 'a map of a completely surveyed country: whereas he should have seen that only the latitude and longitude, and vertebral heights and broken coast lines, were ascertained, and that wide regions remained unexplored, and deep recesses unentered' (*BS* 270, 271). According to Martineau, Combe 'helped to originate a new and pernicious pedantry' and had 'retarded' the development of phrenology as 'a genuine scientific discovery' (*BS* 270).

Martineau's and Atkinson's own elaboration of phrenology made important departures from Spurzheim and Combe, the most significant of which was that it did not organize faculties hierarchically. It, too, was a doctrine of the head, but not one which exalted reason, and not one which, as a consequence, justified the exploitation of manual labourers. Instead, Atkinson's 'catalogue' presents 'the mutual relations of the faculties' (*LLMND* 74). His nearest approximation to hierarchical arrangement is to designate certain faculties as 'centres,' but not only are these 'centres' so diffuse as to suggest that the centre is everywhere in the brain, many of these 'centres' are chiefly important to Atkinson for their roles in mesmeric phenomena. For example, in the cerebrum, beneath a 'central organ of Comparison' is what a som-nambule termed 'the Eye of the Mind,' or the 'Intuitive faculty; for it is this which is chiefly concerned in *clairvoyance*' (*LLMND* 76). The fac-ulty of Consciousness is described as the 'most central faculty of all,' being situated in that part of the brain which is 'the most sensitive we can apply ourselves to for the purpose of waking a somnambule, or casting him into a deeper sleep, or changing his conscious state' (*LLMND* 85, 82). Other 'central organs' include all of those extending 'from Individuality over the nose round over the head to Love' (*LLMND* 86). Indeed, Love, which is defined as 'the desire of union with the opposite sex,' is also distinguished as 'the central organ of the cerebrum' and is located above its counterpart in the cerebellum: 'In the central part of the cerebellum is that which relates to the physical conditions of the amative state' (*LLMND* 61). To the extent that 'cen-tres' in Atkinson's system are important, the centrality of sexuality in his phrenological catalogue was innovative. Atkinson had retrieved human passions from their degraded status in earlier phrenological hierarchies and had seen them as participating, without restraint by any 'higher' faculties, within a 'harmony' or 'a consistent whole' (*LLMND* 83).

For Martineau and Atkinson, man's cerebral organization deter-mined, to a considerable extent, his character and behaviour. This had been a basic assumption of phrenology since Gall, who had responded to Lockean sensationalism by arguing that man's mental endowment was innate.[31] At the same time, Martineau and Atkinson perceived that character was also influenced by external conditions, or by environ-ment:

> The tone and power of [a mental] organ depends also on the quality of the
> substance of the brain, arising from original constitution, or from external
> circumstances; the condition of the stomach, for example, or the air we
> breathe: or the mind may be twisted from its proper action and propor-
> tion by the influence of habit or example, or other similar causes.
> (*LLMND* 131)

The mind depended on the condition of the brain; the brain depended on the condition of the body; and the condition of the body was deter-mined by external factors. It was a chain of influence that effectively overturned the head/body hierarchy. If the head was the seat of intel-lect and reason, representing the bourgeoisie rather than the working classes, as Cooter argues, then it was subordinate to the body for Martineau and Atkinson. As the author of *Materialistic Views ... Criticized* perceived, matter was made 'master instead of servant' in the philosophy of the 'pure materialist' (*MVC* 11).

Most importantly, Martineau's and Atkinson's chain of influence denied free will: 'Free will! the very idea is enough to make a Democritus fall on his back and roar with laughter, and a more serious thinker almost despair of bringing men to reason, – to experience the advantages of knowledge, and the calming influence of a recognition of universal law and necessity' (*LLMND* 194–5). An individual's will and character were always already determined, and although society could seek to develop a person's nature to its 'full and truest proportions,' in order to protect itself against others' actions, it was mistaken to hold men responsible for their acts, 'as if they could help their nature':

> ... drunk or sober, mad or idiot, a man is at all times the result of his material condition, and the influences without. Some men are, as it were, a law unto themselves; while others by their nature are disposed to thieve and to murder. Some men are wolves by their nature, and some are lambs: and it is vain to talk of responsibility, as if men made themselves what they are. (*LLMND* 131)

Rewards and punishments for behaviour were wholly inappropriate, being entirely undeserved. The criminal was not 'other' for Martineau and Atkinson: place men in the same circumstances, and they would share the same ideas. As a consequence, the punishment of individuals as 'criminals' did not, as Foucault suggests,[32] contribute to social solidarity in their view. On the contrary, it was socially degrading and had the potential to increase crime: 'Executions diminish the respect for life, and stimulate the morbid tendency to destroy. The descriptions in the newspapers tend to brutalize society, and make us all the worse.' George Combe wrote extensively on the punishment of criminals in the *Constitution of Man*, but Martineau and Atkinson believed that punishment proceeded on the mistaken view that criminals were different from everybody else. They argued that 'knowledge of the Mind's laws, and the law of love, and the exhibition of goodness and mercy' could alone reform men's conduct and create social cohesion (*LLMND* 134).

It was a vision that required for its realization the reformation of society's institutions: 'We must remove the gallows, and no more use the rod; for these are not the instruments of reform and civilization, but the instruments of barbarism and the cause of brutality' (*LLMND* 243). In their place, dialogue was needed, especially between medical practitioners and judicial bodies: 'There is a rivalry going on now between the insanity doctors and the judges. The doctor says, by the laws of mind, this man is not responsible; but the judge insists on opposing the laws of the land to the laws of nature, and declares the man a criminal' (*LLMND* 242). Moreover, the medical profession itself needed to be further educated on the laws of mental phenomena, since universities continued to provide inadequate instruction in the areas of physiology and psychology, or 'Physiology, and Mental and Moral Philosophy,' as Atkinson termed these subjects (*LLMND* 207).[33] Once these reforms were established, Martineau and Atkinson imagined that the current reign of terror would give way to a 'reign of love, when men shall no more be irritated, by notions of free will and responsibility, to revenge, and pride, or be pampered in any foolish longings whatsoever' (*LLMND* 190).

If Martineau and Atkinson supposed that their imagined 'reign of love' was possible, their readers by no means agreed. To most, it seemed that Martineau and Atkinson were endorsing a reign of licence, and their outrage at the authors' ethics was only exceeded by their horror at the pair's atheism. As the author of *Materialistic Views ... Criticized* reasoned, it was assuredly absurd to designate 'tigers and wolves, or lambs and honeybirds' as vicious and virtuous creatures, but it was 'the height of folly to misapply the terms as regards mankind, and not clearly to define the vicious man as vicious, and the good as good' (*MVC* 37). Bushnan concurred and argued further that a 'boundless relaxation of morals' would follow the acceptance of Martineau's and Atkinson's views on the necessity of human actions (Bushnan 156). Moreover, he suggested that Martineau's 'female disciples in particular' might find it 'difficult at first to bring their theory and practice to conform to this standard' (Bushnan 4). Martineau's and Atkinson's views on morality tore apart representations of women in Victorian society: if 'the laws of Mind' dictated that human behaviour was amoral, as Martineau and Atkinson argued, then women could not be described as 'virtuous.' At the same time, because readers feared that a 'relaxation of morals' would likely follow popular assent to Martineau's and Atkinson's view, they also had to suppose that women were capable of 'relaxed' behaviour, which also meant that women could not be supposed to be characterized by innate virtue. In fact, Bushnan's assertions accede to Atkinson's argument that behaviour is influenced by environment: women's behaviour would correspond to, or be determined by, the amorality of society. But Bushnan's observation is also a threat: women would 'at first' find it difficult to make their behaviour conform to this new standard. Eventually, they might enjoy it, which augured the end of patriarchal authority.

Others had different concerns. W.E. Hickson, for example, was less affected by the implications of the doctrine of necessity for sexual difference (and sexual licence) than he was alarmed by the accordance of Martineau's and Atkinson's views with Owenism:

> And here we may take the opportunity to notice a popular fallacy into which many persons have fallen who have but imperfectly mastered the doctrine of philosophical necessity; a fallacy so often repeated by Robert Owen that he may be said to have made it his own, but which we find put forward as an original conception in *'Letters on Man's nature and development.'* It is, that as man is the creature of circumstances, he is not properly the subject of praise or blame, reward, or punishment. (Hickson 211n)

It was indeed the cornerstone of Owenism, and it was because phrenology (as Spurzheim transmitted phrenology) shared this doctrine that Owen was himself drawn to the science.[34] For Hickson, however, Martineau's, Atkinson's, and Owen's concentration on environment meant that the focus was deflected from the individual, and Hickson sought to restore that focus: '"Circumstances," in reference to the human character, are *motives*. Man is the creature of motives: – motives as arising from our own observations and reflections, or as suggested to us by the minds of others: – motives in which considerations of praise and blame, reward and punishment, are largely mingled' (Hickson 211n).

Hickson was not alone in his concern for the status of the individual in the necessarian system. The concept of the individual lay at the heart of bourgeois liberal ideology, and to many it seemed that *Letters* undermined this central concept. Because Martineau and Atkinson denied free will, they were seen to degrade the individual to the level of animals. What was the individual, the conceptual touchstone of bourgeois liberalism? 'A pig with additions and improvements' was one answer, although at times reviews of *Letters* read something like medieval bestiaries: 'Well, then, Mr or Miss Puppet, as the case may be, according to this, your own philosophy, you are by no means superior in your own special nature, power, or private worth, to horse, dog, cat, or wallowing pig ... As the pig is superior to the oyster, so you to the pig' (*MVC* 34–5). Plato, Shakespeare, and Milton were also 'so many oysters or red mullet' if one followed Martineau's path (*MVC* 38). Necessarianism eroded individualism, and it denied man's status as God's special creation. Martineau and Atkinson fully perceived these implications: they not only identified men and animals explicitly, but, as Diana Postlethwaite observes, they adumbrated an evolutionary biology (*MW* 150). Atkinson writes: 'What I wish to indicate in the first place, then, is this: – that Man has his place in natural history: that his nature does not essentially differ from that of the lower animals: that he is but a fuller development and varied condition of the same fundamental nature or cause; of that which we contemplate as Matter, and its changes, relations, and properties' (*LLMND* 16).

Martineau's and Atkinson's view of man's place in the natural world was not considered their sole threat to the concept of the individual. *Letters* also undermined directly the stability of personal identity:

> The sense of Identity seems to follow as a consequence from the sense of Personality or Individuality. It is a fact of the Memory, presenting similitude, or sameness of impression. Memory is a recurrence of impressions. Habit is a form of memory. Fits are a form of habit, and often have relation to time. To identify myself as an Englishman is a habit of thought. (*LLMND* 274)

Atkinson's explanation of identity was a response to one of Martineau's questions. Because Martineau and Atkinson believed that mind was a product of brain and also supposed (wrongly) that the material substance of the brain was in a constant state of renewal, she had asked how a continued sense of personality was possible, given that 'the material of life is incessantly changing' (*LLMND* 250). Memory explained why individuals had the sense of a constant personality, but it did not guarantee that identity was constant. As Atkinson maintained earlier in their correspondence, 'one false case of identity takes away all reliance or argument, as to the continuity or unity of being from the ordinary sense of identity' (*LLMND* 188), and even in his own case, Atkinson felt that he could 'hardly identify [himself] with [his] condition of childhood; nor in a calm moment feel [himself] to be the same as when under the influence of any passion' (*LLMND* 275). Martineau was satisfied with Atkinson's explanation. Four years later, she would complete her *Autobiography*, documenting memories of personal beliefs which she no longer accepted and which could now be accounted for by the understanding that man, as a part of nature, was characterized by 'action, change, and growth' – a condition that is reflected in the seasonal descriptions of her life as periods of 'winter,' 'spring,' 'summer,' and 'autumn.'[35] One's sense of identity was a matter of memory; it was not inherently stable. Moreover, this view of personal identity also provided Martineau with a rationalization of her career. Having dispensed with the idea of a Protector-God who 'ordered' her work (which did not accord with her earlier view that her illness was God's punishment for her violation of his laws),[36] she could now derive comfort from the belief that identity was indeterminate: 'For me it is enough that I am what I am; – something far beyond my own power of analysis and comprehension. By what combination of elements, action of forces, I came to be what I am, does not at all touch my personal complacency, or interfere with my awe of the universe' (*LLMND* 13). The indeterminacy of identity meant that sexual identity was also indeterminate. In other words, the instability of personal and sexual identity combined with the overdetermination of the individual by unknown but omnipotent forces functioned to obviate cultural alienation.[37]

However satisfactory the indeterminacy of personal identity may have been to Martineau, it was not at all satisfactory to *Letters'* readers. In the *Westminster Review* it was argued that the authors' denial of permanent, conscious identity was merely a *reductio ad absurdum* of their denial of '*personal* existence to the Cause of all phenomena.'[38] Bushnan asserted that men had an 'intuitive' knowledge of their personal identity, and he berated the 'flippancy' with which Martineau addressed such a 'solemn topic' (Bushnan 21, 160). Hickson compared Atkinson to the ancient Pyrrhonists, although he could not himself define what was meant by 'I.' There was nothing to which it might be compared, and he concluded: 'We cannot, therefore, in our definition of mind, go beyond the simple process of naming it; and among a great variety of expressions, we may choose whichever we prefer, – life, soul, spirit, mind, consciousness, person, individual, self, and the pronoun I, or the neutral denominative of "*that* which thinks"' (Hickson 218). Personal identity was, at best, a signifying chain. Most disturbing, however, was the idea that an individual's thoughts could be determined by somebody else: the operating principle of phreno-mesmerism was that the stimulation of particular areas of a mesmerized subject's skull resulted in the subject's manifestation of behaviour corresponding to the mental 'organ' excited. For Atkinson, phreno-mesmerism, which constituted much of the empirical basis of his views on man, God, and the nature of the universe, provided the ultimate demolition of the belief that individuals had souls, free will, or stable identity: 'How far a man does resemble an instrument will, I think, be better seen in contemplating the facts of phreno-mesmerism. There, any doubt which might remain in regard to the mind's independent action must, I think, be swept away, and the law of dependence be exhibited as clearly as in regard to all other physical facts' (LLMND 19). In contrast, Froude maintained that phreno-mesmerism provided the best refutation of materialism ever advanced.[39] At best, mesmeric wonders and scientific rationalism were inconsistent; conversely, the wonders of mesmerism provided a significant check to increasing confidence in scientific rationalism.

Mesmeric marvels and supernatural phenomena pervade Letters. Accounts are offered of a female somnambule who sees her own brain and of a blind woman who sees in her sleep and who is naturally clairvoyant.[40] Martineau herself reports swelling of her hand when she mesmerizes persons who are in severe pain and refers to her own sensations when mesmerized after her long-term illness:

> Now, in certain depths of the mesmeric state, I have received knowledge, or formed conceptions, devoid of all perceptible intermixture with sensible impressions. Of course, I cannot explain what they were, because they could be communicated only to a person in a similar state; and not by ordinary language at all. They have since (during five years) been gathering to themselves more and more visual elements; so that the experience remains only an affair of memory. But it is one which assuredly I can never forget. There is no pleasure that I would not forego to experience it again and often; – the conscious exercise of a new faculty. (LLMND 120–1)

The apparent sexuality of Martineau's mesmeric experience has been discussed in chapter 5, and what I wish to focus on here is the irrationality of the phenomenon. Martineau's mesmeric experience escapes and transcends sign systems. She insists that it is 'really vexatious' not to be able to convey it to anyone, but because her experience resists language, it also resists delimitation (LLMND 119). Atkinson suggests that she might be delusional: '... we must regard the fact by the side of other facts, and consider whether it is not likely to be a delusion of the senses; or rather a delusion of the mind when the senses are at rest ... you, as a matter of course, will find it difficult to abstract yourself, and criticise your own case as you would one in which you were only a looker-on' (*LLMND* 152). Atkinson would seek to objectify Martineau's experience, and, of course, he is concerned to police supernatural phenomena that might suggest the existence of supernatural entities at odds with his denial of the existence of God.[41] However, because Martineau's experience constitutes an escape from discourse, it also resists conceptual control (cf. Stockton 118). It continues to be a pleasurable and empowering experience for Martineau precisely to the extent that it remains irrational and unrepresentable.

References to clairvoyant and supernatural phenomena in *Letters* function culturally in the same way that Martineau's own mesmeric experience functions for her personally. According to Diana Postlethwaite, mesmeric marvels in *Letters* provide Martineau and Atkinson with 'a faith consistent with [their] scientific world view' (*MW* 155), but, in contrast, I should like to indicate that *Letters*' readers found its 'faith' and its science fundamentally opposed. Bushnan states the conflict precisely: '... we cannot but think it will appear that Miss Martineau and Mr Atkinson admit their faith in some things commonly called supernatural, the existence of which is incompatible with their dogma, that there is nothing in the universe but the workings of the physics and chemistry of matter' (Bushnan 139). In certain respects, accounts of supernatural phenomena in *Letters* were at least as countercultural as the text's advocacy of materialism. Because *Letters* presented its 'supernaturalism' as the basis of empirical 'science,' it threatened the science/occult binary established by Newtonian mechanists and, thus, the cornerstone of scientific rationalism.[42] Quite simply, there seemed to be no discursive framework in which these ideas might be contained, controlled, or, indeed, discredited. As Froude argued:

> We have no doubt at all that from time to time very strange things indeed take place in this world, which defy explanation by ordinary causes; but until these new powers can be put to some broad, open proof, – until they have ceased to show themselves only in private society, or in the irregular abnormal way in which they have appeared hitherto, it is premature to bring them forward for purposes of science, and to expect us to submit to have our whole system of thought revolutionized on the faith of facts in themselves so unsatisfactory. (Froude 426)

Because clairvoyant and mesmeric phenomena often exceeded consciousness, not to mention reason and interpretation, these phenomena repudiated 'the rational' at the same time that they were advanced to uphold and promote it. Because supernaturalism was irrational, it always already escaped linguistic, conceptual, and cultural control.

Increasingly, cultural control in Victorian society was exercised by secular rather than by religious authority. Froude perceived that practical atheism had become abundant in England by mid-century, which means that the controversy generated by *Letters* was caused chiefly by its articulation of issues already concerning Victorians, rather than by its engendering of new anxieties. It was the kind of work at which Martineau excelled, and it was also a profitable business. Assessing the consequences of the publication of *Letters* four years later in her *Autobiography*, she asserts that, with regard to her fortunes, her 'latest years have been the most prosperous since the publication of my Political Economy Series' (*HMA* 2:357–8). As was the case with so much of Martineau's work, *Letters*, however distressing to the public, did not destroy her career because, as Froude perceived, it could not be simply ignored:

> Such a book as this is a strange echo of [awful] forebodings. We may turn away from it, affect a horror of it, slight it, laugh at it; but it is a symptom of a state of things, it is the first flame of a smouldering feeling now first gaining air, and neither its writers, nor we, nor any one, well know how large material of combustion there may be lying about ready to kindle. (Froude 433)

Conclusion

In 1877, one year after Harriet Martineau's death, Florence Fenwick Miller delivered a speech before the Sunday Lecture Society on the significance of Martineau's life and work. She described Martineau as 'one of the most remarkable women that ever lived': born to a middle-class family, she became a political power in England; born a member of a sex supposedly '"incapable of understanding politics,"' she demonstrated the fallacy of denying political existence to women.[1] Miller also perceived that Martineau had suffered from such 'torture as could be inflicted on such a mind by misrepresentation, slander, and abuse of her convictions' (Miller 5). Not only were Martineau's life and career considered remarkable, she was also seen to have endured an inordinate amount of hostile criticism.

This study has been chiefly concerned to understand the nature of this criticism and, in particular, the hostile responses to Martineau's most controversial texts. I have focused on those texts which Martineau herself regarded as her most polemical, and, indeed, the public reception of her works in Victorian periodicals justifies fully her opinion. In addition, I have considered her two ground-breaking novels. *Deerbrook* and *The Hour and the Man* are important in literary history for their introduction to prose fiction of middle-class and black heroes, and it is to be hoped that the outrage of her contemporary readers will be succeeded by the increased interest of literary scholars concerned with matters of class and race. It is, of course, impossible to do justice to the range of Martineau's prolific literary output in a single volume, and this study has not considered her publications subsequent to her writing her *Autobiography* in 1855. These texts include *The Factory Con-*

troversy: A Warning against Meddling Legislation (1855), *Suggestions towards the Future Government of India* (1858), *England and Her Soldiers* (1859), *Endowed Schools of Ireland* (1859), and numerous articles for the *Westminster Review*, the *Edinburgh Review*, *Household Words*, the *Leader*, *Macmillan's Magazine*, *Cornhill Magazine*, the *Spectator*, the *Atlantic Monthly*, *Once a Week*, and, of course, the *Daily News*. It was in a letter to the *Daily News* (2 July 1864) that Martineau initiated the feminist attack on the Contagious Diseases Bill, aimed at curtailing the spread of vene-real disease by empowering the police to arrest and examine suspected prostitutes. In her letter, she defended the rights of all women citizens, but because the bill applied exclusively to garrison towns, it attracted little public notice and was passed notwithstanding her protest.[2] Indeed, the works listed above, unlike her earlier publications, gener-ated comparatively little controversy and therefore do not fit within the scope of this study.

Much of the criticism endured by Martineau was the consequence of her commitment to social change. Following her necessarian princi-ples, she believed that society was advancing according to natural, irreversible laws, and she was optimistic about the development of social relations and institutions. A tireless advocate of representative democracy, she stressed the importance of extending the franchise to all persons, regardless of sex, race, or class, and in her autobiography she maintains that her society was preparing for a war against patriar-chy. In a letter to an abolitionist friend in America, she writes:

> This corrupted 'patriarchal' system of society, (but little superior to that which exists in your slave States) occupies one-half of the great battle-field where the hosts are gathering for the fight. On the other, the forces are ill-assorted, ill-organised, too little prepared; but still, as having the better cause, sure, I trust, of final victory. The conflict must be long, because our constitutions are, like yours, compromises, our governments as yet a mere patch-work, our popular liberties scanty and adulterated, and great masses of our brethren hungry and discontented. (*HMA* 2:453)

Martineau's eclecticism always resists simplification, but much of her work was aimed at preparing the 'ill-organised' for the conflict she anticipates. Education was central to this agenda from the beginning of her career with publication of *Illustrations of Political Economy*, designed to teach the principles of political economy to the middle and lower classes.[3] An advocate of laissez-faire economics, she endorsed Smith's theory of identitical interests, believing that many working-class problems arose from a failure to perceive that the interests of workers and manufacturers were the same. A staunch supporter of free trade, she illustrated the need for repealing the Corn Laws, and, indeed, in 1846 she played a crucial role in ameliorating relations between Sir Robert Peel and Richard Cobden of the Anti-Corn Law League.

The *Illustrations*, in addition to launching Martineau's career, established her fame as a contentious writer. The 'population numbers' of her *Illustrations* showed that the reproduction and popularization of society's dominant discourses could expose tensions and contradictions within those discourses. The science of political economy was supposed to uphold and advance prevailing social structures and imperatives, but Malthus's 'preventive check' on overpopulation challenged the domestic ideal that centred nineteenth-century society. Even after her death, Martineau's population stories continued to cause distress, and one reviewer of her autobiography could not resist a final riposte: 'The tables might be turned against the population-principle by contrasting a testy old bachelor or crabbed old maid, "doom'd to a lone and loveless bed," with a young couple, poor but happy, blest with a brace of babes and looking hopefully to a full quiver.'[4]

That a science designed to promote and explain socio-economic norms should, in particular instances, threaten those norms is ironic. As Martineau's interest in science expanded into other areas, however, it became clear that political economy was not the only science with the potential to act as a socially disruptive force. Martineau's advocacy of mesmerism embroiled her in a controversy about women's sexuality. Her phrenological studies led to her making an explicit statement of atheism in *Letters on the Laws of Man's Nature and Development*, although her religious scepticism had been fuelled several years earlier by her research on Egyptian mythology and Christian dogma. In Victorian society, religious authority was increasingly being superseded by secular power, and Martineau endorsed secular ascendancy. At the same time, she was equally concerned that the new social order should not replicate the iniquities of the old. *Deerbrook* promotes the professionalization of medical practitioners and, simultaneously, interrogates the relation of women to medicine; *Letters on the Laws of Man's Nature and Development* advances empiricism and inductive reasoning, but because it also insists on the importance of supernatural phenomena, the book was seen to undermine, or check, scientific rationalism.

Florence Miller described Martineau as intellectually intrepid: 'Harriet Martineau never shrank from giving any work to the world for fear of the criticism it might receive' (Miller 23). Most of Martineau's work involved popularizing her views on vital matters that were gaining currency in her society, and although she was very much of her age, she was also, paradoxically, ahead of it. As a radical, she shared the fringes of Victorian society with other notable, radical thinkers, but as a successful popular writer she disseminated her radical views to a new market of readers from all classes, and, eventually, her views were considered mainstream. It was a lucrative business, and she earned over ten thousand pounds during the course of her career. More significant is her evident enjoyment of her life's work: 'My business in life has been to think and learn, and to speak out with absolute freedom what I have thought and learned. The freedom is itself a positive and never-failing enjoyment to me, after the bondage of my early life' (*HMA* 1:133). Martineau distinguishes her professional life from the trials of a childhood which, in her opinion, was characterized most notably by maternal neglect. I suspect that she courted notoriety as a writer to compensate for her marginalized and unhappy youth, and she learned other lessons from her early life. In her autobiography, she describes herself as a child who would ask strangers for 'a maxim': 'The family story about me was that I came home [from a cottage at Carleton] the absurdest little preacher of my years (between two and three) that ever was. I used to nod my head emphatically, and say "Never ky for tyfles": "Dooty fust, and pleasure afterwards"' (*HMA* 1:12). They were words to live by.

Notes

Introduction

1 Harriet Martineau, *Harriet Martineau's Autobiography,* 3 vols (London: Smith, Elder, & Co., 1877), 1:199 (hereafter cited as *HMA*). Elsewhere in her *Autobiography,* Martineau refers to four of these publications: 'the Population number of my Political Economy, and the Women and Marriage and Property chapters in my American books, and the Mesmerism affair ... [and] those Egyptian and Mosaic subjects' (*HMA*, 2:345). The fifth is her *Letters on the Laws of Man's Nature and Development* (1851) (a joint publication with Henry George Atkinson) – it was her anticipation of the storm of controversy it might bring that caused her to recollect her earlier trials.
2 Mary Poovey, *Uneven Developments: The Ideological Work of Gender in Mid-Victorian England* (Chicago: University of Chicago Press, 1988), 3.
3 Valerie Sanders, *Reason over Passion: Harriet Martineau and the Victorian Novel* (Sussex: Harvester Press, 1986); R.K. Webb, *Harriet Martineau: A Radical Victorian* (London: Heinemann, 1960); Valerie Kossew Pichanick, *Harriet Martineau: The Woman and Her Work, 1802–76* (Ann Arbor: University of Michigan Press, 1980); Gillian Thomas, *Harriet Martineau* (Boston: Twayne Publishers, 1985); Shelagh Hunter, *Harriet Martineau: The Poetics of Moralism* (Aldershot: Scolar Press, 1995).
4 Martineau met Henry Atkinson in 1845. Atkinson (?1815–84) was a mesmerist and phrenologist.
5 I am indebted to David Shaw for directing my attention to E.D.H. Johnson, *The Alien Vision of Victorian Poetry: Sources of the Poetic Imagination in Tennyson, Browning and Arnold* (Princeton: Princeton University Press, 1952).

Johnson considers (without reference to Martineau) subversive tendencies of representative thinkers in the Victorian period.

1: Gendered Discourses and a Sociology of Texts

1 *Illustrations of Political Economy,* 9 vols (London: Charles Fox, 1834).
2 See Jane Marcet, *Conversations on Political Economy, in Which the Elements of That Science Are Familiarly Explained* (London: Longman, Hurst, Rees, Orme & Brown, 1816).
3 Harriet Martineau, 'An Autobiographic Memoir,' in *HMA* 3:461–2.
4 See Linda H. Peterson, 'Harriet Martineau: Masculine Discourse, Female Sage,' in *Victorian Sages and Cultural Discourse: Renegotiating Gender and Power,* ed. Thaïs E. Morgan (New Brunswick: Rutgers University Press, 1990), 182; Deirdre David, *Intellectual Women and Victorian Patriarchy: Harriet Martineau, Elizabeth Barrett Browning, George Eliot* (London: Macmillan, 1987), 31.
5 Harriet Martineau, Preface, *Illustrations of Political Economy,* Vol. 1 (London: Charles Fox, 1832), xvii.
6 *HMA* 1:274, 276; 'Literary Lionism' is reprinted in Martineau's autobiography.
7 See chapter 7, below, for a more complete discussion of Martineau's views on necessarianism and environmental determinism.
8 M.L.G., 'Miss Martineau – Intellectual Women,' *Tatler* 59 (Oct. 1832): 478.
9 David Simpson, *Romanticism, Nationalism, and the Revolt against Theory* (Chicago: University of Chicago Press, 1993), 126–7. See also David Shaw, *The Lucid Veil: Poetic Truth in the Victorian Age* (London: Althone Press, 1987). Shaw examines J.S. Mill's association of poetry with the female temperament: the poet's substitutions of ideas, influenced by dominant feelings, are feminine, whereas the scientist's method of associating ideas successively is masculine. Mill's distinction between two ways of associating ideas is likely indebted to his father, James Mill, who contrasts synchronous association of ideas with spatial and temporal association. As Shaw argues, 'Mill is anticipating, without in any way influencing, Roman Jakobson's influential distinction between metonymic combination of ideas and metaphoric substitution of them' (Shaw 23).
10 See Peterson 180; David 39.
11 Jerome McGann, *A Critique of Modern Textual Criticism* (Chicago: University of Chicago Press, 1983), 48.
12 That bankruptcy enabled Martineau to pursue a professional literary career may also explain in part her enthusiasm for political economy. See Elaine

Freedgood, 'Banishing Panic: Harriet Martineau and the Popularization of Political Economy,' *Victorian Studies* 39.1 (Autumn 1995): 38. Freedgood maintains that, 'for Martineau, the invisible hand of the market was mercifully impartial. It brought disaster down upon her and her family, but it also allowed for her, as a middle-class woman, to regain financial security and attain literary celebrity through writing a series of tales which explain and defend the system by which she has been paradoxically both victimized and liberated.'

13 [Anonymous], '*Life in the Wilds*,' *Spectator* 188 (Feb. 1832): 112.

14 See, for instance, Nassau William Senior's *Two Lectures on Population Delivered before the University of Oxford in Easter Term, 1828. To Which Is Added a Correspondence between the Author and the Rev. T.R. Malthus* (London: Saunders and Otley, 1829).

15 G. Poulett Scrope, 'Malthus and Sadler: Population and Emigration,' *Quarterly Review* 45 (April 1831): 98.

16 Christian Johnstone, 'Miss Martineau's *Illustrations of Political Economy*,' *Tait's Edinburgh Magazine* 1 (Aug. 1832): 614.

17 William Empson, '*Illustrations of Political Economy*: Mrs Marcet – Miss Martineau,' *Edinburgh Review* 115 (April 1833): 9.

18 Mercurius Rusticus [T. Frognall Dibdin], *Bibliophobia, Remarks on the Present Languid and Depressed State of Literature and the Book Trade. In a Letter Addressed to the Author of the Bibliomania* (London: Henry Bohn, 1832); cited in James J. Barnes, *Free Trade in Books: A Study of the London Book Trade since 1800* (Oxford: Clarendon Press, 1964), 114.

19 Henry R. Plomer, *A Short History of English Printing 1476–1900* (London: Kegan Paul, Trench, Trübner & Co., Ltd, 1915), 252. Plomer notes that by 1840, Clowes had nineteen of Applegarth's and Cowper's machines at work in his printing house (Plomer 253). These four-cylinder machines could print both sides of a sheet simultaneously and were capable of printing 5000 copies per hour (Plomer 241). For a comprehensive description of Clowes's printing house, see Francis B. Head, 'The Printer's Devil,' *Quarterly Review* 65 (Dec. 1839): 1–30.

20 'Junius Redivivus' mentions the price at the end of his letter 'To the Tatler,' *Tatler* 483 (20 March 1832): 270.

21 Charles Knight, *The Old Printer and the Modern Press* (London: Murray, 1854), 246; quoted in Barnes 113.

22 Paul de Man, 'The Rhetoric of Temporality,' in *Blindness and Insight: Essays in the Rhetoric of Contemporary Criticism* (Minneapolis: University of Minnesota, 1983), 189.

23 [Anonymous], 'Glances at New Books,' *Tatler* 34 (19–20 June 1832): 253.

24 Sheila M. Smith, *The Other Nation: The Poor in English Novels of the 1840s and 1850s* (Oxford: Clarendon Press, 1980).

25 Smith does mention a 'comfortable optimism concerning political economy as an infallible science' that informs the *Illustrations* (Smith 37). Valerie Sanders discusses social realism in the *Illustrations*. See Sanders 30–47.

26 Harriet Martineau, 'A Manchester Strike,' in *Illustrations of Political Economy*, Vol. 3 (London: Charles Fox, 1834), 2, 3–4. Hereafter cited as MS.

27 [Anonymous], 'Homes Abroad,' *Spectator* 227 (3 Nov. 1832): 1046; [Anonymous], 'Cousin Marshall,' *Spectator* 219 (8 Sept. 1832): 853.

28 My view departs from Freedgood's view that 'Martineau, like many of her fellow Britons, failed or refused to know the actual conditions of what Disraeli aptly named the "other nation" of the poor' (Freedgood 43).

29 [Anonymous], 'Cinnamon and Pearls,' *Spectator* 271 (7 Sept. 1833): 834.

30 Peterson 175; the positions are held by Joyce Carol Oates, Ellen Moers, and Mary Ellman respectively. Peterson refers the reader to Mary Eagleton, ed., *Feminist Literary Theory* (Oxford: Basil Blackwell, 1986), 208–13.

31 D.F. McKenzie, *The Panizzi Lectures* (London: The British Library, 1985), 50.

32 Catherine Belsey, 'Constructing the Subject: Deconstructing the Text,' in *Feminist Criticism and Social Change*, ed. Judith Newton and Deborah Rosenfelt (New York: Methuen, 1985).

33 Harriet Martineau, 'Demerara,' in *Illustrations of Political Economy*, Vol. 2 (London: Charles Fox, 1834), 141.

34 John Wilson Croker and G. Poulett Scrope, 'Miss Martineau's *Monthly Novels*,' *Quarterly Review* 49 (April 1833): 139.

35 Although 'Cousin Marshall' discredits the rationale of eighteenth-century poor laws, it is noteworthy that Martineau relaxed her stance on charity soon after the story's publication. Henry Broughman (of the Society for the Diffusion of Useful Knowledge) commissioned Martineau to write a series of stories on the New Poor Law of 1834, and her *Poor Laws and Paupers Illustrated* (1833–4) favours government intervention in the free market to provide relief, albeit less than was provided by earlier legislation. Sheila Smith describes these tales as 'ephemeral propaganda' (Smith 9). See also Freedgood 47–9.

36 William Maginn [prob.], 'On National Economy (No. III): Miss Martineau's "Cousin Marshall" – the Preventive Check,' *Fraser's Magazine* 6 (Nov. 1832): 403.

37 William Maginn, 'Gallery of Literary Characters No. XLII: Miss Harriet Martineau,' *Fraser's Magazine* 8 (Nov. 1833): 576. The 'Tory songster' to whom Maginn refers was the poet Moore, who wrote satirical verses on Martineau entitled 'She Politician.' Cf. Maginn's 'Gallery of Literary Characters No.

LXIV: Michael Thomas Sadler, Esq.,' *Fraser's Magazine* 12 (Sept. 1835): 280, where Maginn laments the death of one 'who put an end to' the Malthusian theory.

38 John Ham, 'The Prudential Check – Marriage or Celibacy,' *Tait's Edinburgh Magazine* 3 (June 1833): 318.

39 Scrope argues that population increase is 'expressly commanded in the Scriptural exhortation, "Increase, and multiply, and replenish the earth"' (Scrope 108).

40 Michel Foucault, *The Order of Things: An Archaeology of the Human Sciences* (New York: Pantheon Books, 1971), 255–60; originally published as *Les mots et les choses* (Paris: Editions Gallimard, 1966). Hereafter cited as *OT*.

2: The Linguistic Structure of American Society

1 Harriet Martineau, *Society in America*, 3 vols (London: Saunders and Otley, 1837), 3:205–6. Hereafter cited as *SA*.

2 'Utterance' is the title of Martineau's chapter on American literature. See *SA* 3:205–23.

3 [Anonymous], 'Miss Martineau on America,' *American Quarterly Review* 22 (Sept. 1837): 43. Martineau considered this periodical to be 'uninteresting from the triteness of its morals, and a general dearth of thought, amid a good deal of cleverness' (*SA* 3:216).

4 Martineau declared that 'the American manners please me, on the whole, better than any that I have seen' (*SA* 3:70).

5 Frances Milton Trollope, *Domestic Manners of the Americans* (Dover: Alan Sutton, 1984; first pub. London: Whittaker, Treacher, & Co., 1832). Hereafter cited as *DMA*.

6 Trollope compared her opinion to that of Captain Basil Hall, for whom the greatest difference between the two countries was 'want of loyalty.' See Captain Basil Hall, *Travels in North America in the Years 1827 and 1828*, 3 vols (Edinburgh: Cadell and Co., 1829).

7 Alexis de Toqueville, *Democracy in America* (London: Saunders and Otley, 1836). Hereafter cited as *DA*.

8 Francis Grund, *Aristocracy in America, from the Sketch-book of a German Nobleman* (New York: Harper Torch Books, 1959; first pub. London: R. Bentley, 1839), 162.

9 Seymour Martin Lipset, 'Harriet Martineau's America,' in *Society in America*, ed. Seymour Martin Lipset (New York: Anchor Books, 1962), 24.

10 Christian Johnstone, 'Miss Martineau's Society in America, and Grund's American Society,' *Tait's Edinburgh Magazine* 8 o.s., 4 n.s. (July 1837): 409.

11 John Wilson Croker, 'Dickens's *American Notes*; Mann's *Anniversary Oration*,' *Quarterly Review* 71 (March 1843): 522. See Charles Dickens, *American Notes for General Circulation*, ed. John S. Whitley and Arnold Goldman (London: Penguin Books, 1972; first pub. London: Chapman and Hall, 1842), 288; hereafter cited as *AN*.

12 Archibald Alison, 'Democracy,' *Blackwood's Magazine* 41 (Jan. 1837): 71–90.

13 [Anonymous], 'Miss Martineau's Society in America,' *North American Review* 45 (Oct. 1837): 435.

14 According to Trollope's reviewer in the *North American Review*, Americans did not notice travellers until their 'libels had been endorsed by the Quarterly, and we are grieved to add, sometimes by the Edinburgh Review, or by some other responsible English authority. Then, when the leading journals in Europe had done their best to authenticate the slander, we have thought it sometimes deserving refutation.' See [Anonymous], 'Prince Pückler Muscau and Mrs. Trollope,' *North American Review* 36 (Jan. 1833): 42.

15 See Michel Foucault, *Discipline and Punish: The Birth of the Prison*, trans. Alan Sheridan (London: Penguin Books, 1977), 195–228; originally published as *Surveiller et punir: naissance de la prison* (Paris: Editions Gallimard, 1975). Hereafter cited as *DP*.

16 See Jerome Meckier, *Innocent Abroad: Charles Dickens's American Engagements* (Lexington: University Press of Kentucky, 1990), 75–132, esp. 103.

17 *Third Report of Inspectors of Prisons* (1838), 181. See Sophia Elizabeth DeMorgan, 'Reform of Prisons,' *Monthly Chronicle* 3 (Feb. 1839): 177.

18 See Charles Edward Dodd, 'Punishment of Death – Wakefield on Newgate,' *Quarterly Review* 47 (March 1832): 212.

19 Harriet Martineau, *How to Observe Morals and Manners* (London: Charles Knight and Co., 1838), 125–6.

20 Martineau believed that capital punishments would soon be abolished in the northern states of America. See *SA* 3:188.

21 See Harriet Martineau, *Retrospect of Western Travel*, 2 vols (London: Saunders and Otley, 1838), 2:130. Hereafter cited as *RWT*.

22 Martineau and Dickens agreed on the importance of Braille for the blind. In *Retrospect of Western Travel*, Martineau appeals to the friends of the blind for help in the distribution of Braille texts that she possessed, including six sets of all that had been printed by the Boston Press. At the request of Howe, Dickens spent $1,700 to pay for 250 copies of *The Old Curiosity Shop* for the blind. See Elizabeth G. Gitter, 'Charles Dickens and Samuel Gridley Howe,' *Dickens Quarterly* 8.4 (Dec. 1991): 162–7.

23 Dickens would reiterate the point: 'Their education is much as with us; neither better nor worse' (*AN* 106).

24 Margaret Fuller, *Woman in the Nineteenth Century* (New York: Greeley & McElrath, 1845), 84. Hereafter cited as *WNC*.

25 Martineau was pleased to note that divorces, at least, were obtained with greater freedom in America. She notes the barbarous practice of granting divorces only to the rich in England and holds up Swiss legislation for emulation: in Zurich, couples have 'liberty to divorce themselves without any appeal to law, on showing that they have legally provided for the children of the marriage' (*SA* 3:126). Martineau was also glad to acknowledge women's property rights in some southern states, such as Louisiana and Missouri.

26 Martineau thought that New England women were especially suited to manufacturing work. There was a large population of 'odd women' in that area as a result of the emigration of New England men to the south and west.

27 See Jean Fagan Yellin, *Women and Sisters: The Antislavery Feminists in American Culture* (New Haven: Yale University Press, 1989), 36–45.

28 See 'Miss Martineau on America,' p. 27: 'Nothing daunted her; she could rise up in the midst of a public meeting and give her assent to doctrines, which, if she had a grain of common sense in her composition, she must know would dissever the Union if carried into effect.'

29 Ibid., p. 38.

30 [Anonymous], 'Practical Reasoning *versus* Impracticable Theories,' *Fraser's Magazine* 19 (May 1839): 566. This review mocks Martineau's constitution as evidenced by her shooting with a rifle, cutting wood, and walking.

31 Ibid., p. 567.

32 Ibid., pp. 567, 569.

33 See above, chapter 1. It should be observed that Martineau's commitment to laissez-faire economics was never rigid; rather, she recognized the importance of government interference in certain areas, most notably education and public works.

34 See 'Miss Martineau's *Society in America*,' p. 445: 'We are content here, for the most part, with living in the good old Christian way of "a state of division into families," with our own wives, children, and household stuff'; see also 'Practical Reasoning *versus* Impracticable Theories,' p. 565.

35 Valerie Kossew Pichanick, *Harriet Martineau: The Woman and Her Work, 1802–76* (Ann Arbor: University of Michigan Press, 1980), 80–1.

36 See Catherine Gallagher, *The Industrial Reformation of English Fiction: Social Discourse and Narrative Form 1832–1867* (Chicago: University of Chicago Press, 1980), 1–35.

37 Jane Moore, 'Sex, Slavery and Rights in Mary Wollstonecraft's *Vindications*,' *The Discourse of Slavery: Aphra Behn to Toni Morrison*, ed. Carl Plasa and Betty J. Ring (London: Routledge, 1994), 18–39.

38 At one point, Jackson endeavoured to make a binary distinction between local and general improvements that Martineau could easily deconstruct: '... a thousand positions of circumstances may be imagined by which local advantages may become general, and general local, so as to confound the limitation altogether' (*SA* 2:212). She cited the Erie Canal as an improvement that benefited the whole country although it lay wholly in New York State.

39 Jacques Lacan, *Ecrits: A Selection*, trans. A. Sheridan (London: Tavistock, 1977), 140. See also Moore 26.

40 Thomas Jefferson, *Correspondence*, 4:295; quoted in *SA* 1:201.

41 See Moira Ferguson, *Subject to Others: British Women Writers and Colonial Slavery, 1670–1834* (London: Routledge, 1992).

42 See Carl Plasa, '"Silent Revolt": Slavery and the Politics of Metaphor in *Jane Eyre*,' in *The Discourse of Slavery: Aphra Behn to Toni Morrison*, ed. Carl Plasa and Betty J. Ring (London: Routledge, 1994), 58. Plasa cites part of a lecture by Frederick Douglas given in 1846 to a meeting in Newcastle-upon-Tyne about the detraction from 'the dreadful horror' of American slavery caused by the application of the term to other systems.

43 See Ferguson 176, 197. Hannah More's 'Slavery, A Poem,' written at the request of the newly founded Abolition Committee to promote the 1788 Abolition Bill, began this discourse of objectification, replacing the named, voiced, and resistant slaves of earlier texts, such as Behn's *Oroonoko* (1688), with unnamed, unvoiced, unproblematized victims. See Hannah More, *Slavery: A Poem* (London: T. Cadell, 1788); see also Ferguson 146–54.

44 See Mary Louise Pratt, 'Scratches on the Face of the Country; or, What Mr. Barrow Saw in the Land of the Bushmen,' in *'Race,' Writing, and Difference*, ed. Henry Louis Gates, Jr (Chicago: University of Chicago Press, 1986), 139.

45 Of course, there were exceptions to this objectification and totalization of slaves. Eliza Haywood, Rachel Wilson, Ann Yearsley, Elizabeth Bentley, Mary Darby Robinson, and Mary Birkett did not tend to view slaves as unproblematized victims. See Ferguson 165–83, 197.

46 Again, poems such as Ann Yearsley's 'A Poem on the Inhumanity of the Slave-Trade,' featuring a rebellious slave hero named Luco, are exceptions to the norm. See Moira Ferguson, ed., *First Feminists: British Women Writers, 1578–1799* (Bloomington: Indiana University Press, 1985), 382–96.

47 [Anonymous], 'Slavery and the New Slave Trade,' *Monthly Chronicle* 1 (April 1838): 126–38.

48 Abolitionists tended to think that Congress did have that authority, since according to U.S. Const. Art. 1, s. 8, cl. 3, Congress has power 'to regulate commerce with foreign nations, and *among the several States,* and with the Indian tribes.' Moreover, s. 9, cl. 1 only restricts Congress from prohibiting migration or importation of persons into any State until the year 1808. See Henry Broughman, 'American Slavery,' *Edinburgh Review* 63 (April 1836): 138. On 16 April 1862 it was decided that Congress did indeed have this power, and Martineau hailed the abolition of slavery in the District of Columbia as 'the greatest event in the history of the American Republic.' See Harriet Martineau, 'The Brewing of the American Storm,' *Macmillan's Magazine* 6 (June 1862): 97.

49 See chapter 1, above.

50 Although Martineau certainly believed that free labour was better than slave labour, she was by no means insensitive to the hard conditions of the working classes in England: 'You [the abolitionists] are strengthening us for conflicts we have to enter upon. We have a population in our manufacturing towns almost as oppressed, and in our secluded rural districts almost as ignorant as your negroes. These must be redeemed.' See Harriet Martineau, 'The Martyr Age of the United States,' *London and Westminster Review* 32 (Dec. 1838): 1–59.

51 See Ferguson 273–81.

52 Preface, 'Demerara,' xii.

53 For example, see Frances Green, 'The Slave-Wife,' in *Liberty Chimes* (Providence: Ladies Anti-Slavery Society, 1845), 82: '[Laco Ray] was black, the skin soft and glossy; but the features had none of the revolting characteristics which are supposed by some to be inseparable from the African visage. On the contrary they were remarkably fine – the nose aquiline – the mouth even handsome – the forehead singularly high and broad.' Karen Sánchez-Eppler discusses Laco Ray and the configuration of traits in anti-slavery stories in 'Bodily Bonds: The Intersecting Rhetorics of Feminism and Abolition,' *Representations* 24 (Fall 1988): 28–59.

54 Cultural mimicry lacks this sense of parody in the post-emancipation context of *The Hour and the Man.* Cf. chapter 4, below.

55 Martineau's view of Christianity accords with its representation in *The Hour and the Man.* Cf. chapter 4, below.

56 See Sánchez-Eppler 33.

57 Martineau was attacked by the *American Quarterly Review* for being both an amalgamationist and a Malthusian. See 'Miss Martineau on America,' p. 26.

58 See Louise H. Johnson, 'The Source of the Chapter on Slavery in Dickens' *American Notes,' American Literature* 14 (Jan. 1943): 427–30.

59 See Croker, 'Dickens's *American Notes*; Mann's *Anniversary Oration*,' p. 519.

60 See 'Practical Reasoning *versus* Impracticable Theories,' p. 587.

61 Elizabeth Eastlake, 'Lady Travellers,' *Quarterly Review* 76 (June 1845): 99–100.

62 See Janet Giltrow, '"Painful Experience in a Distant Land": Mrs Moodie in Canada and Mrs. Trollope in America,' *Mosaic: A Journal for the Interdisciplinary Study of Literature* 14.2 (Spring 1981): 131–44; Kris Lackey, 'Eighteenth-Century Aesthetic Theory and the Nineteenth-Century Traveler in Trans-Allegheny America: F. Trollope, Dickens, Irving and Parkman,' *American Studies* 32.1 (Spring 1991): 33–48.

63 [Anonymous], 'Dickens's *American Notes*,' *Fraser's Magazine* 26 (Nov. 1842): 617.

64 See Croker, 'Dickens's *American Notes*; Mann's *Anniversary Oration*,' pp. 506, 507. See also [Anonymous], 'Dickens's *Notes on America, for General Circulation*,' *Tait's Edinburgh Magazine* 13 o.s., 9 n.s. (Nov. 1842): 744.

65 In fact, Trollope's *A Visit to Italy* and Dickens's *American Notes* were the subject of an article entitled 'Superficial Travelling,' *Dublin Review* 14 (Feb. 1843): 256–62.

66 See James Buzard, *The Beaten Track: European Tourism, Literature, and the Ways to 'Culture'* (Oxford: Clarendon, 1993).

3: Realism and Feminism

1 Martineau is presumably referring to *Tales of My Landlord, Collected and Arranged by Jedediah Cleishbotham* (Edinburgh: William Blackwood; London: John Murray, 1816).

2 Valerie Sanders considers the novel's historical background in her fine study *Reason over Passion*, but she is chiefly concerned to examine *Deerbrook* as source material for later Victorian novels.

3 G.S. Venables, 'Miss Martineau – *Deerbrook*,' *Blackwood's Magazine* 47 (Feb. 1840): 188.

4 Harriet Martineau, *Deerbrook: A Novel*, 3 vols (London: Edward Moxon, 1839), 1:1.

5 See chapter 1, above.

6 Henry Byerley Thomson, *Choice of a Profession: A Concise Account and Comparative Review of the English Professions* (London: Chapman & Hall, 1857), 162; quoted in M. Jeanne Peterson, *The Medical Profession in Mid-Victorian London* (London and Berkeley: University of California Press, 1978), 92.

7 Arthur Buller, 'Bribery and Intimidation at Elections,' *London and Westminster Review* 3 and 25 (July 1836): 485–6.

8 The Anatomy Bill passed the House of Lords on 19 July 1832. In 1829 the bill put forward to regulate anatomical research was opposed by both the Royal College of Surgeons and the archbishop of Canterbury and was rejected by the House of Lords. Valerie Sanders observes that 'Deerbrook was published only seven years after the 1832 Anatomy Act provided for the supply of bodies suitable for dissection, and when the notorious case of Burke and Hare had made people doubly suspicious of bodysnatchers' (Sanders 75).

9 Matthew Baillie was made Fellow of the Royal College of Surgeons in 1790. In his important work, Morbid Anatomy of Some of the Most Important Parts of the Human Body (London: J. Johnson and G. Nicol, 1793), he shows how a knowledge of anatomy assists in the process of diagnosis.

10 See Neil Arnott, 'Regulation of Anatomy,' Westminster Review 16 (April 1832): 484.

11 In the case of Rex vs. Lynn (1788), the court decided that the exhumation of bodies for the purposes of dissection was an indictable offence. A statute of James I had made it illegal to steal bodies for witchcraft but specified nothing concerning dissection. See Thomas Southwood Smith, 'Use of the Dead to the Living,' Westminster Review 2 (July 1824): 88.

12 Robert Gooch, 'Unlawful Disinterment of Human Bodies,' Quarterly Review 42 (Jan. 1830): 5. For a recent discussion of dissection in the nineteenth century, see Ruth Richardson, Death, Dissection and the Destitute (London: Routledge & Kegan Paul, 1987).

13 See also Gooch 12: 'If you dislocate a joint, and cannot get it set, or break a limb, and find on your recovery that you have a shortened thigh, or a bandy leg ... do not complain; it is not his fault, but yours; – at any rate, do not prosecute him: the law which prohibits him from studying anatomy ought not to punish him for the consequences of being ignorant of it.'

14 That Dr Levitt, the rector, arrives at the Hopes too late to be of any assistance anticipates the growing distance between science and religion as separate spheres.

15 See Jacques Derrida, 'Plato's Pharmacy,' in Dissemination, trans. Barbara Johnson (Chicago: University of Chicago Press, 1981). See also James C. Cowan, 'The Pharmakos Figure in Modern American Stories of Physicians and Patients,' Literature and Medicine 6 (1987): 94–7. When Hope previously enjoys popularity with the villagers, it is said that 'the poor folks take him for a sort of magician' (1:27).

16 Consider Tzetzes' account of the rite in his Thousand Histories: 'seven times they smote him with leeks and wild figs and other wild plants. Finally they burnt him with fire with the wood of wild trees and scattered the ashes into

the sea and to the winds, for a purification, as I said, of the suffering city'
(Derrida 133).

17 Theodora Bosanquet, *Harriet Martineau: An Essay in Comprehension* (London: Frederick Etchells & Hugh Macdonald, 1977), 126.

18 See Buller 505.

19 Southwood Smith also refers to violence against an anatomist in Glasgow:
'... in spite of the exertions of the police, aided by those of the military, this
gentleman's premises and their contents, which were valuable, were
entirely destroyed by the mob' (Southwood Smith 84).

20 Thomas Southwood Smith, 'Medical Reform,' *London and Westminster
Review* 4 and 26 (July 1836): 89. Hereafter cited as MR.

21 See also Peterson 22.

22 See also Sanders 71: 'Edward Hope is a surgeon-apothecary, the early nineteenth-century equivalent of the modern general practitioner, whose evolution, as a member of the professional middle class, had at this time reached
a critical point.'

23 Hester echoes this sentiment later in the text when she declares: 'I dare not
and do not wish for anything otherwise than as we have it now. Persecu-
tion seems to have made us wiser, and poverty happier' (3:195).

24 [Anonymous], '*Deerbrook*: A Novel,' *Athenaeum* 597 (6 April 1839): 255.

25 See Venables 185.

26 John Thomson, 'On the Causes, Cure, and Prevention of Contagious Fever,'
Edinburgh Review 31 (March 1819): 415.

27 According to the Medical Act of 1858, a General Council of Medical Education and Registration (or the GMC) would publish annually a register of
qualified medical men without specifying distinctions between ranks. See
Peterson 35.

28 Neil Arnott, 'Professional Morality,' *Westminster Review* 14 (April 1831): 475.
Hereafter cited as PM. Cf. Peterson 31.

29 St John Long was a quack who maintained that all diseases are caused by a
fluid like mercury and that a certain liniment could discover this fluid,
remove it, and heal the body. See PM 467.

30 See also William Maginn [prob.], 'On Quackery, Twaddle, and Other
Offences,' *Fraser's Magazine* 3 (April 1831): 372.

31 See Theodore M. Brown, 'The Changing Self-Concept of the Eighteenth-
Century London Physician,' *Eighteenth Century Life* 7.2 (Jan. 1982): 36–7.
See also Thomson, 438: '... the Association [for the Suppression of Fever]
will find they have but half accomplished their duty if they neglect
cleansing those hot-beds of contagion, the dirty and infected hovels of the
poor.'

32 T.H. Lister [prob.], 'Miss Martineau's *Deerbrook*,' *Edinburgh Review* 69 (July 1839): 502.

33 See Brown, 31. See also Michel Foucault, *The Birth of the Clinic*, trans. A.M. Sheridan Smith (New York: Vintage Books, 1973), 180–1; first published as *Naissance de la clinique* (Paris: Presses Universitaires de France, 1963). Hereafter cited as *BC*. As Foucault points out, Maximilian Stoll recognized at least twelve different 'fevers' in his *Aphorismes sur la connaisance et la curation des fièvres* (1801).

34 Lawrence Rothfield, *Vital Signs: Medical Realism in Nineteenth-Century Fiction* (Princeton: Princeton University Press, 1992), 9–10.

35 See *HMA* 2:108: 'I felt myself in danger of losing nerve, and dreading criticism on the one hand, and of growing rigid and narrow about accuracy on the other. I longed inexpressibly for the liberty of fiction.'

36 Both formal realism and critical realism share, however, what Rothfield calls a 'will-to-mimesis' (Rothfield 6). Georg Lukács champions the idea of 'critical realism' in *The Historical Novel*, trans. Hannah Mitchell and Stanley Mitchell (London: Merlin Press, 1962; first published in Moscow, 1937).

37 Cf. chapter 7, below.

38 See *BC* 139–40.

39 This is, of course, the subject of Foucault's *Discipline and Punish: The Birth of the Prison*.

40 The concept of a pathologically organic narrative derives from Rothfield, who analyses Lydgate, Rosamond, and Bulstrode in *Middlemarch* as pathological characters. Tertius is his case study in the Lydgates' relationship.

41 In tracing this process, I wish to depart from the prevailing view that Hester is simply a bad wife married to a good husband. See Sanders 170.

42 Chapter 7 considers the importance of this gaze to Martineau's phrenological investigations, which endeavour to explain behaviour by relating it to cerebral 'organs' located beneath the cranium.

43 On only one occasion does Margaret appear as a double entity. Upset about Mrs Rowland's pronouncement that Philip is to marry a Miss Bruce, Margaret is invaded by a spirit that whispers to her to deceive everybody about her affection for Philip, but 'the abode was too lowly and too pure for the evil spirit of defiance: the demon did not wait to be cast out; but as Margaret sat down in her chamber, alone with her lot, to face it as she might, the strange inmate escaped, and left her at least herself' (2:89).

44 In marrying Hester, Hope is, in fact, misled by his clinical perspective: '... too many superficial feelings mingled with the sacredness of the transaction, and impaired its integrity' (1:225).

45 It is noteworthy that the crime committed ostensibly by a woman follows a

discussion between Margaret and Maria of how women can make money. It may also be significant that culpability belongs, in fact, to a man. That the only thing 'scarcely terrifying' about the incident is 'the woman's clothes' suggests a fear of the wrong attribution of social crimes to women (3:175).

46 Margaret's and Philip's reunion seems as overdetermined as a ballad that Mrs Enderby recites about a rose and a brier that grow from two graves to form a 'true-lover's knot': 'I did not make it,' Mrs Enderby declares (1:171). Frustration with inherited conventional narratives is suggested by Mrs Platt's strange behaviour when Margaret puts on her restored ring and hides it with a pair of gloves: 'The mother, suddenly awakened, groaned and screamed, so that it was fearful to hear her. All efforts to restore quiet were in vain. Margaret was moved, shocked, terrified. She could not keep her own calmness in such a scene of confusion: but, while her cheeks were covered with tears, while her voice trembled as she implored silence, she never took off her glove' (3:252–3).

47 Cf. Thomas 99.

48 In chapter 7, below, I argue that supernatural phenomena also qualify the authority of scientific rationalism in *Letters on the Laws of Man's Nature and Development*.

49 See M. Jeanne Peterson, 'The Victorian Governess: Status Incongruence in Family and Society,' in *Suffer and Be Still: Women in the Victorian Age*, ed. Martha Vicinus (Bloomington: Indiana University Press, 1972), 3–19; and Poovey, 126–63.

50 Because middle-class women were dependent on their fathers' prosperity, any middle-class woman could be required to earn her own money, as Lady Eastlake recognized: 'We need the imprudencies, extravagancies, mistakes, or crimes of a certain number of fathers, to sow that seed from which we reap the harvest of governesses.' See Elizabeth Eastlake, '*Vanity Fair* – and *Jane Eyre*,' *Quarterly Review* 84 (Dec. 1848): 176. The 1851 Census records only 25,000 governesses. See also Poovey 132, 127.

51 Twenty years later, Martineau would propose a cure for the problem identified in her novel: 'The only certain remedy is to leave open every possible way to employments of the most various kinds that are suitable to the abilities of women.' See 'Female Industry,' *Edinburgh Review* 109 (April 1859): 330.

52 Harriet Martineau, 'The Governess: Her Health,' *Once a Week* 3 (1 Sept. 1860): 269. Hereafter cited as *GHH*.

53 As a developmental character, Maria corresponds to Will and Dorothea in Rothfield's study.

4: History and Romance

1 See Toussaint Louverture (1743?–1803), *Mémoires du général Toussaint-L'Ouverture: écrits par lui-même pouvant servir à l'histoire de sa vie ... Précédés d'une étude historique et critique par Saint-Remy. Suivis de notes et renseigne-ments. Avec un appendice contenant les opinions de l'empereur Napoléon 1er sur les évènements de Saint-Domingue* (Paris: Pagnerre, 1853; repr. Port-au-Prince, Haiti: Fardin, 1982); J.R. Beard, *Life of Toussaint Louverture* (London: Ingram, Cooke, and Co., 1853); C.L.R. James, *The Black Jacobins: Toussaint L'Ouverture and the San Domingo Revolution*, 2nd ed., rev. (New York: Vintage Books, 1963; reissued 1989); Ralph Korngold, *Citizen Toussaint* (London: Victor Gollancz, 1945; reissued 1979); and T. Lothrop Stoddard, *The French Revolution in San Domingo* (Boston and New York: Houghton Mifflin Company, 1914; repr. 1970).
2 Harriet Martineau, *The Hour and the Man: A Historical Romance*, 3 vols (London: Edward Moxon, 1841).
3 Jeffrey's letter to Mr Empson is reprinted in *HMA* 3:234.
4 To Mrs Emerson, 21 Feb. 1841, *Carlyle-Emerson Letters*, 317–18; quoted in R.K. Webb, *Harriet Martineau: A Radical Victorian* (London: Heinemann, 1960), 191.
5 [Anonymous], 'The Hour and the Man,' *Spectator* 649 (5 Dec. 1840): 1167.
6 Christian Johnstone, 'New Novels: The Hour and the Man,' *Tait's Edinburgh Magazine* 12 o.s., 8 n.s. (Jan. 1841): 9.
7 [Anonymous], 'The Hour and the Man: A Historical Romance,' *Athenaeum* 684 (5 Dec. 1840): 958, 959.
8 Vera Wheatley, *The Life and Work of Harriet Martineau* (London: Secker & Warburg, 1957), 218.
9 'The Hour and the Man,' *Spectator* 649 (5 Dec. 1840): 1167.
10 See above, pp. 44–5.
11 See preface to 'Demerara,' xii.
12 See Ferguson, *Subject to Others*, 238. Ferguson notes that pidgin English was used in abolitionist writing around the time of the revolution in St Domingo. See also Amelia Opie, *The Negro Boy's Tale: A Poem Addressed to Children* (London: Harvey and Darton, 1795; repr. 1824).
13 See above, chapter 2.
14 [Anonymous], 'Miss Edgeworth's Tales and Novels,' *Fraser's Magazine* 6 (Nov. 1832): 547.
15 J.A. Heraud, 'Historical Romance,' *Quarterly Review* 35 (March 1827): 527, 528.
16 See Bill Ashcroft, Gareth Griffiths, and Helen Tiffin, *The Empire Writes Back:*

Theory and Practice in Post-Colonial Literatures (London: Routledge, 1989), 77.

17 Gillian Beer, *The Romance* (London: Methuen, 1970), 4.

18 *Biographie universelle, ancienne et moderne* (Paris: L.G. Michaud, 1826), 400. It is added later in the entry on Toussaint L'Ouverture that 'réduit dans ses lettres à employer le style d'autrui, le fond des pensées lui appartenait en propre. Pour rien au monde il n'eût signé une lettre dont il n'aurait point conçu ou pesé chaque expression' (415).

19 Helen Hughes, *The Historical Romance* (London: Routledge, 1993), 1.

20 See Stephen Bann, *The Clothing of Clio* (Cambridge: Cambridge University Press, 1984), 5; see also Hughes 8.

21 Thomas Carlyle, *Selected Writings*, ed. Alan Shelston (Harmondsworth: Penguin, 1988), 40.

22 Theodor Adorno, *Minima Moralia: Reflections from a Damaged Life*, trans. E.F.N. Jephcott (London: Verso, 1974), 54; quoted in Jim Reilly, *Shadowtime: History and Representation in Hardy, Conrad and George Eliot* (London: Routledge, 1993), 4.

23 *OT* 369; also quoted in Reilly 5.

24 Italo Calvino, 'Right and Wrong Political Uses of Literature,' in *The Literature Machine*, trans. Patrick Creagh (London: Picador, 1989), 90–1; quoted in Reilly 6.

25 Beer quotes Erich Auerbach, *Mimesis: The Representation of Reality in Western Literature*, trans. Willard R. Trask (Princeton: Princeton University Press, 1953), 127: 'The Fairy-tale atmosphere is the true element of the courtly romance, which after all is not only interested in portraying external living conditions in the feudal society of the closing years of the twelfth century but also and especially in expressing its ideals.' See also Beer 24.

26 See Beer's references to and quotations from Lukács's *The Historical Novel*, 65–6. It is important to note that Beer sees Scott's historical realism as exceptional: 'When that accuracy [of Scott's historicism] is missing, as in the work of many later novelists, the historical novel does become a lax type of romance' (Beer 66).

27 Harriet Martineau, 'The Achievements of the Genius of Scott,' *Tait's Edinburgh Magazine* 10 (Jan. 1833): 445–60. Hereafter cited as AGS.

28 Sir Walter Scott, *Waverley; or, 'Tis Sixty Years Since*, ed. Claire Lamont (Oxford: Oxford University Press, 1986; orginally pub. Edinburgh: printed by J. Ballantyne for A. Constable, 1814), 193.

29 It is important not to forget the distinction between romance and romantic love; nonetheless, 'sexual love is one of the great themes of the romance' (Beer 3).

30 [Anonymous], 'Past and Present State of Hayti,' *Quarterly Review* 21 (April 1819): 430–60. Other sources Martineau claims to have used include Marcus Rainsford's *Historical Account of the Black Empire of Hayti, Comprehending a View of the Principal Transactions* (London: Cunder, 1805), and Bryan Edward's *An Historical Survey of the French Colony in the Island of St. Domingo* (London: J. Stockdale, 1797). She also admired Wordsworth's sonnet 'To Toussaint L'Ouverture' (1802), which she deemed a fitting tribute to Toussaint.

31 John Cranstoun Nevill, *Harriet Martineau* (London: Frederick Muller, 1943), 76.

32 Theodor Adorno, *Prisms*, trans. Samuel and Shierry Weber (Cambridge: MIT Press, 1983), 55; Reilly 4.

33 This imagery may also suggest Martineau's own confinement during her illness, discussed in chapter 5, below.

34 See Christian Johnstone's review for *Tait's*, p. 9: 'There were, in short, then three parties in St. Domingo, each jealous and watchful of the other two; and not unlike, in some of their ideas, the men we see around us. There were the pure aristocrats, or *whites*; the ten-pound voters, or *mulattoes*; and the *chartists*, those who claim the suffrage, or *negroes*.' See also Sanders 119.

35 Archibald Alison, 'The Chartists and Universal Suffrage,' *Blackwood's Edinburgh Magazine* 46 (Sept. 1839): 289.

36 Joseph Mazzini, 'Is It a Revolt or a Revolution?' *Tait's Edinburgh Magazine* (Aug. 1840): 386, 385.

37 See 1:6.

38 The term is Althusser's. See Hayden White, 'Getting Out of History,' *Diacritics* 12.3 (Fall 1982): 5–6.

39 George Moir [prob.], 'Recent English Romances,' *Edinburgh Review* (April 1837): 181. See also J.A. Heraud, 'Historical Romance,' *Quarterly Review* 35 (March 1827): 546–7: 'Diderot well observes, that the connexion of events frequently escapes our observation in nature, for want of knowing the entire combination of the circumstances: in real facts we only see the accidental occurrence of things; but the poet wishes to show, in the texture of his work, an apparent and sensible connexion; so that, if really less true, he has more the appearance of truth than the historian.'

40 The correspondence is copied from *Haytian Papers*, ed. Prince Sanders (London, 1816; Westport: Negro Universities Press, 1969), 4–54.

41 [Anonymous], 'Revival of the Slave Trade,' *Edinburgh Review* 23 (April 1814): 136.

42 See Henry Broughman, 'The Foreign Slave Trade,' *Edinburgh Review* 72 (Oct. 1840): 179–93.

43 It is worth noting that when the World's Convention of the British and Foreign Anti-Slavery Society was held in London in 1840, Martineau was named a delegate from Massachusetts. This was a 'typically Garrisonian assertion of principle,' as Webb observes, since the convention did not seat women. Around this time, Martineau also raised money for Oberlin College in Ohio, the first college to admit women and blacks. See Webb 189.

44 Of course, the Church was exerting itself against Chartism at the time of publication of *The Hour and the Man*. See, for example, [Anonymous], 'The Church and the Chartists,' *Fraser's Magazine* 20 (Nov. 1839): 619–29. Chartists were frequently encouraged to regard class difference as an appointment of Providence.

45 The conflicting representation of Christianity in this novel may also reflect Martineau's own fraught relation to orthodox religion. See especially chapter 6, below.

46 *Erythrophlæum guineense.* See below.

47 Martineau concedes that Flora Mac-Ivor, Die Vernon, Rebecca, and Jeanie Deans are exceptions, indicating what women may become 'having escaped from the management of men' (AGS 456).

48 Cf. Ashcroft et al. 9.

49 See, for example, Broughman 179–80.

50 See her Appendix, 266–7.

51 Emily Miller Budick considers these issues in relation to Nathaniel Hawthorne's *The Scarlet Letter* in 'Hester's Scepticism, Hawthorne's Faith: or, What Does a Woman Doubt? Instituting the American Romance Tradition,' *New Literary History* 22.1 (1991): 200.

52 Nurses are not simply represented as ministering angels in the novel. Génifrède, who does not want to be a nurse, recalls 'what some nurses did in the plague at Milan – in the plague in London – in the night – with wet cloths' (3:122). The ministering angel can also be demonic. It is also important to note that Martineau turns the nurse motif on its head: in historical romances generally, nursing culminates in the marriage of the nurse and (male) patient, who have been equalized by the process (see Hughes 135). In *The Hour and the Man*, Papalier dies and Thérèse is unambiguously empowered by the experience.

53 See 1:50. It is important to realize that it is not miscegenation itself that is objected to since the marriage of M. Pascal, a white, and Aphra Raymond, a mulatto, is celebrated by everyone in the text.

54 See Leslie G. Desmangles, *The Faces of the Gods: Vodou and Roman Catholicism in Haiti* (Chapel Hill: University of North Carolina Press, 1992), 1–16. It will

be recalled that Génifrède has already been associated with red water and an ivory charm.

5: Invalidism, Mesmerism, and the Medical Profession

1 Alison Winter, *Mesmerized: Powers of Mind in Victorian Britain* (Chicago: University of Chicago Press, 1998).
2 T.M. Greenhow, *Medical Report of the Case of Miss H– M–* (London: Samuel Highley, 1845). Webb also relies on articles by Greenhow and T. Spencer Wells in the *British Medical Journal* published after Martineau's death. See 'Termination of the Case of Miss Harriet Martineau,' *British Medical Journal* (8 July 1876): 64; (14 April 1877): 449–50; (21 April 1877): 496; (5 May 1877): 543–50. Martineau had a twelve-inch ovarian tumour at the time of her death, supposed generally to be identical with the tumour that incapacitated her in 1839; however, chronic ovarian cystitis should not be ruled out in her case.
3 Letter to T.M. Greenhow, dated 14 June 1839; discussed in Greenhow 9–10.
4 See chapter 3, above.
5 Quoted in Elizabeth Barrett to Mary Russell Mitford, 30 Nov. 1844, in *The Brownings' Correspondence*, ed. Philip Kelley and Scott Lewis (Winfield: Wedgestone Press, 1991), 253.
6 M. Baillie, *Morb. Anat.* (1807), 367: 'By a polypus is meant a diseased mass, which adheres to some part of the cavity of the uterus, by a sort of neck or narrower portion' (quoted in *OED*, 2nd ed.).
7 See Miriam Bailin, *The Sickroom in Victorian Fiction: The Art of Being Ill* (Cambridge: Cambridge University Press, 1994), 9.
8 Dr G. Oakley Heming, 'Practical Facts and Observations on Diseases of Women, and Some Subjects Connected with Midwifery,' *Lancet* 1 (24 Aug. 1844): 672.
9 See, for example, [Anonymous], 'Uterine Polypi Expelled by the Aid of Ergot of Rye,' *Lancet* 1 (3 Dec. 1842): 347.
10 Dr Marshall Hall, 'Lectures on the Theory and Practice of Medicine,' *Lancet* 2 (7 July 1838): 503.
11 Greenhow 16. In fact, Clarke recommended the external application of iodine ointment, which Martineau refused to use. Greenhow (21–2) appends a full list of prescriptions employed.
12 [Anonymous], 'Miss Martineau and Her Traducers,' *Zoist* 3.9 (April 1845): 93.
13 See *HMA* 2:191; and Harriet Martineau, 'Miss Martineau on Mesmerism,' *Athenaeum* 891 (23 Nov. 1844): 1070.

14 Dr William MacDonald, 'Clinical Discourse Concerning a Polypus of the Womb,' *Lancet* 1 (14 Jan. 1843): 575.
15 Spencer T. Hall, *Mesmeric Experiences* (London: H. Balliere, 1845), 75.
16 I shall discuss Martineau's behavioural abnormalities below.
17 Harold Merskey and Paul Potter, 'The Womb Lay Still in Ancient Egypt,' *British Journal of Psychiatry* 154 (June 1989): 753.
18 Mark S. Micale provides a brief 'history' of hysteria in *Approaching Hysteria: Disease and Its Interpretations* (Princeton: Princeton University Press, 1995), 19–29. I am indebted to Micale for the outline of hysteria's history presented here.
19 Foucault, *OT* xxiii. See chapter 4, above.
20 Janet Oppenheim, *Shattered Nerves: Doctors, Patients, and Depression in Victorian England* (Oxford: Oxford University Press, 1991), 181; Carroll Smith-Rosenberg, 'The Hysterical Woman: Sex Roles and Role Conflict in Nineteenth-Century America,' in *Disorderly Conduct: Visions of Gender in Victorian America* (New York: Alfred A. Knopf, 1985), 197.
21 The unwillingness of Martineau's doctors to diagnose her case as hysterical and my explanations for this unwillingness contrast with Carroll Smith-Rosenberg's view that in the nineteenth century, 'ailments as varied as menstrual pain and irregularity, prolapsed or tipped uterus, uterine tumor, vaginal infections and discharges, sterility, could all – doctors were certain – cause hysteria' (Smith-Rosenberg 206).
22 [Anonymous], 'Medical Societies,' *Lancet* 1 (13 April 1844): 109–10.
23 John C.W. Lever, *A Practical Treatise on Organic Disease of the Uterus* (London: Longman and Co., 1843). Lever was assistant-accoucheur at Guy's Hospital.
24 [Anonymous], 'Review of Dr Lever on the Diseases of the Uterus,' *Lancet* 1 (17 Aug. 1844): 639.
25 Ibid. 640.
26 For example, Valerie Pichanick contends that Martineau's deafness might be attributed to hysteria, but that hysteria 'was certainly not the cause of the disease that laid her low in 1839,' which according to Greenhow's *Report* was of a more definitively clinical nature (Pichanick 122). Webb also backs away from the hysteria diagnosis: 'It should be said at once that Miss Martineau was really ill. Her invalidism was not simply hysteria or hypochondria or an excuse to escape, however much all of them may have entered into the situation' (Webb 193). A discussion of Martineau's hysterical need for escapism follows below.
27 Elaine Showalter, *The Female Malady: Women, Madness and English Culture, 1830–1980* (New York: Pantheon Books, 1985), 121.

28 See T.S. Clouston, 'The Psychological Dangers to Women in Modern Social Development,' in *The Position of Women: Actual and Ideal*, ed. Sir Oliver Lodge (London: James Nisbet, 1911), 109–10; see also Showalter 123.

29 Henry Maudsley, 'Sex in Mind and in Education,' *Fortnightly Review* 15 (1874): 466–83; see also Showalter 124–5.

30 See Oppenheim 186.

31 Henry had been a problem in the family since 1829, when he began to drink heavily after the failure of the family business. In 1834 Martineau attempted, unsuccessfully, to have him appointed an assistant poor law commissioner. In 1838, having moved in with his sister, he worked as a clerk at Somerset House. The family later funded his emigration to New Zealand. See Webb 197.

32 See *HMA* 1:29.

33 Harriet Martineau, *Household Education* (London: 1849; repr. Boston: Houghton, Osgood, 1850), 286.

34 [Harriet Martineau], *Life in the Sick-Room* (London: Edward Moxon, 1844), 7. Hereafter cited as *LS*.

35 Harriet Martineau, *The Playfellow*, 4 Parts (London: Charles Knight, 1841). Indeed, in this context, Martineau's concerns in *The Hour and the Man* with history and romance, actuality and aspiration, possibly ordained Fate and actual fortune assume a whole new significance. And, of course, *The Hour and the Man* is also a tragedy with a highly ironic title that conceals the hero's identity (and complexion).

36 See chapter 2, above.

37 Diana Postlethwaite, 'Mothering and Mesmerism in the Life of Harriet Martineau,' *Signs: Journal of Women in Culture and Society* 14.3 (Spring 1989): 598.

38 Martineau describes her reaction to a visitor who saw 'no brightness' in her condition and thought she would never be well again: 'How my spirits rose in a moment at this recognition of the truth!' (*LS* 15).

39 See Smith-Rosenberg 205–6: 'In an age when will, control, and hard work were fundamental social values, this hypothetical etiology necessarily implied a negative evaluation of those who succumbed to hysteria. Such women were described as weak, capricious, and, perhaps most important, morbidly suggestible.' See also Showalter 134: 'Hysterics also expressed "unnatural" desires for privacy and independence.' Showalter also shows how Darwinian psychiatrists later in the century defined 'morbid intro-spection and solitary habits' as the most distinguishing features of mental disturbance. The Maréville alienists later in the century would see hysteria

as characterized by excessive self-dramatization, excessive sentiment, and excessive religiosity; see Micale 124.

40 For a full discussion of Mesmer and a detailed history of animal magnetism, see Adam Crabtree, *From Mesmer to Freud: Magnetic Sleep and the Roots of Psychological Healing* (New Haven: Yale University Press, 1993). I am indebted to Crabtree for the discussion of Mesmer and the history of mesmerism in France that follows. See also Alan Gauld, *A History of Hypnotism* (Cambridge: Cambridge University Press, 1992).

41 Puységeur discovered artificial somnambulism when magnetizing Victor Race, a peasant on his estate who was suffering from fever and congestion. To Puységeur's surprise, Race fell asleep in the midst of proceedings. Puységeur described this condition as that of a sleep-waking consciousness in which the subject is susceptible to suggestions and experiences amnesia in the waking state for events when magnetized. See Crabtree 38–53.

42 J.C. Colquhoun, *Report on the Experiments on Animal Magnetism, Made by a Committee of the Medical Section of the French Royal Academy of Sciences: Read at the Meetings of the 21st and 28th of June, 1831, Translated, and Now for the First Time Published; with an Historical and Explanatory Introduction, and an Appendix* (Edinburgh: Robert Cadell, 1833). Colquhoun's one-hundred-and-five-page introduction to this translation subsequently swelled to almost six hundred pages. He published this enlarged version as *Isis Revelata; an Inquiry into the Origin, Progress & Present State of Animal Magnetism*, 2 vols (Edinburgh: Maclachlan & Stewart, 1836).

43 Elliotson had witnessed and was impressed by experiments in mesmerism conducted by Richard Chevenix at St Thomas's Hospital in London. Chevenix was an Irish chemist and mineralogist trained in the tradition of Puységeur, and the results of his work were published in the *London Medical and Physiological Journal* (March, June, Aug., and Oct. 1829) and reported unfavourably in the *Lancet* (13 June 1829). Elliotson later recorded his impressions in *Human Physiology* (London: Longman, Orme, Brown, Green and Longmans, 1840). Elliotson's growing interest in mesmerism led to his inviting Baron Jules Du Potet de Sennevoy to demonstrate the importance of mesmerism at the University College Hospital. Du Potet's experiments had been partly responsible for the establishment of the 1826 commission, and when the Hospital Committee put an end to his demonstrations, Elliotson himself began to conduct experiments in the manner of Du Potet. See Crabtree 145–6.

44 I will consider the reasons for this rift below.

45 The Paris-born Lafontaine arrived in England in 1841 and gave mesmeric performances throughout England, Scotland, and Ireland.

46 Greenhow had been appointed chair of the proceedings at Newcastle and was sufficiently impressed by Hall's demonstration to persuade him to visit Martineau at Tynemouth. For a full account of the exchanges between Hall and Greenhow, see Hall 63–75.

47 'Miss Martineau on Mesmerism,' *Athenaeum* 891 (23 Nov. 1844): 1070–1.

48 See Joseph Philippe Deleuze, *Instruction pratique sur le magnétisme animal, suivie d'une lettre écrite à l'auteur par un médecin étranger* (Paris: Dentu, 1825). Deleuze's manual was the most popular of the period.

49 'Miss Martineau on Mesmerism,' *Athenaeum* 891 (23 Nov. 1844): 1071.

50 Ibid., p. 1072.

51 'Miss Martineau on Mesmerism,' *Athenaeum* 892 (30 Nov. 1844): 1093.

52 Martineau reprinted the letters in a pamphlet that sold out in four days. See Harriet Martineau, *Letters on Mesmerism* (London: Edward Moxon, 1844).

53 [Charles Wentworth Dilke], 'A Few Words by Way of Comment on Miss Martineau's Statement,' *Athenaeum* 896 (28 Dec. 1844): 1198.

54 [Charles Wentworth Dilke], 'Miss Martineau in Reply to our Few Words of Comment,' *Athenaeum* 897 (4 Jan. 1845): 14.

55 [Charles Wentworth Dilke], 'Miss Martineau and Mesmerism,' *Athenaeum* 907 (15 March 1845): 268.

56 [Charles Wentworth Dilke], 'Miss Martineau and Mesmerism,' *Athenaeum* 908 (22 March 1845): 291

57 [Charles Wentworth Dilke], 'Miss Martineau and Mesmerism,' *Athenaeum* 909 (29 March 1845): 311.

58 'Miss Martineau on Mesmerism,' *Athenaeum* 892 (30 Nov. 1844): 1093.

59 'Miss Martineau on Mesmerism,' *Athenaeum* 894 (14 Dec. 1844): 1144.

60 [Anonymous], 'Correspondence on Animal Magnetism,' *Lancet* 1 (22 Sept. 1838): 35.

61 Dr John Leeson, 'Objections to the Reality of Phenomena in Animal Magnetism,' *Lancet* 2 (18 Aug. 1838): 728, 727.

62 John Eagles, 'What Is Mesmerism?' *Blackwood's Magazine* 70 (July 1851): 84.

63 William Benjamin Carpenter, 'Electro-Biology and Mesmerism,' *Quarterly Review* 93 (Sept. 1853): 511.

64 Robert Ferguson, 'Animal Magnetism,' *Quarterly Review* 61 (April 1838): 275.

65 Harriet Martineau, 'Letter to John Elliotson,' *Zoist* 4.14 (July 1846): 276–7.

66 The *OED* defines seton as 'a thread, piece of tape, or the like, drawn through a fold of skin so as to maintain an issue or opening for discharges, or drawn through a sinus or cavity to keep this from healing up.'

67 Dionysius Lardner and E.L. Bulwer, 'Animal Magnetism,' Part ii, *Monthly Chronicle* 1 (June 1838): 20.

68 [Anonymous], 'The Experiments on the Two Sisters, O'Key,' *Lancet* 2 (15 Sept. 1838): 874.

69 Harriet Martineau, 'Miss Martineau on Mesmerism,' *Athenaeum* 893 (7 Dec. 1844): 1118.

70 John Neal, 'Men and Women,' *Blackwood's Magazine* 16 (Oct. 1824): 392. Neal cites the example of Sir Isaac Newton, who would unknowingly 'suffer [his] shins to be roasted alive' in front of a fire when he was lost in profound meditation.

71 George Sandby, quoted in William Nelson, *Mesmerism and Its Relation to Health and Disease and the Present State of Medicine* (Edinburgh: Shepherd & Elliot, 1855), 60.

72 Rev. Hugh M'Neile, 'Satanic Agency and Mesmerism,' *Penny Pulpit* (1842); see also G[eorge] S[andby], *Mesmerism the Gift of God: In Reply to 'Satanic Agency and Mesmerism,' a Sermon Said to Have Been Preached by the Rev. Hugh M'Neile: in a Letter to a Friend by a Beneficed Clergyman* (London: William Edward Painter, 1843). By the time Sandby responded to M'Neile's sermon, a thousand copies of it had already been sold and a reprint demanded. Proponents of mesmerism also compared mesmerism to witchcraft, but they used the former to explain the latter phenomena. See John William Jackson, *Mesmerism in Connection with Popular Superstitions* (London: H. Bailliere, 1858), 25–31.

73 Elizabeth Barrett, in a letter to Mary Russell Mitford in which she discusses Martineau's recovery by mesmerism, writes: 'Who will dare to doubt anymore the existence of the agency [mesmerism] – as my own father has done hitherto? What will Mr. May say, – he, who used to talk of hysteria? The phenomena of hysteria are morbid symptoms in themselves, & not *correctives* of morbidity' (*The Brownings' Correspondence*, 9:150).

74 J. Allison, *Mesmerism: Its Pretensions As a Science Physiologically Considered* (London: Whittaker and Co., 1844), 18.

75 According to Showalter, 'the hysterical attack generally began with pain in the uterine region, and with a sense of obstruction in the chest and throat. At its height, the victim alternately sobbed and laughed; she might have convulsive movements of the body, heart palpitations, impaired hearing and vision, or unconsciousness' (Showalter 130). Smith-Rosenberg's list of hysterical symptoms includes 'loss of sensation in part, half, or all of the body, loss of taste, smell, hearing, or vision, numbness of the skin, inability to swallow, nausea, headaches, pain in the breast, knees, hip, spine, or neck, as well as contracture or paralysis of virtually any extremity' (Smith-Rosenberg 202).

76 Sydenham described hysteria as 'a farrago of disorderly and irregular phe-

nomena.' See Thomas Sydenham's *Epistolary Dissertation* (1685), in *The Works of Thomas Sydenham*, 2 vols (London: Sydenham Society, 1830), 2:90. According to Sydenham, hysteria was unsurpassed in its capacity to imitate the symptoms of other diseases. See also Micale 22, 109n3.

77 'Experiments on the Two Sisters, O'Key,' p. 874.

78 A clinical neurologist, Charcot (1825–93) used hypnosis to show that mental factors were responsible for hysterical symptom formation. He conducted his popular public experiments in hysteria at the Salpêtrière and accomplished his most important work in this area between 1878 and 1893. See Micale 88–97. O'Key may be compared to Blanche Whitmann, known as 'Queen of the Hysterics' at the Salpêtrière. Hypnotized, Whitmann would perform spectacular shows at Charcot's public lectures, culminating in a full hysterical fit. See Showalter (147–54) on Charcot and the *Iconographie photographique de la Salpêtrière*.

79 George Sandby, *Mesmerism and Its Opponents: With a Narrative of Cases* (London: Longman, Brown, Green, and Longmans, 1844), 124.

80 [Anonymous], 'On the False Lights of Medical Science, As Obstacles to Medical Reform,' *Lancet* 1 (4 Feb. 1843): 685. Cf. Hope's representation in *Deerbrook*, considered in chapter 3, above.

81 Ibid., p. 686.

82 Jean Sylvain Bailly, 'Rapport secret sur le mesmérism,' *Le conservateur ... de N. François (de Neufchateau)* (1800) 1:150; quoted in Crabtree 93.

83 Thomas Wakley, *Lancet* (11 Nov. 1848); quoted in *Zoist* 7.28 (Jan. 1850): 377.

84 'Miss Martineau on Mesmerism,' *Athenaeum* 891 (23 Nov. 1844): 1071. Deleuze recommended that women be magnetized by women.

85 [Anonymous], 'Mesmerism, Miss Martineau, and the "Great New Idea,"' *Lancet* (30 Nov. 1844): 291; emphasis in the *Lancet*.

86 Elizabeth Barrett to Mary Russell Mitford, 16 Dec. 1844, in *The Brownings' Correspondence*, 9:280.

87 Harriet Martineau, 'Miss Martineau on Mesmerism,' *Athenaeum* 895 (21 Dec. 1844): 1174.

88 [Anonymous], 'The Animal Magnetism Fraud and Humbug,' *Lancet* 1 (1 Dec. 1838).

89 Quoted in John Elliotson, 'London College of Physicians and Mesmerists,' *Zoist* 6.24 (Jan. 1849): 404.

90 *Mesmerism and Its Opponents*, 191.

91 See [Anonymous], 'Labour in the Mesmeric State,' *Zoist* 2.5 (April 1844): 121–2.

92 Initially, the medical community refused to countenance Braid's experiments, as well. Braid proposed to read a paper to the Medical Section of the

British Association on his new discovery and sent them a manuscript. The manuscript was returned to Braid in an unsealed envelope, with a statement on the back in pencil that it was rejected as unsuitable. See R.S.S., 'Animal Magnetism and Neurhypnotism,' *Fraser's Magazine* 29 (June 1844): 690–1.

6: History and Religious Faith

1 Harriet Martineau, *Eastern Life, Present and Past*, 3 vols (London: Edward Moxon, Son, and Co., 1848). Hereafter cited as *EL*.

2 See, for example, Philippa Levine, *The Amateur and the Professional: Antiquarians, Historians and Archaeologists in Nineteenth-Century England, 1838–1886* (Cambridge: Cambridge University Press, 1986); and Rosemary Jann, *The Art and Science of Victorian History* (Columbus: Ohio State University Press, 1985). See also Maria H. Frawley, 'Desert Places / Gendered Spaces: Victorian Women in the Middle East,' *Nineteenth-Century Contexts* 15.1 (1991): 50–1.

3 See John Barrell, 'Death on the Nile: Fantasy and the Literature of Tourism 1840–1860,' *Essays in Criticism* 41.2 (April 1991): 101; see also Anthony Sattin, *Lifting the Veil: British Society in Egypt 1768–1965* (London: Dent, 1988) 44–63.

4 Cf. chapter 4, above.

5 See [Sophia Poole], *The Englishwoman in Egypt: Letters from Cairo, Written during a Residence in 1842, 1843, and 1844, with E.W. Lane, Esq., Author of The Modern Egyptians*, By his Sister (London: C. Knight, 1844). For Poole, the harem was a cultural 'contact zone,' although not one in which her relations with harem women were characterized by conflict. The term 'contact zone' is Mary Louise Pratt's. See *Imperial Eyes: Travel Writing and Transculturation* (New York: Routledge, 1992). Mrs Dawson Damer also visited harems during her travels in the East and published her *Diary of a Tour in Greece, Turkey, Egypt, and the Holy Land* (London: Henry Colburn, 1841). Lady Mary Wortley Montagu visited harems in Turkey in the early eighteenth century.

6 Billie Melman examines mixed attitudes of attraction and repulsion in travel writing on the harem in *Women's Orients: English Women and the Middle East, 1718–1918* (London: Macmillan, 1992), chapters 3–5. My own analysis of Martineau's view of the harem departs from Melman's assertion that Martineau's is one of 'the most glaring examples of racism and cultural narcissism' (Melman 63). Although Melman's study considers the ways in which British women's contact with the East caused them to reassess sexual

politics in the West, for Melman, Martineau's 'racism' renders her an exception to this tendency.

7 Jill Matus, 'The "Eastern-Woman Question": Martineau and Nightingale Visit the Harem,' *Nineteenth-Century Contexts* 21.1 (1999): 65.

8 Martineau's unwillingness to discuss sexuality explicitly here nonetheless departs from a tendency of much women's travel writing to maintain absolute silence on sexual matters. See Sara Mills, *Discourses of Difference: An Analysis of Women's Travel Writing and Colonialism* (London: Routledge, 1991), 22.

9 For Martineau, children born in these circumstances were literally destroyed, or murdered, by an excess of maternal care. The women she visited in Cairo were mourning the loss of a newly born infant. She argues that in English households that resemble harems, women will nurse a child 'all night in illness, and pamper it all day with sweetmeats and toys; they will fight for possession of it, and be almost heartbroken at its loss: and lose it they must; for the child always dies, – killed with kindness, even if born healthy' (*EL* 2:151).

10 Women in Alexandria, for example, pulled a 'bit of blue rag' half over their faces when approached, but Martineau and her companions found that they 'could generally get a sight of any face we had a mind to see, – excepting, of course, those of mounted ladies.' They found the women more closely veiled as they proceeded into the country to Nubia, 'where we were again favoured with a sight of the female countenance' (*EL* 1:8).

11 Other women travellers, such as Sophia Poole, had adopted Eastern dress when abroad.

12 [Anonymous], 'Miss Martineau's *Eastern Life*,' *Spectator* 1035 (29 April 1848): 419.

13 J.J. Tayler, 'Miss Martineau's *Eastern Life*,' *Prospective Review* 4.6 (Nov. 1848): 524.

14 See chapter 2, above.

15 The first volume of Poole's *Englishwoman in Egypt* (Knight's Weekly Volume, 1845) contains an abstract of Egyptian history, agricultural and general calendars, information on physical features of the country, and various statistics, avowedly taken from her brother's notes. Frederick Holme acknowledged that these dissertations supplied additional information to readers of Lane's *Modern Egyptians*, but he complained that 'they are scarcely "germane to the matter," as interpolations in the work of a lady.' See Frederick Holme, 'Mrs Poole's "Englishwoman in Egypt,"' *Blackwood's Magazine* 57 (March 1845): 287.

16 Martineau contends that it was impossible to obtain reliable information on

the material condition of Egyptians. She observes in her journal that '"even a census does not help. The present census, we are told, will be a total failure – so many will bribe the officials to omit their names, because of the poll-tax"' (*EL* 2:168).

17 T. B. Macaulay, 'History,' *Edinburgh Review* 47 (May 1828): 363–4.

18 J.A. St John [prob.], 'Voyages and Travels. – Public Taste,' *Monthly Chronicle* 2 (Oct. 1838): 367.

19 Francis Ainsworth, 'Oriental Travel,' *New Monthly Magazine* 93 (Sept. 1851): 89.

20 Edward Clarkson [prob.], 'Bunsen's Egypt,' *Fraser's Magazine* 35 (June 1847): 631 (a review of Von Christian Carl Josias Bunsen, *Aegypten's Stelle in der Weltgeschichte*, 3 vols [Hamburg, 1845]).

21 These were that Moxon would accept the risk and that Martineau would be entitled to two-thirds of the profits. The first year's proceeds paid for Martineau's new house in Ambleside and its contents. She donated her share of proceeds from the second edition to the cheapening of the book, believing that its contents would be received more favourably by the lower classes. See *HMA* 2:295–6.

22 Martineau's contributions to the *Monthly Repository* were republished in America as *Miscellanies*, 2 vols (Boston: Hilliard Gray and Co., 1836). See also Pichanick 172.

23 James had introduced his sister to necessarianism. Notwithstanding, in 1833 he expressed reservations about the necessarian school in his essay 'On the Life, Character, and Works of Dr Priestley,' *Monthly Repository* 7 (1833): 19–30, 84–8, 231–41. In 1842 he renounced necessarianism altogether. See Pichanick 173. Pichanick provides an excellent account of the development of Martineau's views on religion.

24 Martineau did not reject Christianity after her visit to America and was an avid Bible-reader up to the time of her illness. The extravagance of her devotion in *Life in the Sick-Room*, however, has no equivalent in the period preceding her sickness.

25 Harriet Martineau to Richard Monckton Milnes, 22 Feb. 1845, in *Harriet Martineau: Selected Letters*, ed. Valerie Sanders (Oxford: Clarendon Press, 1990), 108.

26 David Friedrich Strauss argued that the life of Jesus was a myth unintentionally developed between Jesus' death and the composition of the Gospels in the second century. Martineau was unusual in recognizing the story in Egyptian mythology. Melman charges Martineau with applying the myth 'indiscriminately' to Egyptian thought. See Melman 241.

27 A different solution was that the Egyptian priests were disciples of Plato

and had Platonized the attributes of Osiris, as later Platonizing Christians would Christ's. Martineau refutes this suggestion by noting that the attributes of Osiris were the same in the centuries before the birth of Abraham as they were after the deaths of Plato and Pythagoras. See *EL* 1:248–9.

28 See *EL* 1:330–1.

29 The Egyptians believed that Typho, the brother of Osiris, was the cause of evil. Martineau insists on the absence of an evil spirit in the Mosaic system, maintaining that the serpent in Eden 'is, in the history, a mere serpent, altogether Egyptian in its conception' (*EL* 2:277).

30 Martineau's remarks may be related to debates in England on the growth of Catholicism. Certainly Catholic rituals were opposed to her own Unitarian background. Cf. her exasperation at the superstition of Christian monks at Jerusalem, discussed below.

31 Jesus maintained that a spiritual kingdom would be established within the lifetime of his generation. See Matt. 24:34, 36; Mark, 13:30; Luke, 21:32. See also *EL* 3:174.

32 *OT* xxiii. Cf. chapter 4, above.

33 See Levine 2; see also chapter 5, above.

34 Stephen Bann, 'The Sense of the Past: Image, Text, and Object in the Formation of Historical Consciousness in Nineteenth-Century Britain,' in *The New Historicism*, ed. H. Aram Veeser (New York: Routledge, 1989), 102.

35 Baden Powell, 'Mysticism and Scepticism,' *Edinburgh Review* 84 (July 1846): 201.

36 Of course, the Catholic Church, in establishing ecclesiastical history as the basis of ecclesiastical authority, also declared itself infallible in its historical research, thereby suppressing independent historical investigation of evidence on the part of its adherents.

37 Sir Austen Layard's researches at Nineveh and Nimrud accelerated the popular assimilation of biblical archaeology. Ironically, Layard's researches exonerated Old Testament narratives. See Levine 97. See also Sir Austen Henry Layard, *Nineveh and Its Remains* (London: John Murray, 1849).

38 See Levine 5, 94.

39 For an excellent summary of the 'higher criticism' in Germany and in England, see Robin Gilmour, *The Victorian Period: The Intellectual and Cultural Context of English Literature, 1830–1890* (London and New York: Longman, 1993), 53–62. Gilmour also recognizes that, excepting 'higher criticism,' nineteenth-century historicism tended to exclude Christianity from the scope of its activities: 'Hitherto, scholarship had put a ring-fence around Christianity and its origins. Men like Dr Arnold of Rugby School went at ancient history like an express-train and then pulled up short when

it came to the Old and New Testaments: these belonged in the realm of Revelation rather than history' (Gilmour 54).

40 See also Pichanick: '*Eastern Life* added little to the arsenal of the biblical critics and little that was original to the world view of Christianity. It was primarily one woman's struggle with the awesome revelation that, beside the relics of the ancient Egyptian culture and holding many of the same verities, Christianity could claim no special divine appointment' (Pichanick 181).

41 [Anonymous], 'Fuss in a Book-Club, As Related by a Copy of Miss Martineau's "Eastern Life," ETC. ETC.,' *Fraser's Magazine* 38 (Dec. 1848): 630.

42 This review uses Martineau's text as a persona, recounting the book's sensations and remarks made by its alleged readers, of whom the character of Murray is one. See 'Fuss in a Book-Club' p. 631.

43 George Troup, '*Eastern Life, Present and Past*,' *Tait's Edinburgh Magazine* 19 o.s., 15 n.s. (Sept. 1848): 611.

44 My argument contrasts with Melman's view that Martineau endorsed the 'unarrested progress' of civilizations. See Melman 237. In fairness to Melman, Martineau's stance here is an unusual departure from her generally optimistic view of social development.

45 J.J. Tayler, for example, countered Martineau's statement by insisting on the superiority of Christianity to the 'elementary Monotheism of Moses': 'there is nothing inconceivable in the acceptance of it by an enlightened Jew, who can read the order of providence in a retrospect of human history.' See 'Miss Martineau's *Eastern Life*,' *Prospective Review*, p. 535.

46 See Levine 100. Levine stresses the conservatism of nineteenth-century historicism: 'At no point in the nineteenth century did these groups [historicists] deviate markedly from the expression of the values of their educated and comfortable world.'

47 George Croly, 'Modern Tourism,' *Blackwood's Magazine* 64 (Aug. 1848): 189.

48 'Miss Martineau's *Eastern Life*,' *Spectator* 1035 (29 April 1848): 419.

49 G.W.F. Hegel, *The Philosophy of History*, trans. J. Sibree (New York: Dover Publications, 1956); originally delivered as lectures, 1830–1.

50 Reviewers' insistence on the imaginative quality of Martineau's historicizing suggests her reversion to eighteenth-century historiography.

51 See Lukács 35. Cf. chapter 4, above.

52 Martineau maintained that it required years of learning to learn hieroglyphics. She also despaired that the language had forever lost its power of grammatical inflection. See *EL* 1:177.

53 See *EL* 1:179.

54 Tourists not only stole relics, but they also carved their names into the walls of temples. See *EL* 1:299. Martineau admits to carving her own name on a wild rock beyond the Second Cataract, but she never defaced a temple: 'If we ever do such a thing, may our names be publicly held up to shame, as I am disposed to publish those of the carvers and scribblers who have forfeited their right to privacy by inscribing their names where they can never be effaced!' (*EL* 1:145).

55 Thomas Carlyle, 'On History,' in *Selected Writings*, ed. Alan Shelston (Harmondsworth: Penguin, 1986), 91.

56 Martineau maintains that the 'light-hearted voyager' who sets off on a tour of the ancient monuments returns 'an antique, a citizen of the world of six thousand years ago, kindred with the mummy' (*EL* 1:85).

57 This momentary restoration of Martineau's hearing corroborates Pichanick's view that her deafness was an hysterical symptom. Cf. chapter 5, above. Gillian Thomas also observes that the incident provokes 'speculation about the precise nature and causes of Martineau's deafness' (Thomas 56).

58 See Stendhal, *The Charterhouse of Parma*, trans. Margaret R.B. Shaw (Harmondsworth: Penguin, 1983); originally published as *La Chartreuse de Parme*, 1839. See also Reilly 6–14.

59 Barrell 102. Barrell situates Martineau's description of the Sphinx in an ongoing ethnological debate at that time. When Martineau was writing *Eastern Life*, Samuel George Morton, a Philadelphia craniologist, was engaged in research to discredit the belief that the ancient Egyptians were black – a belief held by the influential British ethnologist James Cowles Prichard – and thereby to provide a scientific justification for slavery. Prichard eventually came to accept Morton's view, and by 1848 'Martineau's belief in the blackness of the Egyptians was becoming increasingly hard to sustain' (Barrell 104). However, given Martineau's unflagging commitment to abolitionism and the racial egalitarianism of *The Hour and the Man*, I find it difficult to accept Barrell's view that Martineau's reaction to the Sphinx reveals 'the anxiety caused by her belief in the blackness of the Ancient Egyptians,' especially when 'what was at stake, of course, was more than the identity of the Ancient Egyptians; it was the humanity of the blacks' (Barrell 105, 104).

60 Martineau's project also recalls the work of the French revolutionary Charles Dupuis. Dupuis argued that all religions could be traced to an Egyptian source. See *The Origin of All Religious Worship* (New York: Garland Publishers, 1984); originally published as *Origine de tous les cultes, ou religion universelle* (Paris: Chez H. Agasse, 1795).

7: Shaking the Faith

1 Henry George Atkinson and Harriet Martineau, *Letters on the Laws of Man's Nature and Development* (London: John Chapman, 1851). Hereafter cited as *LLMND*.

2 Because Martineau assumes responsibility for the publication of *Letters*, my analysis of this text proceeds on the assumption that Atkinson's opinions, as stated in his letters to Martineau, are shared by Martineau herself – an assumption that is supported by her assent to Atkinson's views in their epistolary dialogue.

3 The term 'phrenology' was coined by Thomas Ignatius Maria Forster in the *Philosophical Magazine* in 1815. The *Philosophical Magazine* was the ideological organ of the London Askesian Society and the London Philosophical Society. For a discussion of Forster's contributions to phrenology, see Roger Cooter, *The Cultural Meaning of Popular Science: Phrenology and the Organization of Consent in Nineteenth-Century Britain* (Cambridge: Cambridge University Press, 1984), 59–64. Although Cooter does not consider *Letters on the Laws of Man's Nature and Development*, Cooter's is an excellent study of more than four thousand texts on phrenology.

4 See Harriet Martineau, 'George Combe,' in *Biographical Sketches* (London: Macmillan and Co., 1869), 265. Hereafter cited as *B5*.

5 For J. Stevenson Bushnan, Combe's omission from the *Letters* was unwarranted: 'Alas for George Combe! – a man who has laboured on the subject for a life-time, – who has written books, and good ones too, – who has repeatedly crossed the Atlantic to instruct our brethren of the New World in the mysteries of the callipers! – his name is not even mentioned by Mr. Atkinson; he is lumped among the fortune-telling phrenologists who have disgusted the world. How complacent is self-sufficiency!' See *Miss Martineau and Her Master* (London: John Churchill, 1851), 119.

6 Knight had himself intended to write the *History of the Peace* and to publish it in monthly numbers aimed at middle- and working-class readers. After completing the first instalment, however, other commitments caused him to abandon the scheme, and he persuaded Martineau to finish the project. The *History of the Peace* was so successful that Knight then persuaded Martineau to extend the work, and the following year Martineau produced an *Introduction to the History of the Peace: from 1800 to 1815*, which was published in 1851. A further volume was also planned, but Knight was sufficiently distressed by *Letters on the Laws of Man's Nature and Development* to sell the rights to the entire series, and final chapters were not added to the work until an American edition was published in

1864; see Harriet Martineau, *The History of England from the Commencement of the xixth Century to the Crimean War*, 4 vols (Philadelphia: Porter and Coates, 1864).

7 D.T. Coulton, 'Contemporary History – Mr Roebuck and Miss Martineau,' *Quarterly Review* 91 (June 1852): 161.

8 Cf. chapter 4, above.

9 Martineau did not read Comte's *Cours de philosophie positive* until the spring of 1851, at which time she decided to translate and to condense the work. By 1853, she had reduced Comte's six volumes to two, published by John Chapman. Martineau's translation was favourably reviewed in the *Westminster Review*, and Comte himself wrote Martineau flattering letters and substituted her condensation for his own volumes in the *Positivist Library*. See Richard Congreve [prob.], 'Comte's *Positive Philosophy*,' *Westminster Review* 62 o.s., 6 n.s. (July 1854): 173–94. See also Webb 303–9. Webb attributes the article in the *Westminster Review* to T.H. Huxley.

10 Diana Postlethwaite also considers the importance of Priestley to Martineau in her engaging book, *Making It Whole: A Victorian Circle and the Shape of Their World* (Columbus: Ohio State University Press, 1984), 117–22 (hereafter cited as *MW*). See also Pichanick 185–6.

11 Priestley's edition of Hartley omitted his theory of vibrations, according to which vibrations originating at sense organs are communicated to the brain via the nerves.

12 Joseph Priestley, *Disquisitions Relating to Matter and Spirit: To Which Is Added the History of the Philosophical Doctrine Concerning the Origin of the Soul, and the Nature of Matter, with Its Influence on Christianity*, 2nd ed., improved and enl. (Birmingham: Printed by Pearson and Rollason for J. Johnson, 1782; first pub. London, 1777), iv.

13 Priestley, Preface to *Matter and Spirit*, xi.

14 Combe abhorred the enforced discipline of the Calvinist sabbath and the endless sermons on human sin and misery that had tormented his upbringing, although in many respects his own brand of phrenology was a secularized version of Calvinism. For a full discussion of Combe's background and work, see Cooter 101–33.

15 Like Martineau, Atkinson felt that religion was significant from an historical perspective, although he complained that 'it is hard for reason and for history to struggle against such romance as this' (*LLMND* 235).

16 'How I wonder at myself now for having held (and very confidently held forth upon it, I am ashamed to say) that at all events it was safe to believe dogma: that for instance, whether there was a future state or not, it was safe and comfortable to believe it: – that if, even, there was no God, serving as a

model to Man, – the original of the image, – it was safe and tranquilizing to take for granted that there was' (*LLMND* 282).

17 Elizabeth Gaskell, *The Life of Charlotte Brontë*, ed. Alan Shelston (Penguin Books, 1975; first pub. 1857) 441.

18 John Eagles, 'What Is Mesmerism,' *Blackwood's Magazine* 70 (July 1851): 76n.

19 Surprisingly, this view was stated in *Zoist*. See Anti-Glorioso, 'The Fireaway Style of Philosophy Briefly Examined and Illustrated,' *Zoist* 9.33 (April 1851): 67.

20 James Martineau, 'Mesmeric Atheism,' *Prospective Review* 7.26 (1851): 234.

21 [Anon.], 'Martineau and Atkinson on Man's Nature and Development,' *Westminster Review* 55 (April 1851): 83–92; W.E. Hickson, 'Life and Immortality,' *Westminster Review* 56 (Oct. 1851): 168–228. See also *MW* 148.

22 *Leader*, 1 March 1851; *Reasoner*, 12 March 1851; Martineau to G.J. Holyoake, 7 April 1852, British Museum, quoted in Webb 301.

23 James Anthony Froude, 'Materialism – Miss Martineau and Mr Atkinson,' *Fraser's Magazine* 43 (April 1851): 418.

24 Cf. chapter 6, above.

25 [Anonymous], *Materialistic Views of Professor Tyndall and Miss Harriet Martineau Criticized* (London: Bickers & Son, 1879), 41. Hereafter cited as *MVC*.

26 *MVC* 44. This reference to the mummy was presumably intended to augment the horrors of Martineau's argument by narrowing the gap of cultural difference separating the East and West. At the same time, it clearly occluded the significance of the mummy for ancient Egyptians, who were preoccupied with the afterlife.

27 'Martineau and Atkinson on Man's Nature and Development,' *Westminster Review* 55 (April 1851): 86.

28 [Anonymous], 'Miss Martineau and Her Master,' *British and Foreign Medico-Chirurgical Review* 8 (Oct. 1851): 540.

29 The quotation is taken from 'Combe,' in *Biographical Sketches*, 276.

30 See Cooter 122, 121, 220.

31 Innatism was of primary importance to Gall, although he also recognized that stimuli applied to particular mental organs could also influence behaviour. See Cooter 226.

32 See *DP* 195–228.

33 Cf. chapter 3, above.

34 The doctrine that character was determined by environmental conditions was opposed to Gall's innatist view of character but was developed by Spurzheim in order to enhance phrenology's meliorist potential. For a full discussion of the alliance of Owenism and phrenology, see Cooter, chapter 8. As Cooter suggests, the fact that phrenology could be made to support

such opposed ideologies as Owenism and industrial capitalism indicates the ideological complexity of the science. See also Charles Bray, *The Philosophy of Necessity; or, The Law of Consequences, as Applicable to Mental, Moral, and Social Sciences* (London: Longman, Orme, Brown, Green, and Longmans, 1841). Bray also arrives at an understanding of necessity that incorporates both phrenology's biological determinism and Owen's doctrine of environmental influences.

35 Martineau had made two earlier attempts to write her autobiography. The first was when she was twenty-nine and chiefly known as a contributor to W.J. Fox's *Monthly Repository.* She made her second effort during her illness at Tynemouth. On both occasions she proceeded no further than her childhood.

36 Cf. chapter 5, above.

37 For a discussion of feminist, poststructuralist theorizing on indeterminate (sexual) identity, see Kathryn Bond Stockton, 'Bodies and God: Poststructuralist Feminists Return to the Fold of Spiritual Materialism,' *Boundary 2* 19 (Summer 1992): 122–4.

38 See 'Martineau and Atkinson on Man's Nature and Development,' *Westminster Review* 55 (April 1851): 88.

39 See Froude 428: 'The features and the body are agitated as they usually are by particular emotions. The mesmerists have jumped to the conclusion that such emotions are really felt; and we have to thank them for the most satisfactory confutation of materialism which has yet been offered.' Notwithstanding Froude's protest, he expresses fear at the potential of phreno-mesmerism to manipulate human emotions and to pervert morality: '... shall the mother, weeping at the grave of her child, be suddenly, at the wave of some fool's hand, convulsed with ghastly laughter?' (Froude 429).

40 See *LLMND* 55, 103–5.

41 According to Atkinson, 'When somnambulists think they see into another world, a world of spirits, it may be clearly proved to be delusive dreaming; and yet on such declarations do enthusiasts build up a faith and religion, and are proud of what they call spirituality' (*LLMND* 54).

42 Cooter also considers the significance of the occult to nineteenth-century radicals. See Cooter 203–4.

Conclusion

1 Florence Fenwick Miller, *Lessons of a Life: Harriet Martineau. A Lecture, Delivered before the Sunday Lecture Society* (London: Sunday Lecture Society, 1877), 5, 27.

2 When it was subsequently proposed to extend the scope of the Contagious Diseases Act in 1869, Martineau wrote three more letters to the *Daily News* (28, 29, 30 Dec. 1869) and gave needlework to the Ladies' National Association for fundraising. See Pichanick 234–6 for a full discussion of Martineau's efforts to repeal the Act.

3 For an extensive discussion of the *Illustrations* and Martineau's early fiction, see Claudia Orazem, *Political Economy and Fiction in the Early Works of Harriet Martineau* (New York: P. Lang, 1999).

4 Abraham Hayward, 'Harriet Martineau's *Autobiography*,' *Quarterly Review* 143 (April 1877): 499.

Works Cited

Adorno, Theodor. *Minima Moralia: Reflections from a Damaged Life*. Trans. E.F.N. Jephcott. London: Verso, 1974.

– *Prisms*. Trans. Samuel and Shierry Weber. Cambridge: MIT Press, 1983.

Ainsworth, Francis. 'Oriental Travel.' *New Monthly Magazine* 93 (Sept. 1851): 88–105.

Alison, Archibald. 'The Chartists and Universal Suffrage.' *Blackwood's Edinburgh Magazine* 46 (Sept. 1839): 289–303.

– 'Democracy.' *Blackwood's Magazine* 41 (Jan. 1837): 71–90.

Allison, J. *Mesmerism: Its Pretensions As a Science Physiologically Considered*. London: Whittaker and Co., 1844.

Anonymous. 'The Animal Magnetism Fraud and Humbug.' *Lancet* 1 (1 Dec. 1838).

Anonymous [signed R.S.S.]. 'Animal Magnetism and Neurhypnotism.' *Fraser's Magazine* 29 (June 1844): 681–99.

Anonymous. 'The Church and the Chartists.' *Fraser's Magazine* 20 (Nov. 1839): 619–29.

Anonymous. 'Cinnamon and Pearls.' *Spectator* 271 (7 Sept. 1833): 834–6.

Anonymous. 'Correspondence on Animal Magnetism.' *Lancet* 1 (22 Sept. 1838): 35.

Anonymous. 'Cousin Marshall.' *Spectator* 219 (8 Sept. 1832): 853.

Anonymous. '[Review of] *Deerbrook*: A Novel.' *Athenaeum* 597 (6 April 1839): 255.

Anonymous. 'Dickens's *American Notes*.' *Fraser's Magazine* 26 (Nov. 1842): 617–29.

Anonymous. 'The Experiments on the Two Sisters, O'Key.' *Lancet* 2 (15 Sept. 1838): 873–7.

Anonymous. 'Fuss in a Book-Club, As Related by a Copy of Miss Martineau's "Eastern Life," ETC. ETC.' *Fraser's Magazine* 38 (Dec. 1848): 628–34.

Anonymous. 'Glances at New Books.' *Tatler* 34 (19–20 June 1832): 253–4.

Anonymous. 'Homes Abroad.' *Spectator* 227 (3 Nov. 1832): 1046.

Anonymous. '*The Hour and the Man.*' *Spectator* 649 (5 Dec. 1840): 1167.

Anonymous. '*The Hour and the Man: A Historical Romance.*' *Athenaeum* 684 (5 Dec. 1840): 958.

Anonymous. 'Labour in the Mesmeric State.' *Zoist* 2.5 (April 1844): 121–3.

Anonymous. '*Life in the Wilds.*' *Spectator* 188 (Feb. 1832): 112–15.

Anonymous. 'Martineau and Atkinson on Man's Nature and Development.' *Westminster Review* 55 (April 1851): 83–92.

Anonymous. *Materialistic Views of Professor Tyndall and Miss Harriet Martineau Criticized.* London: Bickers & Son, 1879. Cited as *MVC*.

Anonymous. 'Medical Societies.' *Lancet* 1 (13 April 1844): 109–10.

Anonymous. 'Mesmerism and the Medical Profession?' *Zoist* 7.28 (Jan. 1850).

Anonymous. 'Mesmerism, Miss Martineau, and the "Great New Idea."' *Lancet* (30 Nov. 1844): 291.

Anonymous. 'Miss Edgeworth's Tales and Novels.' *Fraser's Magazine* 6 (Nov. 1832): 541–58.

Anonymous. 'Miss Martineau and Her Master.' *British and Foreign Medico-Chirurgical Review* 8 (Oct. 1851): 538–40.

Anonymous. 'Miss Martineau and Her Traducers.' *Zoist* 3.9 (April 1845).

Anonymous. 'Miss Martineau on America.' *American Quarterly Review* 22 (Sept. 1837): 21–53.

Anonymous. 'Miss Martineau's Deerbrook.' *Spectator* 563 (13 April 1839): 350–1.

Anonymous. 'Miss Martineau's *Eastern Life.*' *Spectator* 1035 (29 April 1848): 419.

Anonymous. 'Miss Martineau's *Society in America.*' *North American Review* 45 (Oct. 1837): 418–60.

Anonymous. 'Miss Martineau's Travels in America.' *Edinburgh Review* 67 (April 1838): 180–97.

Anonymous. 'On the False Lights of Medical Science, As Obstacles to Medical Reform.' *Lancet* 1 (4 Feb. 1843): 685–8.

Anonymous. 'Past and Present State of Hayti.' *Quarterly Review* 21 (April 1819) 430–60.

Anonymous. 'Practical Reasoning *versus* Impracticable Theories.' *Fraser's Magazine* 19 (May 1839): 557–92.

Anonymous. 'Prince Pückler Muscau and Mrs. Trollope.' *North American Review* 36 (Jan. 1833): 1–48.

Anonymous. 'Review of Dr. Lever on the Diseases of the Uterus.' *Lancet* 1 (17 Aug. 1844): 639–41.

Anonymous. 'Revival of the Slave Trade.' *Edinburgh Review* 23 (April 1814): 131–50.

Anonymous. 'Slavery and the New Slave Trade.' *Monthly Chronicle* 1 (April 1838): 126–38.

Anonymous. 'Superficial Travelling.' *Dublin Review* 14 (Feb. 1843): 256–62.

Anonymous. 'Uterine Polypi Expelled by the Aid of Ergot of Rye.' *Lancet* 1 (3 Dec. 1842): 347.

Anti-Glorioso. 'The Fire-away Style of Philosophy Briefly Examined and Illustrated.' *Zoist* 9.33 (April 1851): 65–9.

Arnott, Neil. 'Professional Morality.' *Westminster Review* 14 (April 1831): 463–81. Cited as PM.

– 'Regulation of Anatomy.' *Westminster Review* 16 (April 1832): 482–96.

Ashcroft, Bill, Gareth Griffiths, and Helen Tiffin. *The Empire Writes Back: Theory and Practice in Post-Colonial Literatures.* London: Routledge, 1989.

Auerbach, Erich. *Mimesis: The Representation of Reality in Western Literature.* Trans. Willard R. Trask. Princeton: Princeton University Press, 1953.

Bailin, Miriam. *The Sickroom in Victorian Fiction: The Art of Being Ill.* Cambridge: Cambridge University Press, 1994.

Baillie, Matthew. *Morbid Anatomy of Some of the Most Important Parts of the Human Body.* London: J. Johnson and G. Nicol, 1793.

Bann, Stephen. *The Clothing of Clio: A Study of the Representation of History in Nineteenth-Century Britain and France.* Cambridge: Cambridge University Press, 1984.

– 'The Sense of the Past: Image, Text, and Object in the Formation of Historical Consciousness in Nineteenth-Century Britain.' In *The New Historicism.* Ed. H. Aram Veeser. New York: Routledge, 1989.

Barnes, James J. *Free Trade in Books: A Study of the London Book Trade since 1800.* Oxford: Clarendon Press, 1964.

Barrell, John. 'Death on the Nile: Fantasy and the Literature of Tourism 1840–1860.' *Essays in Criticism* 41.2 (April 1991): 97–127.

Beer, Gillian. *The Romance.* London: Methuen, 1970.

Belsey, Catherine. 'Constructing the Subject: Deconstructing the Text.' In *Feminist Criticism and Social Change.* Ed. Judith Newton and Deborah Rosenfelt. New York: Methuen, 1985.

Biographie universelle, ancienne et moderne. Paris: L.G. Michaud, 1826.

Bosanquet, Theodora. *Harriet Martineau: An Essay in Comprehension.* London: Frederick Etchells & Hugh Macdonald, 1977.

Bray, Charles. *The Philosophy of Necessity; or, The Law of Consequences, As Applica-*

ble to Mental, Moral, and Social Sciences. London: Longman, Orme, Brown, Green, and Longmans, 1841.

Broughman, Henry. 'American Slavery.' *Edinburgh Review* 63 (April 1836): 135–43.

– 'The Foreign Slave Trade.' *Edinburgh Review* 72 (Oct. 1840): 179–93.

Brown, Theodore M. 'The Changing Self-Concept of the Eighteenth-Century London Physician.' *Eighteenth Century Life* 7.2 (Jan. 1982): 31–40.

Budick, Emily Miller. 'Hester's Scepticism, Hawthorne's Faith: or, What Does a Woman Doubt? Instituting the American Romance Tradition.' *New Literary History* 22.1 (1991): 199–211.

Buller, Arthur. 'Bribery and Intimidation at Elections.' *London and Westminster Review* 3 and 25 (July 1836): 485–513.

Bushnan, J. Stevenson. *Miss Martineau and Her Master.* London: John Churchill, 1851.

Buzard, James. *The Beaten Track: European Tourism, Literature, and the Ways to 'Culture.'* Oxford: Clarendon, 1993.

Calvino, Italo. 'Right and Wrong Political Uses of Literature.' In *The Literature Machine.* Trans. Patrick Creagh. London: Picador, 1989.

Carlyle, Thomas. *Selected Writings.* Ed. Alan Shelston. Harmondsworth: Penguin, 1986.

Carpenter, William Benjamin. 'Electro-Biology and Mesmerism.' *Quarterly Review* 93 (Sept. 1853): 501–57.

Clarkson, Edward [prob.]. 'Bunsen's Egypt.' *Fraser's Magazine* 35 (June 1847): 631–8.

Clouston, T.S. 'The Psychological Dangers to Women in Modern Social Development.' In *The Position of Woman; Actual and Ideal.* Ed. Sir Oliver Lodge. London: James Nisbet, 1911.

Colquhoun, J.C. *Isis Revelata; an Inquiry into the Origin, Progress and Present State of Animal Magnetism.* 2 vols. Edinburgh: Maclachlan & Stewart, 1836.

– *Report on the Experiments on Animal Magnetism, Made by a Committee of the Medical Section of the French Royal Academy of Sciences: Read at the Meetings of the 21st and 28th of June, 1831; Translated, and Now for the First Time Published; with an Historical and Explanatory Introduction, and an Appendix.* Edinburgh: Robert Cadell, 1833.

Congreve, Richard [prob.]. 'Comte's *Positive Philosophy.*' *Westminster Review* 62 o.s., 6 n.s. (July 1854): 173–94.

Cooter, Roger. *The Cultural Meaning of Popular Science: Phrenology and the Organization of Consent in Nineteenth-Century Britain.* Cambridge: Cambridge University Press, 1984.

Coulton, D.T. 'Contemporary History – Mr. Roebuck and Miss Martineau.' *Quarterly Review* 91 (June 1852): 160–95.

Cowan, James C. 'The *Pharmakos* Figure in Modern American Stories of Physicians and Patients.' *Literature and Medicine* 6 (1987): 94–109.

Crabtree, Adam. *From Mesmer to Freud: Magnetic Sleep and the Roots of Psychological Healing*. New Haven: Yale University Press, 1993.

Croker, John Wilson. 'Dickens's *American Notes*; Mann's *Anniversary Oration.*' *Quarterly Review* 71 (March 1843): 502–28.

Croker, John Wilson, and G. Poulett Scrope. 'Miss Martineau's *Monthly Novels.*' *Quarterly Review* 49 (April 1833): 136–52.

Croly, George. 'Modern Tourism.' *Blackwood's Magazine* 64 (Aug. 1848): 185–9.

Damer, Mrs Dawson. *Diary of a Tour in Greece, Turkey, Egypt, and the Holy Land.* London: Henry Colburn, 1841.

David, Deirdre. *Intellectual Women and Victorian Patriarchy: Harriet Martineau, Elizabeth Barrett Browning, George Eliot.* London: Macmillan, 1987.

De Man, Paul. 'The Rhetoric of Temporality.' In *Blindness and Insight: Essays in the Rhetoric of Contemporary Criticism.* Minneapolis: University of Minnesota, 1983.

de Toqueville, Alex. *Democracy in America.* New York: Vintage Books, 1959. Cited as *DA*.

Deleuze, Joseph Philippe. *Instruction pratique sur le magnétisme animal, suivie d'une lettre écrite à l'auteur par un médecin étranger.* Paris: Dentu, 1825.

DeMorgan, Sophia Elizabeth. 'Reform of Prisons.' *Monthly Chronicle* 3 (Feb. 1839): 173–84.

Derrida, Jacques. 'Plato's Pharmacy.' In *Dissemination.* Trans. Barbara Johnson. Chicago: University of Chicago Press, 1981.

Desmangles, Leslie G. *The Faces of the Gods: Vodou and Roman Catholicism in Haiti.* Chapel Hill: University of North Carolina Press, 1992.

Dickens, Charles. *American Notes for General Circulation.* Ed. John S. Whitley and Arnold Goldman. London: Penguin Books, 1972. First published, London: Chapman and Hall, 1842. Cited as *AN*.

Dilke, Charles Wentworth. 'A Few Words by Way of Comment on Miss Martineau's Statement.' *Athenaeum* 896 (28 Dec. 1844): 1198–9.

– 'Miss Martineau and Mesmerism.' *Athenaeum* 907 (15 March 1845): 268–9; 908 (22 March 1845): 290–1; 909 (29 March 1845): 310–11; 910 (5 April 1845): 333–5; 911 (12 April 1845): 361–3.

– 'Miss Martineau in Reply to Our Few Words of Comment.' *Athenaeum* 897 (4 Jan. 1845): 14–15.

Dodd, Charles Edward. 'Punishment of Death – Wakefield on Newgate.' *Quarterly Review* 47 (March 1832): 170–216.

Dupuis, Charles. *The Origin of All Religious Worship*. New York and London: Garland Publishers, 1984. First published as *Origine de tous les cultes, ou Religion universelle*. Paris: 1795.

Eagles, John. 'What Is Mesmerism?' *Blackwood's Magazine* 70 (July 1851): 70–83.

Eagleton, Mary ed. *Feminist Literary Theory*. Oxford: Basil Blackwell, 1986.

Eastlake, Elizabeth. 'Lady Travellers.' *Quarterly Review* 76 (June 1845): 98–136.

– 'Vanity Fair – and *Jane Eyre*.' *Quarterly Review* 84 (Dec. 1848): 153–85.

Edwards, Bryan. *An Historical Survey of the French Colony in the Island of St. Domingo*. London: J. Stockdale, 1797.

Elliotson, John. *Human Physiology*. London: Longman, Orme, Brown, Green and Longmans, 1840.

– 'London College of Physicians and Mesmerists.' *Zoist* 6.24 (Jan. 1849): 399–405.

Empson, William. '*Illustrations of Political Economy*: Mrs Marcet – Miss Martineau.' *Edinburgh Review* 115 (April 1833): 1–39.

Ferguson, Moira. *Subject to Others: British Women Writers and Colonial Slavery, 1670–1834*. London: Routledge, 1992.

– ed. *First Feminists: British Women Writers, 1578–1799*. Bloomington: Indiana University Press, 1985.

Ferguson, Robert. 'Animal Magnetism.' *Quarterly Review* 61 (April 1838): 273–301.

Foucault, Michel. *The Birth of the Clinic*. Trans. A.M. Sheridan Smith. New York: Vintage Books, 1973. First published as *Naissance de la clinique*. Paris: Presses Universitaires de France, 1963. Cited as *BC*.

– *Discipline and Punish: The Birth of the Prison*. Trans. Alan Sheridan. London: Penguin Books, 1977. First published as *Surveiller et punir: naissance de la prison*. Paris: Editions Gallimard, 1975. Cited as *DP*.

– *The Order of Things: An Archeology of the Human Sciences*. New York: Pantheon Books, 1971. First published as *Les mots et les choses*. Paris: Editions Gallimard, 1966. Cited as *OT*.

Frawley, Maria H. 'Desert Places / Gendered Spaces: Victorian Women in the Middle East.' *Nineteenth-Century Contexts* 15.1 (1991): 49–64.

Freedgood, Elaine. 'Banishing Panic: Harriet Martineau and the Popularization of Political Economy.' *Victorian Studies* 39.1 (Autumn 1995): 33–53.

Froude, James Anthony. 'Materialism – Miss Martineau and Mr. Atkinson.' *Fraser's Magazine* 43 (April 1851): 418–34.

Fuller, Margaret. *Woman in the Nineteenth Century*. New York: Greeley & McElrath, 1845. Cited as *WNC*.

G., M.L. 'Miss Martineau – Intellectual Women.' *Tatler* 59 (Oct. 1832): 478.

Gallagher, Catherine. *The Industrial Reformation of English Fiction: Social Dis-*

course and Narrative Form 1832–1867. Chicago and London: University of Chicago Press, 1980.

Gauld, Alan. *A History of Hypnotism*. Cambridge: Cambridge University Press, 1992.

Gilmour, Robin. *The Victorian Period: The Intellectual and Cultural Context of English Literature, 1830–1890*. London and New York: Longman, 1993.

Giltrow, Janet. '"Painful Experience in a Distant Land": Mrs. Moodie in Canada and Mrs. Trollope in America.' *Mosaic: A Journal for the Interdisciplinary Study of Literature* 14.2 (Spring 1981): 131–44.

Gitter, Elizabeth G. 'Charles Dickens and Samuel Gridley Howe.' *Dickens Quarterly* 8.4 (Dec. 1991): 162–7.

Gooch, Robert. 'Unlawful Disinterment of Human Bodies.' *Quarterly Review* 42 (Jan. 1830): 1–17.

Greenhow, T.M. *Medical Report of the Case of Miss H– M–*. London: Samuel Highley, 1845.

Greenhow, T.M., and T. Spencer Wells. 'Termination of the Case of Miss Harriet Martineau.' *British Medical Journal* (8 July 1876): 64; (14 April 1877): 449–50; (21 April 1877): 496; (5 May 1877): 543–50.

Grund, Francis. *Aristocracy in America*. New York: Harper Torch Books, 1959. First published, London: R. Bentley, 1839.

Hall, Basil. *Travels in North America in the Years 1827 and 1828*. 3 vols. Edinburgh, 1829.

Hall, Dr Marshall. 'Lectures on the Theory and Practice of Medicine.' *Lancet* 2 (7 July 1838): 497–504.

Hall, Spencer T. *Mesmeric Experiences*. London: H. Balliere, 1845.

Ham, John. 'The Prudential Check – Marriage or Celibacy.' *Tait's Edinburgh Magazine* 3 (June 1833): 316–20.

Hayward, Abraham. 'Harriet Martineau's *Autobiography*.' *Quarterly Review* 143 (April 1877): 484–526.

Head, Francis B. 'The Printer's Devil.' *Quarterly Review* 65 (Dec. 1839): 1–30.

Hegel, G.W.F. *The Philosophy of History*. Trans. J. Sibree. New York: Dover Publications, 1956). Originally delivered as lectures, 1830–1.

Heming, Dr G. Oakley. 'Practical Facts and Observations on Diseases of Women, and Some Subjects Connected with Midwifery.' *Lancet* 1 (24 Aug. 1844): 670–3.

Heraud, J.A. 'Historical Romance.' *Quarterly Review* 35 (March 1827): 518–66.

Hickson, W.E. 'Life and Immortality.' *Westminster Review* 56 (Oct. 1851): 168–228.

Holme, Frederick. 'Mrs Poole's "Englishwoman in Egypt."' *Blackwood's Magazine* 57 (March 1845): 286–97.

Hughes, Helen. *The Historical Romance*. London: Routledge, 1993.

Hunter, Shelagh. *Harriet Martineau: The Poetics of Moralism*. Aldershot: Scolar Press, 1995.

Jackson, John William. *Mesmerism in Connection with Popular Superstitions*. London: H. Bailliere, 1858.

Jann, Rosemary. *The Art and Science of Victorian History*. Columbus: Ohio State University Press, 1985.

Johnson, E.D.H. *The Alien Vision of Victorian Poetry: Sources of the Poetic Imagination in Tennyson, Browning and Arnold*. Princeton: Princeton University Press, 1952.

Johnson, Louise H. 'The Source of the Chapter on Slavery in Dickens' *American Notes*.' *American Literature* 14 (Jan. 1943): 427–30.

Johnstone, Christian. 'Dickens' *Notes on America, for General Circulation*.' *Tait's Edinburgh Magazine* 13 o.s., 9 n.s. (Nov. 1842): 737–46.

– 'Miss Martineau's *Illustrations of Political Economy*.' *Tait's Edinburgh Magazine* 1 (Aug. 1832): 612–18.

– 'Miss Martineau's Society in America, and Grund's American Society.' *Tait's Edinburgh Magazine* 8 o.s., 4 n.s. (July 1837).

– 'New Novels: *The Hour and the Man*.' *Tait's Edinburgh Magazine* 12 o.s., 8 n.s. (Jan. 1841).

Kelley, Philip, and Scott Lewis, eds. *The Brownings' Correspondence*. Winfield: Wedgestone Press, 1991.

Lacan, Jacques. *Ecrits: A Selection*. Trans. A. Sheridan. London: Tavistock, 1977.

Lackey, Kris. 'Eighteenth-Century Aesthetic Theory and the Nineteenth-Century Traveler in Trans-Allegheny America: F. Trollope, Dickens, Irving and Parkman.' *American Studies* 32 (Spring 1991): 33–48.

Lardner, Dionysius, and E.L. Bulwer, 'Animal Magnetism.' Part II *Monthly Chronicle* 2 (July 1838): 11–30.

Layard, Sir Austen Henry. *Nineveh and Its Remains*. London: John Murray, 1849.

Leeson, Dr John. 'Objections to the Reality of Phenomena in Animal Magnetism.' *Lancet* 2 (18 Aug. 1838.

Lever, John C.W. *A Practical Treatise on Organic Disease of the Uterus*. London: Longman and Co., 1843.

Levine, Philippa. *The Amateur and the Professional: Antiquarians, Historians and Archaeologists in Nineteenth-Century England, 1838–1886*. Cambridge: Cambridge University Press, 1986.

Lipset, Seymour Martin. 'Harriet Martineau's America.' In *Society in America*. Ed. Seymour Martin Lipset. New York: Anchor Books, 1962.

Lister, T.H. [prob.]. 'Miss Martineau's *Deerbrook*.' *Edinburgh Review* 69 (July 1839): 494–502.

Lukács, Georg. *The Historical Novel*. Trans. Hannah and Stanley Mitchell. London: Merlin Press, 1962. First published in Moscow, 1937.

M'Neile, Rev. Hugh. 'Satanic Agency and Mesmerism.' *Penny Pulpit* (1842).

Macaulay, T.B. 'History.' *Edinburgh Review* 47 (May 1828): 331–67.

MacDonald, Dr William. 'Clinical Discourse Concerning a Polypus of the Womb.' *Lancet* 1 (14 Jan. 1843): 574–7.

Maginn, William. 'Gallery of Literary Characters No. LXIV: Michael Thomas Sadler, Esq.' *Fraser's Magazine* 12 (Sept. 1835): 280.

– 'Gallery of Literary Characters No. XLII: Miss Harriet Martineau.' *Fraser's Magazine* 8 (Nov. 1833): 576.

– [prob.] 'On National Economy (No. III): Miss Martineau's "Cousin Marshall" – "The Preventive Check."' *Fraser's Magazine* 6 (Nov. 1832): 403–13.

[prob.] 'On Quackery, Twaddle, and Other Offences.' *Fraser's Magazine* 3 (April 1831): 368–75.

Marcet, Jane. *Conversations on Political Economy, in Which the Elements of That Science Are Familiarly Explained*. London: Longman, Hurst, Rees, Orme & Brown, 1816.

Martineau, Harriet. 'The Achievements of the Genius of Scott.' *Tait's Edinburgh Magazine* 10 (Jan. 1833): 445–60.

– *Biographical Sketches*. London: Macmillan and Co., 1869.

– 'The Brewing of the American Storm.' *Macmillan's Magazine* 6 (June 1862): 97–107.

– *Deerbrook: A Novel*. 3 vols. London: Edward Moxon, 1839.

– *Eastern Life, Present and Past*. 3 vols. London: Edward Moxon, Son, and Co., 1848. Reprinted with plates, 1875.

– 'Female Industry.' *Edinburgh Review* 109 (April 1859): 293–336.

– 'The Governess: Her Health.' *Once a Week* 3 (1 Sept. 1860). Cited as *GHH*.

– *Harriet Martineau's Autobiography*. With memorials by M.W. Chapman. 3 vols. London: Smith, Elder, & Co., 1877). Cited as *HMA*, followed by the volume number.

– *The History of England from the Commencement of the XIXth Century to the Crimean War*. 4 vols. Philadelphia: Porter and Coates, 1864.

– *The Hour and the Man: A Historical Romance*. 3 vols. London: Edward Moxon, 1841.

– *Household Education*. London: 1849; Boston: Houghton, Osgood, 1850.

– *How to Observe Morals and Manners*. London: Charles Knight and Co., 1838.

- *Illustrations of Political Economy.* 9 vols. London: Charles Fox, 1834.
- 'Letter to John Elliotson.' *Zoist* 4.14 (July 1846): 276–7.
- *Letters on Mesmerism.* London: Edward Moxon, 1844.
- *Life in the Sick-Room.* London: Edward Moxon, 1844. Cited as *LS.*
- 'The Martyr Age of the United States.' *London and Westminster Review* 32 (Dec. 1838): 1–59.
- *Miscellanies.* 2 vols. Boston: Hilliard Gray and Co., 1836. First published in *Monthly Repository* 3 (1829): 521–6, 599–606, 707–12, 745–57, 817–22.
- 'Miss Martineau on Mesmerism.' *Athenaeum* 891 (23 Nov. 1844): 1070–2; 892 (30 Nov. 1844): 1093–4; 893 (7 Dec. 1844): 1117–18; 894 (14 Dec. 1844): 1144–5; 895 (21 Dec. 1844): 1173–4.
- *The Playfellow.* 4 parts. London: Charles Knight, 1841.
- *Retrospect of Western Travel.* 2 vols. London: Saunders and Otley, 1838.
- *Society in America.* 3 vols. London: Saunders and Otley, 1837. Cited as *SA.*
- trans. *The Positive Philosophy of Aug. Comte.* London: John Chapman, 1853.
Martineau, Harriet, and Henry George Atkinson. *Letters on the Laws of Man's Nature and Development.* London: John Chapman, 1851. Cited as *LLMND.*
Martineau, James. 'Mesmeric Atheism.' *Prospective Review* 7.26 (1851): 224–62.
- 'On the Life, Character, and Works of Dr. Priestley.' *Monthly Repository* 7 (1833): 19–30, 84–8, 231–41.
Matus, Jill. '"The Eastern-Woman Question": Martineau and Nightingale Visit the Harem.' *Nineteenth-Century Contexts* 21.1 (1999): 65.
Maudsley, Henry. 'Sex in Mind and in Education.' *Fortnightly Review* 15 (1874): 466–83.
Mazzini, Joseph. 'Is It a Revolt or a Revolution?' *Tait's Edinburgh Magazine* 11 o.s.; 7 n.s. (June 1840): 385–90.
McGann, Jerome. *A Critique of Modern Textual Criticism.* Chicago: University of Chicago Press, 1983.
McKenzie, D.F. *The Panizzi Lectures.* London: The British Library, 1985.
Meckier, Jerome. *Innocent Abroad: Charles Dickens's American Engagements.* Lexington: University Press of Kentucky, 1990.
Melman, Billie. *Women's Orients: English Women and the Middle East, 1718–1918.* London: Macmillan, 1992.
Merskey, Harold, and Paul Potter. 'The Womb Lay Still in Ancient Egypt.' *British Journal of Psychiatry* 154 (June 1989).
Micale, Mark S. *Approaching Hysteria: Disease and Its Interpretations.* Princeton: Princeton University Press, 1995.
Miller, Florence Fenwick. *Lessons of a Life: Harriet Martineau. A Lecture, Delivered before the Sunday Lecture Society.* London: Sunday Lecture Society, 1877.
Mills, Sara. *Discourses of Difference: An Analysis of Women's Travel Writing and Colonialism.* London: Routledge, 1991.

Moir, George [prob.]. 'Recent English Romances.' *Edinburgh Review* 65 (April 1837): 180–204.

Moore, Jane. 'Sex, Slavery and Rights in Mary Wollstonecraft's *Vindications*.' In *The Discourse of Slavery: Aphra Behn to Toni Morrison*. Ed. Carl Plasa and Betty J. Ring. London: Routledge, 1994. 18–39.

More, Hannah. *Slavery: A Poem*. London: T. Cadell, 1788.

Neal, John. 'Men and Women.' *Blackwood's Magazine* 16 (Oct. 1824): 387–94.

Nelson, William. *Mesmerism and Its Relation to Health and Disease and the Present State of Medicine*. Edinburgh: Shepherd & Elliot, 1855.

Nevill, John Cranstoun. *Harriet Martineau*. London: Frederick Muller, 1943.

Opie, Amelia Alderson. *The Negro Boy's Tale: A Poem Addressed to Children*. London: Harvey and Darton, 1795. Reprinted S. Wilkin, Norwich, 1824.

Oppenheim, Janet. *Shattered Nerves: Doctors, Patients, and Depression in Victorian England*. Oxford: Oxford University Press, 1991.

Orazem, Claudia. *Political Economy and Fiction in the Early Works of Harriet Martineau*. New York: P. Lang, 1999.

Peterson, Linda H. 'Harriet Martineau: Masculine Discourse, Female Sage.' In *Victorian Sages and Cultural Discourse: Renegotiating Gender and Power*. Ed. Thaïs E. Morgan. New Brunswick: Rutgers University Press, 1990. 171–86.

Peterson, M. Jeanne. *The Medical Profession in Mid-Victorian London*. London and Berkeley: University of California Press, 1978.

– 'The Victorian Governess: Status Incongruence in Family and Society.' In *Suffer and Be Still: Women in the Victorian Age*. Ed. Martha Vicinus. Bloomington: Indiana University Press, 1972. 3–19.

Pichanick, Valerie Kossew. *Harriet Martineau: The Woman and Her Work, 1802–76*. Ann Arbor: University of Michigan Press, 1980.

Plasa, Carl. '"Silent Revolt": Slavery and the Politics of Metaphor in *Jane Eyre*.' In *The Discourse of Slavery: Aphra Behn to Toni Morrison*. Ed. Carl Plasa and Betty J. Rigg. London: Routledge, 1994.

Plomer, Henry R. *A Short History of English Printing 1476–1900*. London: Kegan Paul, Trench, Trübner & Co., Ltd, 1915.

Poole, Sophia. *The Englishwoman in Egypt: Letters from Cairo, Written during a Residence in 1842, 1843, and 1844, with E.W. Lane, Esq., Author of The Modern Egyptians*. By his Sister. London: C. Knight, 1844.

Poovey, Mary. *Uneven Developments: The Ideological Work of Gender in Mid-Victorian England*. Chicago: University of Chicago Press, 1988.

Postlethwaite, Diana. *Making It Whole: A Victorian Circle and the Shape of Their World*. Columbus: Ohio State University Press, 1984. Cited as MW.

– 'Mothering and Mesmerism in the Life of Harriet Martineau.' *Signs: Journal of Women in Culture and Society* 14.3 (Spring 1989): 583–609.

Powell, Baden. 'Mysticism and Scepticism.' *Edinburgh Review* 84 (July 1846): 195–223.

Pratt, Mary Louise. *Imperial Eyes: Travel Writing and Transculturation*. New York: Routledge, 1992.

– 'Scratches on the Face of the Country: or, What Mr. Barrow Saw in the Land of the Bushmen.' In *'Race,' Writing, and Difference*. Ed. Henry Louis Gates, Jr. Chicago: University of Chicago Press, 1985. 119–43.

Priestley, Joseph. *Disquisitions Relating to Matter and Spirit: To Which Is Added the History of the Philosophical Doctrine Concerning the Origin of the Soul, and the Nature of Matter, with Its Influence on Christianity.* 2nd ed., improved and enlarged. Birmingham: printed by Pearson and Rollason for J. Johnson, 1782. First published, London: printed for J. Johnson, 1777.

– *The Doctrine of Philosophical Necessity Illustrated: Being an Appendix to the Disquisitions Relating to Matter and Spirit. To Which Is Added an Answer to the Letters on Materialism and on Hartley's Theory of the Mind.* London: printed for J. Johnson, 1777.

Rainsford, Marcus. *Historical Account of the Black Empire of Hayti, Comprehending a View of the Principal Transactions*. London: Cunder, 1805.

Redivivus, Junius. 'To the Tatler.' *Tatler* 483 (20 March 1832): 270.

Reilly, Jim. *Shadowtime: History and Representation in Hardy, Conrad and George Eliot*. London: Routledge, 1993.

Richardson, Ruth. *Death, Dissection and the Destitute*. London: Routledge & Kegan Paul, 1987.

Robertson, John. 'Miss Martineau's Western Travel.' *London and Westminster Review* 6 and 28 (Jan. 1838): 470–502.

Romer, Isabella Frances. *A Pilgrimage to the Temples and Tombs of Egypt, Nubia, and Palestine, in 1845–6*. 2 vols. London: R. Bentley, 1846.

Rothfield, Lawrence. *Vital Signs: Medical Realism in Nineteenth-Century Fiction*. Princeton: Princeton University Press, 1992.

Sánchez-Eppler, Karen. 'Bodily Bonds: The Intersecting Rhetorics of Feminism and Abolition.' *Representations* 24 (Fall 1988): 28–59.

Sandby, George. *Mesmerism and Its Opponents: With a Narrative of Cases*. London: Longman, Brown, Green, and Longmans, 1844.

– *Mesmerism the Gift of God: In Reply to 'Satanic Agency and Mesmerism,' a Sermon Said to Have Been Preached by the Rev. Hugh M'Neile: In a Letter to a Friend by a Beneficed Clergyman*. London: William Edward Painter, 1843.

Sanders, Prince, ed. *Haytian Papers*. London, 1816; Westport: Negro Universities Press, 1969.

Sanders, Valerie. *Reason over Passion: Harriet Martineau and the Victorian Novel*. Sussex: Harvester Press, 1986.

– ed. *Harriet Martineau: Selected Letters*. Oxford: Clarendon Press, 1990.

Sattin, Anthony. *Lifting the Veil: British Society in Egypt 1768–1965*. London: J.M. Dent, 1988.

Scott, Walter. *Waverley; or, 'Tis Sixty Years Since*. Ed. Claire Lamont. Oxford: Oxford University Press, 1986. First published, Edinburgh: printed by J. Ballantyne for A. Constable, 1814.

Scrope, G. Poulett. 'Malthus and Sadler: Population and Emigration.' *Quarterly Review* 45 (April 1831): 97–145.

– 'The Political Economists.' *Quarterly Review* 44 (Jan. 1831): 1–52.

Senior, Nassau William. *Two Lectures on Population Delivered before the University of Oxford in Easter Term, 1828. To Which Is Added a Correspondence between the Author and the Rev. T.R. Malthus*. London: Saunders and Otley, 1829.

Shaw, David. *The Lucid Veil: Poetic Truth in the Victorian Age*. London: Althone Press, 1987.

Showalter, Elaine. *The Female Malady: Women, Madness and English Culture, 1830–1980*. New York: Pantheon Books, 1985.

Simpson, David. *Romanticism, Nationalism, and the Revolt against Theory*. Chicago: University of Chicago Press, 1993.

Smith, Sheila M. *The Other Nation: The Poor in English Novels of the 1840s and 1850s*. Oxford: Clarendon Press, 1980.

Smith, Thomas Southwood. 'Medical Reform.' *London and Westminster Review* 4 and 26 (July 1836): 58–92. Cited as MR.

– 'Use of the Dead to the Living.' *Westminster Review* 2 (July 1824): 59–97.

Smith-Rosenberg, Carroll. 'The Hysterical Woman: Sex Roles and Role Conflict in Nineteenth-Century America.' In *Disorderly Conduct: Visions of Gender in Victorian America*. New York: Alfred A. Knopf, 1985.

St John, J.A. [prob.]. 'Voyages and Travels. – Public Taste.' *Monthly Chronicle* 2 (Oct. 1838): 366–80.

Stendhal. *The Charterhouse of Parma*. Trans. Margaret R.B. Shaw. Harmondsworth: Penguin, 1983. First published as *La Chartreuse de Parme*. Paris: Calmann-Levy, 1839.

Stockton, Kathryn Bond. 'Bodies and God: Poststructuralist Feminists Return to the Fold of Spiritual Materialism.' *Boundary 2* 19 (Summer 1992): 113–49.

Tayler, J.J. 'Miss Martineau's *Eastern Life.*' *Prospective Review* 4.6 (Nov. 1848): 524–38.

Thomas, Gillian. *Harriet Martineau*. Boston: Twayne Publishers, 1985.

Thomson, John [prob.]. 'On the Causes, Cure, and Prevention of Contagious Fever.' *Edinburgh Review* 31 (March 1819): 413–40.

Trollope, Frances Milton. *Domestic Manners of the Americans*. Dover: Alan Sutton, 1984. First published, London: Whittaker, Treacher, & Co., 1832. Cited as *DM*.

Troup, George. '*Eastern Life, Present and Past.*' *Tait's Edinburgh Magazine* 19 o.s., 15 n.s. (Sept. 1848): 604–15.

Venables, G.S. 'Miss Martineau – *Deerbrook.*' *Blackwood's Magazine* 47 (Feb. 1840): 177–88.

Webb, R.K. *Harriet Martineau: A Radical Victorian.* London: Heinemann, 1960.

Wheatley, Vera. *The Life and Work of Harriet Martineau.* London: Secker & Warburg, 1957.

White, Hayden. 'Getting Out of History.' *Diacritics* 12.3 (Fall 1982): 2–13.

Winter, Alison. *Mesmerized: Powers of Mind in Victorian Britain.* Chicago: University of Chicago Press, 1998.

Yellin, Jean Fagan. *Women and Sisters: The Antislavery Feminists in American Culture.* New Haven: Yale University Press, 1989.

Index